YARD
STREET
PARK

YARD
STREET
PARK

The Design of Suburban Open Space

Cynthia L. Girling
Kenneth I. Helphand

John Wiley & Sons, Inc.
New York • Chichester • Brisbane • Toronto • Singapore

This text is printed on recycled paper.

Copyright © 1994 by John Wiley & Sons, Inc.

All rights reserved. Published simultaneously in Canada.

Reproduction or translation of any part of this work beyond
that permitted by Section 107 or 108 of the 1976 United
States Copyright Act without the permission of the copyright
owner is unlawful. Requests for permission or further
information should be addressed to the Permissions Department,
John Wiley & Sons, Inc., 605 Third Avenue, New York, NY
10158-0012.

This publication is designed to provide accurate and
authoritative information in regard to the subject
matter covered. It is sold with the understanding that
the publisher is not engaged in rendering legal, accounting,
or other professional services. If legal advice or other
expert assistance is required, the services of a competent
professional person should be sought.

Library of Congress Cataloging-in-Publication Data
Girling, Cynthia L., 1952–
    Yard, street, park : the design of suburban open space / Cynthia
L. Girling and Kenneth I. Helphand.
        p.   cm.
    Includes bibliographical references and index.
    ISBN 0-471-55600-9
    1. Suburbs—United States—Planning.   2. Open spaces—United
States—Planning.   I. Helphand, Kenneth I.   II. Title.
HT352.U6G57   1994
307.1'214'0973—dc20   93-49454

Printed in the United States of America

10 9 8 7 6 5 4 3 2 1

IN HONOR OF OUR PARENTS

Doreen Lillian Girling
Leslie Francis Girling

Ruth Kavesh Helphand—*in loving memory*
Lewis Helphand

CONTENTS

ACKNOWLEDGMENTS

Many persons contributed to the creation of this book. We would like to thank the Department of Landscape Architecture and the University of Oregon for their support. Robert Melnick, the department chair, and our colleagues in the department worked hard to open our schedules and provide office support for this project. Our students in design studios and seminars have contributed fresh ideas and insights about the suburban landscape. The Office of the Provost provided support through a Scholarship and Creative Development Award, which gave Cynthia Girling release time and supported Kate Van Rooy.

The drawings of the houses and their yards and maps of open space systems were created by Kate Van Rooy of Eugene, Oregon. We thank her for adding a distinctive, insightful, and humorous graphic quality to the book.

All of the readers and critics of the manuscript helped us to work raw ideas into a synthetic piece. Dan Sayre was an exemplary editor, providing informed and constructive critiques, always finding the threads that weave the chapters together. Allison Morvay has deftly shepherded the book production. Russell Till has created a superb design which allows text and graphics to emerge as one. Our other readers asked hard questions about biases and unsubstantiated thoughts, alerting us to weaknesses. Thanks to Ron Kellett, Linda Girling, Michael Martin, and Stan Jones.

Our manuscript assistants, Cathleen Corlett and Andrene Hyatt, deserve the warmest thanks for doggedly sticking with us through to the last citation and permission, and we also thank Susan Dolan for uncovering historical information about Vermont Hills.

We have tapped the resources of several design firms for ideas and graphic materials. Thanks to Phil Erickson and Cathleen Chang at Calthorpe Associates; Tom Lamb and Bob Jacob at The SWA Group, Laguna Beach; and Xavier Inglesias at Duany and Plater-Zyberk, Architects and Town Planners. We would also like to thank the residents of Vermont Hills who graciously opened their homes, memories, and old files to our inquisitions. Fred and Peg Lofsvold provided valuable insights into life in Levittown. These and many other persons, including family and friends, have contributed to our ideas about the suburban landscape; however, the final product of this book is our own and we accept responsibility for its contents.

INTRODUCTION

The suburbs are a middle ground, located between city and country-side, promising a combination of the "best of both worlds." Ideally a union of the virtues of the urban and the rural, the civilized and the natural, they are intended to be without the vices of either. A utopian strain and a degree of naiveté is part of their history. Their location places them at two edges. Viewed from the city side, suburbs are the urban perimeter, but they are equally found at the rural periphery. The American suburbs have historically defined the urban frontier. Their character has always been fundamentally related to their position in space and to the quality of that space. Part of what makes a suburb a suburb is open space. At the heart of the suburban ideal is the promise of living within green open spaces. One of the reasons that people move to the suburbs is a desire for more personal space and an expansiveness not found amid urban congestion and density. An equal desire is for a private domain of house and lot, a combination of built and natural space, that one could call one's own, care for, and trans-form. The wish rarely recognized the need for the types of open spaces left behind, the community of street and public places.

The study of suburban design necessitates an understanding of the power of cultural images, the influence of policy, the pattern of design, and the veracity of experience. Recent scholarship about suburbs has primarily focused on their urbanization, related demographic shifts, and metropolitan morphology. It has observed that many suburban areas have become city-like, offering the full range of urban services: home, work, school, shopping, recreation, entertainment, and civic life. New terminology has been coined for these emerging forms: Fishman's "technoburb,"[1] Muller's "mini-city,"[2] and Garreau's "Edge City."[3] In this changing landscape American sentiment in favor of single-family detached-home ownership remains strong and is unlikely to undergo significant change in the near future. However, the appeal of traditional suburban forms and lifestyles is tempered by economic and social costs and by changing social structures. Suburbs conceived around traditional households have proven to be less supportive for other groups and serve an increasingly narrow segment of the population. There are substantial costs associated with low-density suburbs: a loss of agri-cultural land, a decline in air and water quality, and exorbitant costs for sewers, power, and roads. As a consequence, metropolitan regions are reex-amining their philosophy and attitudes toward growth. Planners and de-signers are responding to this evolving circumstance through changes in policy, land use and transportation planning, and site and building design.

Suburban settlers have tended to assume that the periphery was fixed, that both city and countryside would remain in their current configuration. Geographical stability would prove to be illusory, however, as metropolitan

Suburbs Timeline: 1900–1990. All plans except Vermont Hills from Keller Easterling, American Town Plans: A Comparative Timeline. *New York: Princeton Architectural Press, 1993.*

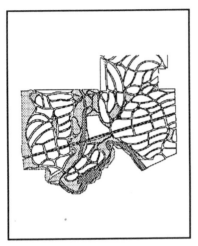

Pre-1910
Olmstedian Planned Suburb
Riverside, IL

Picturesque landscape style
Streets follow landscape contours

Parks connected by boulevards
Linear park along river corridor

Each yard is an estate

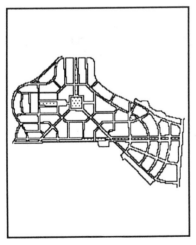

1910s
War Housing/Nolen Towns
Yorkship Village, NJ

Orderly plans. Geometry diminishes as town meets countryside.

Squares, parks, and landmarks were civic sites linked by boulevards.

areas continued to grow and expand into rural areas. As the suburbs grew, their character inexorably changed. People were attracted to the suburbs to be in a more natural setting, yet at a certain point overdevelopment destroyed that initial appeal. People moved to the suburbs to be near the countryside, but new development often left them surrounded by more suburbs. These effects were accomplished not by a single catastrophe, but by incremental effect, making it difficult to react to such changes, on either an individual or a community basis. Suburban development proved to be a classic example of "the tragedy of the commons."[4] Problems were not anticipated, and once recognized they were often beyond solution.

The physical environment is an active ingredient of our existence. Individual, family, and community life is enhanced by experiencing a variety of environments, which requires access to a diversity of open spaces. The functioning, or the failure to function, of open spaces is one determinant to the success or failure of a suburb, both as a private home and as a public community. The contemporary American suburb is seldom successful at providing "the best of both worlds." Suburbs have developed into a new amalgam, one that not only partakes of the extremes but has an independent identity. As a combination of city and country, the suburb includes elements of their open spaces, of urban civic spaces, along with rural and natural amenity. However, their identities change in the suburban landscape. In the suburbs, the greatest time and attention has gone into enriching and embellishing the outdoor space of the private yard, at the expense of the public landscapes of street and park. These shared places can foster a sense of community. Streets are not only for cars. We have lost sight of the fact that they are also important public spaces, which should equally accommodate bikes and pedestrians. Suburban residents need not be as dependent on the automobile as they now are. This is particularly true for those who commute and those who chauffeur children on their daily rounds, as well as those who must, or will choose, to stay home if a ride is not available. Ideally, the tasks of daily life should be within walking distance—a trip to buy groceries, get a haircut, rent a video, or play baseball. Plazas and centers, from the neighborhood scale to the civic center, may be even more necessary in the highly privatized and automobile-dependent suburb. Parks are not needed in the suburbs as a relief from urban density and congestion, but they are still necessary as places for recreation and contact with natural areas. What is perhaps more critical in the suburbs is a system of open space connections. As streets in the urban environment provide the primary pedestrian linkages, creative ways are needed in the lower-density suburbs to bring together dispersed populations and open space opportunities. One reason suburbs fail to live up to their advertising hyperbole is that they fail to provide an open space system offering residents proper access to the variety of outdoor and indoor experiences. A combination of intensified densities and more extensive and inviting open space networks can be one component to enriching suburban life. Networks can facilitate access to leisure and recreational amenity, as well as to employment and local shopping and services, and can offer transportation alternatives to rush hour car commuting.

In the past 40 years suburbs have expanded, but they have also matured. Land uses and building types have evolved that were not previously planned for: the shopping mall, corporate headquarters, and highway development. Unanticipated problems have arisen, such as increased traffic, the overdevelopment of land, and the depletion of scarce landscape resources of

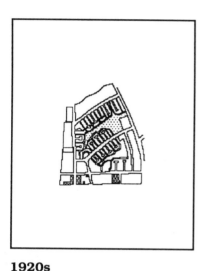

1920s
Radburn Introduced
Radburn, NJ

Open space backbone linking parks, schools

Dual "front" yards

Cul-de-sac service lane for cars

1930s
Greenbelt Towns
Greenbelt, MD

Park networks with interconnecting paths

Parking lots instead of local streets

Small yards face onto narrow walkways

wetlands, woods, soils, and streams. The lawn, a seemingly benign personal patch of greenery, when aggregated across the landscape, pollutes through the overuse of pesticides and fertilizers. Moreover, social problems are not confined to urban political boundaries. A sense of community is difficult to sustain in our modern mobile culture.

Urban and suburban landscapes are not independent of nature. Rather, they are part of their region's ecology. It is possible for them to maintain an ecological balance, but current patterns of development sap resources and damage ecosystems.[5] The design of the suburban landscape is not just a scenic amenity; it contributes to the quality of life, it can provide the structure and frame for a richer existence. It can offer access to diverse opportunities and ease the accomplishment of daily tasks. A well-designed open space system can decrease automobile use, enable people to walk more and drive less, preserve natural land, and provide connections from developed to undeveloped land. It can contribute to social interaction and community sensibility, as space is actively used and shared. It is a necessary ingredient in the fulfillment of the suburban promise.

The house and its accompanying yard are at the core of suburban ideology. In the framework of American culture, the individualistic ideal has manifested itself in a quest for a small piece of a dream: owning a home and a surrounding piece of land. Suburbs offer a response to that desire. Although some suburban communities have certainly been elitist and exclusive, the suburban ideal has at its heart a democratic flavor. However, suburbs have been less successful at providing the connective tissue necessary to create communities of individual home owners. Yards, the private landscape, have succeeded in fulfilling household functions and desires, whereas streets and parks, the public landscape, have too often been ignored or devalued. Physical connections, spaces for mobility and passages of open spaces, provide the means for weaving a landscape together. These connections provide opportunities for persons to move through space. They also provide a social context within which people can explore, play, and engage in commerce or neighboring. Successful open spaces encourage people to use them, provide rich structured and unstructured opportunities, and give order to a community.

To create a suburban landscape supportive of individual fulfillment, community life, and environmental sustainability requires a broader, more comprehensive view of open space. The suburban yard is not just an autonomous private piece of property, but part of a larger community landscape structure. The suburban street is typically conceived exclusively as a conduit for movement and rarely as a community network. Similarly, suburban parks are neglected as places of repose, recreation, and contact with nature, perhaps because these needs are seen as being accommodated in each person's backyard. There is a paradox. Open space defines the suburbs, but the suburbs also have redefined open space. Suburban society is neither urban nor rural, and the suburbs are still in the throes of constructing their own identity. As a result, suburban open space has taken on distinctive patterns and forms. This landscape is still emerging; its mores are still in flux. As the suburbs now dominate much of the metropolitan landscape, they demand our attention.

In this book we define three open space types as a way of understanding suburban open space. These are broad, encompassing categories; their names are commonplace: yard, street, and park. Each of these types is inclusive, with much overlap between them. It is important to keep in mind that

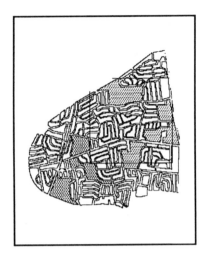

1940s
Post-war Planned
Subdivisions
Levittown, NY

Parks, schools, and shopping spread about the neighborhood

Continuous fabric of curvilinear streets—few sidewalks

Spacious yards

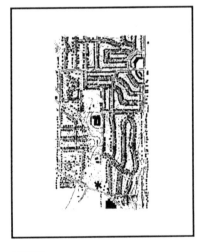

1950s
FHA Model Subdivisions
Vermont Hills, OR

Isolated parks, schools, shopping Occasional streams or lakesides reserved

Curvilinear streets or loops and culs-de-sac, often no curbs or sidewalks

Spacious, wide yards

when we discuss open space, the reference is not only to green spaces or to nature, but includes the entire outdoor continuum, spanning the domestic private space of the yard to the public landscapes of street and park. Streets should be considered at all scales, from cul-de-sac to highway and parks in their myriad varieties, from the neighborhood tot lot thorough the grander scope of greenway systems. We emphasize the opportunities created by spaces that are aggregates of these types, the linkages between them, and their hybrid forms. Thus, along the street front, yards coalesce into continuous semipublic yardscapes, whereas backyards are defined private fragments. Driveways join yard to street, and their hard surfaces offer distinctive possibilities. Parks conjoin into park systems and networks. In thinking about open space, it is imperative that this full range is encompassed. A richness of opportunity is a sign of suburban health, its lack a deficiency.

This study cuts across disciplines and genres. It offers a historical study, but one that seeks to learn and glean from past lessons. It is a cultural study sympathetic to suburban dwellers and aspirants. As landscape architects, we have tried to bring to bear the theory and practice of other disciplines, but to emphasize our area of expertise in open space design and planning. This is not a design casebook, but it partakes of that methodology. We speak in the language of planning and design, a style that integrates words and images. Merging graphics and text, we provide examples of the application of theory to practical work. There are project plans, diagrams, and maps that demonstrate the designer's intentions as well as interpretive diagrams emphasizing key ideas. A comparative series of drawings of houses and yards runs throughout the book. These examples provide a structure to compare disparate locations. Along with photographs, they also give a flavor of daily life, a sense of how places are used and lived in. As we have dealt with open space at multiple scales, so too the graphic material ranges from domestic detail to general theory. We hope that mixture adds depth to the discussion of these essential matters.

Throughout the text are case studies of places conceived in each decade since the 1920s. We begin in the nineteenth century and discuss the formative impact of early designs, but our focus is on the automobile suburb, for how to design in response to the automobile is surely one of the questions of the twentieth century for all forms of settlement. All too often design has been exclusively for the accommodation of the automobile, with little recognition of the automobile's (and the road's) effect on people, places, or resources. Our emphasis is on the planned suburban community, although there are lessons here for even the most modest subdivision and for communities of all sizes. Our analysis ranges from places where dozens dwell to areas for tens of thousands. We look at places in all regions of the nation. We explore those that have acted as positive models and those that have provided negative lessons. We look at the familiar and the ordinary, as well as places that are part of the canon of modern community design. We have tried to be observant, approaching old places with a fresh eye and new places with an eye to their improvement. Our intention is not to extol the superiority of the suburban way of life over the city or rural environment, nor to bemoan the opposite. Each type of settlement has rich possibilities. In a critical review of the strengths and weaknesses of a century of suburban planning, we argue for specific measures, particularly for effective open space planning, that will make the suburbs, both existing and new, deliver on their promise of providing the "best of both worlds." Well-conceived

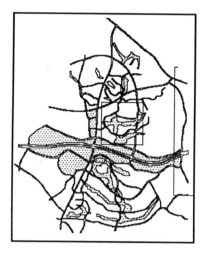

1960s
The New Towns
Reston, VA

Connected recreational networks

Loop and cul-de-sac streets

Multifamily housing with common space linked to networks

Private yards abutting recreational networks

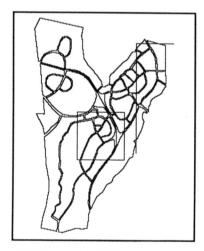

1970s and 1980s
Master Planned
Communities
Rancho Santa Margarita, CA

Themed recreational networks displaying a corporate image

Loop and cul-de-sac streets

Gated neighborhoods introduced

Fenced yards separated from common spaces

open space systems connecting yard to neighborhood to suburb to city can provide a network in the suburbs for socialization, recreation, education, and mobility. The struggle for those who design, build, finance, and legislate is to help suburbs reach their potential.

In Chapter 1 we begin with a discussion of the suburbs and suburban open space and try to sort out the complexities of language and history. Chapter 2 is a discussion and critique of common suburban open space types: yards, streets, and parks. Particular attention is paid to those aspects of the landscape that act as connectors, whether driveways or open space networks; to the aggregate collections of yards into yardscapes and streets into streetscapes; and to the neglected places. Many of America's best designers have responded to the suburban challenge. In Chapter 3 we proceed to examine three designs by some of America's greatest designers: Frederick Law Olmsted and Calvert Vaux's plan for Riverside, Illinois; Clarence Stein and Henry Wright's Radburn plan; and Frank Lloyd Wright's unrealized proposal of Broadacre City. Each offers valuable lessons in the creation of park and parkway systems, the relationships between houses, cars, parks and the rural landscape within the context of suburban design. Following this historical introduction we proceed in Chapter 4 to look at the first great wave of post-World War II suburbanization, the impact of the Federal Housing Administration on housing policy and design, and the development of Levittown, perhaps the archetypal suburb. Levittown's initial plan is considered, as well as how residents became the cobuilders of that community. Chapter 5 discusses a series of reactions to the excesses of suburbanization and a resurgence of community planning in the 1960s. During that decade "open space communities," planned communities that included commonly held open space, became popular. These were cluster subdivisions, planned unit developments (PUDs) and the New Towns of Reston, Virginia, and Columbia, Maryland. Throughout the book our focus is on a comprehensive look at the open space patterns and systems in these communities. Chapter 6 discusses the next generation of development trends, master-planned communities (MPCs). Developers of MPCs used the planning lessons of the New Towns era and, in an increasingly competitive market, blended sophisticated marketing strategy into the design process. We examine the full range of MPCs, from "technoburbs" such as Irvine, California, to the "ecoburbs" of Village Homes in Davis, California, and The Woodlands of Texas. Chapter 7 considers the designs of Miami architects Andres Duany and Elizabeth Plater-Zyberk, along with those of California architect Peter Calthorpe. The work of these designers, sometimes called neotraditional communities, represents the current condition of thoughtful suburban design development. These designers have consciously turned to the careful study of traditional communities and suburban designs of the past to learn valuable lessons. Having rediscovered Ebenezer Howard's brilliant insights into the suburban condition, they attempt to ameliorate the effects of unregulated suburban sprawl, to foster the sense of community that is often advertised but not always present, and to conserve scarce human and natural resources. We document and evaluate these new strategies. In the concluding chapter we examine the retrofitting of Bellevue, Washington, and how that community is both becoming more urban and simultaneously seeking to incorporate nature within its midst.

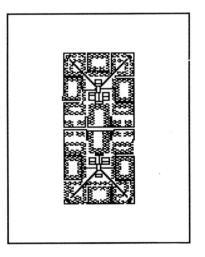

1990s
Traditional Neighborhoods and Pedestrian Pockets
Pedestrian Pockets

Public open space includes streets that connect centers and parks

Pedestrian-friendly streets directly connect civic spaces

Yards are small; front porches overlook streets

The suburbs of the late twentieth century have evolved from bedroom communities served by and serving a central city to minicities in their own right. Suburban planning strategies are responding to this fundamental change. The suburban middle ground, between city and country, was once at the periphery. It is now at the core of our concerns. The historical polarization between city and country, humans and nature, is outmoded. The suburb is part of the continuums of both urban life and nature. A comprehensive view is needed, one that looks at all scales of open space, from yard to street to park. The physical environment, our habitations and settlements, should aspire to enrich the human condition, providing opportunities for self-fulfillment, community life, and connection to the natural world.

NOTES

1. Robert Fishman, *Bourgeois Utopias: The Rise and Fall of Suburbia* (New York: Basic Books, 1987), p. 17.
2. Peter O. Muller, *Contemporary Suburban America* (Englewood Cliffs, NJ: Prentice-Hall, 1981).
3. Joel Garreau, *Edge City: Life on the New Frontier* (New York: Doubleday, 1991).
4. Garrett Hardin, "The Tragedy of the Commons," *Science* **162** (13 December 1968):1243–1248.
5. Anne Spirn, *The Granite Garden: Urban Nature and Human Design* (New York: Basic Books, 1984); Michael Hough, *City Form and Natural Processes: Toward a New Urban Vernacular* (New York: Routledge, 1984); and Ian McHarg, *Design with Nature* (New York: John Wiley & Sons, 1992).

1
SUBURB

The skyline is slowly shrinking in the rearview mirror. You have just passed the Tri-State Mall. Keep a watchful eye for the exit signs and try to remember the directions: Take a left, go under the highway, go right at the third traffic light, go two miles and turn in at the stone gate, just past the school (if you see silos on the left, you've gone too far), take the loop road to the right, look for the signs to the "Estates." We're number 36, the blue one with the window boxes. Just come around back—we'll be there. You all know the place; you've been there many times before. One hundred million of us live here and millions more aspire to residence. We are in the suburbs.

Suburban meaning and character are elusive. In the late fourteenth century *suburb* first appeared in the English language. The word referred to residential areas outside, but adjacent to, the bounds or wall of the city, occupying what was then a narrow band between city and countryside. The etymology describes a modification of an urban place; a concentration of humanity associated with civilization and culture. *Sub* referred to being up against, near, or beneath. *Sub*-urb was a locale less than urban, at the fringe and beneath the city in significance. The city occupied the center of a planetary system, with the suburbs dependent on the urban sun for their life-sustaining energy.

Part of our dilemma in dealing with the suburbs is the residue of this etymology. City and suburb are, and always have been, tied together in a mutual regional dependency, a set of economic and social relationships that extend far beyond the bounds of the suburbs into a resource hinterland.[1] Suburbs were subordinate as they emerged and remained so in much of North America until the 1970s, but this is no longer the case. The hierarchical relationship between city and suburb has also been one of geography, value, and function. The city is described as the center of culture, civilization, and commerce. It is the world of work and, historically, of men. The suburb is a residential appendage, as if a person's dwelling were a less significant aspect of human life. It is the realm of women and children. Suburbs have been ignored, devalued, and, when dealt with seriously, all too often approached with an apologetic tone—this despite the fact that for several generations millions of Americans have made these places their home, and a culture and way of life distinctive from that of the city or the countryside has developed within their borders.

CHARACTER AND APPEAL

Precise contemporary definitions of a suburb are difficult, for there are multiple components that characterize the modern American "automobile suburb." The suburbs were to be places distinct from the city and country, yet they have struggled with defining their own peculiar identity. Certain characteristics, however, are evident. Suburbs are situated in a peripheral location, at the urban edge. The aggregate collections of subdivisions (the typical forms for suburban expansion) create a sprawling pattern splayed across the landscape. They have lower population densities than older core areas, with residents dwelling predominantly in single-family, owner-occupied houses (this is true of many American urban areas as well). People journey to work as commuters, originally to central cities. However, commuting is now frequently between the suburban communities encircling the urban core. This contemporary pattern of settlement is a product of modern technology. Its origins were in the rail era, but it is now dependent on automobile transportation. Technological umbilicals—pipe, wire, and highway—transmit services, information, products, and waste to and from the home.

While remaining predominantly middle class (like the nation), suburbs are pluralistic, spanning all social classes, ethnicities, and races. However, these differences are not typical within individual suburban communities, which remain economically and racially homogeneous. The postwar American automobile suburb has been supported and developed by national government policy, which offered financial incentives and the material resources for suburban settlement patterns and highway building while ignoring the needs of inner cities.[2] These landscapes, although developed on lands that real estate developers see as virgin territory at the urban "frontier," are intrusions into predominantly rural areas and small towns. Modern locales are part of a longer historical scheme. They follow the ample precedent of the romantic nineteenth-century suburbs—street car and trolley suburbs, planned communities, and urban expansion by additions—along with the substantial ideological heritage that supports a suburban landscape. Suburbs began as residences of the elite, but since becoming available to the middle class, their appeal to Americans appears to be virtually universal.

Half of the nation now dwells in suburbs, but what do their locations—for instance, Mount Vernon (New York), Schaumberg (Illinois), Aurora (Colorado), and Woodbridge (California)—have in common? Suburbs are more than addresses. They represent in physical form the enactment of cultural ideals, embodying philosophies and images of what constitutes the good life.[3] In the marketplace they are the collective preferences of home buyers, who are purchasing both dwellings and a way of life. All suburbs lie along a spectrum between the worlds of city and country. Their occupying this broad middle ground complicates matters of definition. Each suburb, in its distinctive fashion, combines aspects of the city, its urbanity, convenience, and energies, with aspects of an idealized nature, its beauty, physical elements, and the psychological distance it affords from people and the world of human affairs and artifice. This nature is not wilderness, but the rural landscape of agricultural countryside, small town, and village life. At a deep level, suburbs combine the pastoral longing for an idealized past associated with the natural world, and a hoped-for future associated with the progressive, technological promise of the city. In American culture, suburbs constitute a "middle landscape," which mediates between a polarization of places and ideas.[4] In the American vernacular of place types, the suburbs are a place distant from, but accessible to, downtown, where "Main Street" meets "Four Corners."

While sharing common ingredients, each suburb manifests its uniqueness. Specific places gravitate toward the sharp intensity of either end of the city-country cultural spectrum, but most occupy a comfortable middle position. For each locale the reading of the suburban spectrograph will be distinctive, and one should be cautious about generalizations and oversimplifications. The roots of the suburban idea share much with the classical villa. In many ways, the villa is a suburb ideologically concentrated within a single property. The term *villa* referred to an entire estate—buildings and grounds—not just a single structure. So too *suburb* is an inclusive, not purely an architectural, term. Classical ideology emphasized the role of the farm and a domesticated landscape. In the eastern United States the model of the "gentleman farmer" is part of this heritage. In the American West, it is the ranch with its expansive territory, frontier ideology, and sprawling architecture—miniaturized and captured in the "ranch-style" home. Garden cities, greenbelt towns, PUDs, New Towns, and neotraditional communities all seek, in some variant, an ancient promise, the classical ideal of a golden mean, the best of both worlds, an equal opportunity for cultural connectedness and pastoral privacy. The cultural formulas are occasionally articulated, but the realities are enacted at all levels and in everyday events: the drive home, the walk to school, the trip to the store, the chance encounter with neighbors.

WELLINGTON.THE KIND OF NEIGHBORHOOD YOU THOUGHT DISAPPEARED A HUNDRED YEARS AGO.

Wellington, Manassas, Virginia.
Advertisement, The Washington Post, *8 July 1989. Wellington by Kettlet & Scott.*

Advertising reveals fundamental appeals. Motivated by a desire to sell products and services, advertising is an enticement, a commercial aphrodisiac, selling entire "project personalities" and lifestyles.[5] In real estate advertising the messages can be subliminal, but they are often a direct, even forthright, reflection of desires. (Advertisers also use code words and images for neighborhoods that are exclusive by race, religion, ethnicity, or social class.) Advertising confirms the polarities that form the basis of suburban appeal. Many communities claim to offer "Country living, close in"; Forest Heights in Portland, Oregon, is "Away from it all, 4 Miles to Town"; Wild Harbour Estates, North Falmouth, Massachusetts, is simply "A best of both worlds community"; and at Conashaugh Lakes, Pennsylvania "Your neighbors aren't neighbors—they're trees!" At the extreme, where communities are designed with themes, the boundaries are blurred between promotion and property, design and lifestyle. The tenor of the times is clear in communities where "nature is protected from man, and man is protected from man"; or in Reston, Virginia: "For times like these . . . designed to combine the best features of living in the city, country or suburbs and claiming to have in fact become much more."[6] Garden City pioneer Ebenezer Howard used the imagery of three magnets pulling upon "the people." "Where will they go?" he asked. The Town and Country magnets had positive and negative poles and a corresponding list of virtues and vices. The Town-Country magnet defied science and had only positive poles—it was a new artifact. Reminiscent of Howard's magnets of a century ago, Reston offers "the convenience of the city without the pollution or the noise. The tranquility of the country without the feeling of isolation. And the recreation of the suburbs without the unpleasant sprawl." The new town of Columbia, Maryland, lauded itself as "a city built to be enjoyed . . . not perfect, but a few steps

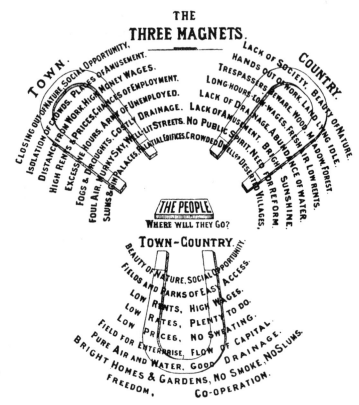

The Three Magnets. Garden City Diagram.
Ebenezer Howard, 1902. From F. J. Osborn,
ed., *Garden Cities of To-Morrow,*
Cambridge: MIT Press 1965, p. 46.

removed from the crush and bother of today's living. It's trees and parks and lush fields and beauty and just about everything you've always wanted your own city to be." The advertisements appeal to deep desires. Wellington, near Old Manassas, Virginia offers "a neighborhood like they used to make" just 30 minutes from Union Station, Washington D.C.. Here, "as the end of the century approaches," you are asked to "revisit the beginning of it," along its newly constructed Main Street. Fulfilling a nostalgic desire for a rewritten past, at The Woodlands near Houston, Texas, "you will feel peace and be reminded of the neighborhood you *might* [author's emphasis] have grown up in."

As Robert Wood noted 25 years ago, suburbanites may be re-creating and reconfiguring, not small cities, but small town and village life.[7] Too often we look to a suburb and are disappointed because we do not see a "city." Our images are conditioned by expectations. If, more modestly, we look for an updated town or village, or accept the suburb on its own terms,

Forest Heights, Portland, Oregon.
Advertisement, The Oregonian, 5 July 1992.

AWAY FROM IT ALL,

4 MILES TO TOWN.

Only Forest Heights is this close to town yet a Walden world of its own. One acre in three is being preserved in natural areas, hiking trails—and get-away places like Mill Pond park (shown). The best builders in town are crafting beautiful homes here. Or, choose a lot and have your own dream built. (Ask about direct financing on lots.

Very easy.) Forest Heights is the creative expansion of Portland's close-in west hills, the heights. Just possibly the best place to live <u>anywhere</u>. *Entry on NW Cornell Rd where NW Miller and Cornell meet. From town take west Burnside to Miller. Turn right. From Sunset Hwy or 217 take East Barnes Rd to Miller, turn left.*

FOREST ❀ HEIGHTS

Forest Heights Realty, Gary Locker, J.R. Figurski—297-1919

we may discover more. The marketers are well aware of this, even if critics are not. Thus, The Woodlands, was marketed as a "New Hometown"; the innovative ecoburb of Davis, California, is "Village Homes," and Fisher's Landing in Camas, Washington, is "A Town to Come Home To." Across the nation there are thousands of "Villages," "Towns," "Greens," "Woods," "Fields," and "Lands," but few mini-"Cities."[8]

Combining the best of both worlds is not the blending of a simple dichotomy, but has multiple meanings beyond the complex of categories associated with city and country. It also refers to the balancing of individualistic desire with community responsibility, their mutual obligations, and the satisfactions of both. As historian Joel Schwartz has noted, "The suburbanization of America has meant more than physical removal beyond the built up portions of the city; it has also included a pervasive yearning, often frustrated by an individualistic ethos, for some attachment to a covenanted community."[9] The move to the suburbs has been characterized as a flight from the city, but it was equally a passage to a promised land, not unlike the pioneer migrations of the nineteenth century. The conscious neglect of the inner city was the result of a long-held American ideological heritage of antiurbanism.[10] The city, with its density and difficulties, appeared dangerous, crime ridden, populated by persons seen as undesirable—the poor and the minorities—with inferior schools and inadequate services. The suburb lured people with the promise of being a place without these problems, offering a better place for their children, safety and security, and the simplicities of a more homogenous community.[11] It also enticed them by appealing to the American cultural habit of equating personal progress with moving, whereby physical mobility equals social mobility.

Contemporary technology, especially the automobile, enabled these desires to become actuality. Developers showcased homes, models equipped with all the latest technology. The dreams of a World's Fair exhibit could be yours in "all-electric kitchens" and homes where modern machines would do all the work smoothly, sleekly, and effortlessly. Prospective buyers were welcomed guests into the domestic worlds of model homes complete with the furnishings, decor, and landscaping of an aspired-to way of life. The postwar suburb coupled the promise of modernity and technological facility with the national cure-all, the elixir of nature—truly "a machine in a garden." All of this could be had within the privacy of one's own house and yard.

In Barry Levinson's autobiographical film saga, *Avalon,* his extended family makes the suburban exodus from Baltimore's row houses in the 1950s. "What does it mean, the suburbs?" a young Mike asks his mother. "It's just a nicer place to live," she replies. "Yes, nicer. Its got lawn and big trees." A skeptical Mike queries his aunt, "Is this a good thing that's happening? Is this a good thing, going to the suburbs? Am I going to like it there?" Later in the film, nature shows a side of the suburbs rarely noted in the omnipresent green of the large yards. Attacked and stung by a swarm of bees lurking beneath the house, Mike declares, "I hate the suburbs." However, the adults, his father and uncle, as their business expands, toast their intertwined social and physical mobility. If we don't make it, they say, "We're out of the suburbs and back in the row houses."[12]

"Suburbia" has an iconic quality, with instant images and stereotypes: lines of identical houses, curving streets, backyard swing sets, kids biking down the street, smiling faces of white families eating on outdoor patios. A Little League game might appear in this picture, a minivan trip to the market, a wife waiting at the train station to chauffeur her commuting husband. Domestic life predominates, and work takes place somewhere else. In the image there is an overriding sense of facade, a picture of a pleasant way of life, yet with something lurking beneath the surface or in the distance, a gloss over difficulties and dissatisfactions. The image lags behind the reality, and only in recent years has it incorporated the actualities of shopping mall commerce, roadside enterprises, and office parks. Yet the stereotype lingers.

The portrait of the bedroom community or commuter suburb, especially prevalent in the 1950s, concentrated on limited factors and did little justice to the full range of suburban life. It was also insidious, for it allowed the house and the community to be defined as the exclusive domicile of the male "breadwinner" while virtually ignoring the lives of women and children at home, at school, and working in the suburb. It relegated daytime inhabitants of suburbia to a secondary position, those left behind, while the "important" work was pursued elsewhere. Some described suburbs as "ruled" by women, a place with absentee fathers, where the desires and demands of children were the guiding aspect.[13] The picture was more complex. There was no consideration for families and residents who did not fit into the proscribed mold of restrictive domesticity. Limitations on mobility, lack of proximity to services, and insufficient community services added to the burdens of single parents, children, and the elderly. The privatized suburban world made no provision for cooperative endeavors in child care or a liberation from household labors.[14]

Statistically, the average American is now a suburbanite, and even rural and urban dwellers partake of suburban lifestyles. (Perhaps owing to the dilemmas of definition, the census does not refer to suburbs. The closest statistics are for the "urban fringe," areas inside an urbanized area, yet outside the central city.) *Suburban* originally referred to a place *and* a person. People become suburbanites and places become suburbanized. Often the suburban areas were associated with inferior habits or characteristics, in contrast to the city. The multiple, encompassing, and adaptable meanings of suburban terminology are not absolute. For example, for many urban Easterners, western cities seem "suburban" in character. Building types that originated in suburbia—franchise restaurants, condominiums, and enclosed shopping malls—have now infiltrated downtowns. More apartment houses are now built in suburbs than in central cities, which have declining densities and abandoned lands. New thinking is called for.

Suburbia has become a national landscape type. Geographer D. W. Meinig has written that there are three symbolic landscapes that constitute the geography of places that unite the nation. They signify not only locations, but a constellation of values. First is the New England village as an ideal of community and traditional values. Second, Main Street exemplifies the entrepreneurial spirit, middle America, and the virtues of small-town life. Third is suburbia, particularly that of Southern California, made possible by the automobile and founded on a new lifestyle of informal leisure.[15] Significantly, some modern suburbs have attempted to appropriate the traditional village and Main Street small-town ideals and to subsume both into their symbolic programs. Thus the lines between these complex cultural symbols are blurred, in what may be a sign of the maturation and increased sophistication of suburban design.

Historian Kenneth Jackson, author of *Crabgrass Frontier: The Suburbanization of the United States,* notes that "suburbia has become the quintessential physical achievement of the United States. . . . Suburbia symbolizes

People are still heading for the suburbs to fulfill their dreams, but no longer are they dreaming of a private house.

Today people would rather spread up than out. They'd rather get above it all and make their home in an apartment.

These are people who think being tied down to a house with all its headaches is crazy. They think that having more than one child in a family is too big a family. And they believe the right time to get married is after you've had enough time to discover yourself.

And because these people have completely different values and life styles than people who own houses—they have more time and money to spend as they choose.

We write the only regularly published national magazine specially designed for apartment people.

Our name is Apartment Life and our February/March issue will deliver 500,000 copies to the fastest growing segment of the home market—the apartment market.

And by chance, if you don't know that much about us, we're published bi-monthly and our parent company is the Meredith Corporation.

So if you want to talk to people who live in apartments, you should talk to us.

We're in on the ground floor.

The suburbs are spreading up.

Apartment Life
The magazine for 20 million Americans.

Apartment Life, 750 3rd Ave., New York, N.Y. 10017

Issue on sale

"The Suburbs Are Spreading Up"
advertisement for *Apartment Life*,
November 1974, in *New York Magazine*.

the fullest, most unadulterated embodiment of contemporary culture; it is a manifestation of such fundamental characteristics of American society as conspicuous consumption, a reliance upon the private automobile, upward mobility, the separation of family into nuclear units, the widening division between work and leisure, and a tendency towards racial and economic exclusiveness."[16] Although undoubtedly true, these largely negative attributes ignore other critical aspects of American culture embodied in suburbia, to which Jackson gives less attention. There is a continuing need to find a mediating position between individualistic desire and the efforts of building community. There is the struggle to find a place in Daniel Boorstin's "Everywhere Community," the desire to feel at home everywhere, perhaps essential in a large, mobile, pluralistic society such as ours.[17] There is the traditional adaptability of the wood frame house and its accompanying lot to individualization. There are the virtues of personal freedoms, the pleasures of privacy, and the satisfactions and achievement of upward social mobility. Individuals personalized their dreams into visions of home—dream houses. A 1980s real estate advertisement said, "The American Dream is very simple. A better house and a new car." At first glance this appears simplistic and even insulting, yet it touches basic chords. The desire for change, the promise of the future, is present in the optimistic "better" and the desire for the "new." The pairing of house and car appeal to American individualism and the quest for private happiness (with the implication that the house is part of a community). The car appeals to the desire for mobility and change, a compulsion to get up and go—if it does not work out, move on.

The image of suburbia is still subject to a 40-year-old stereotype. Certainly, there are aspects of suburbia that fit these attributes, but the suburbs have also changed, many would say "matured," beyond an adolescent period into a developing communal adulthood, exploring their identities, dealing with their complexities. A comparison of the original raw, denuded construction sites with the tree-shaded landscape of a generation later is symbolic of this shift. The geographical and political boundaries have been blurred, and the identities of city and suburb are ill defined. Suburbs become cities and cities are suburbanized. Suburbs are no longer relegated to a secondary, subordinate, satellite status, but are entities which, at least at the prosaic level of daily activity, strive for a degree of self-sufficiency. These are Robert Fishman's "Technoburbs," constituting a decentralized city made possible by contemporary technology, an area where there is urban diversity without urban concentrations.[18] They are now "Edge Cities," reporter Joel Garreau's term for these dramatic peripheral agglomerations, symbolized by the surprising eruption of skylines at freeway interchanges.[19]

As suburbia matures, it is being reconceived and reconfigured. In this process, ideas, inspiration, and models are sought by those who plan, design, and build communities. They are all looking to the lessons of the suburban past with a new-found interest in its, until recently, neglected history. Urban neighborhoods, small towns, and village life are all scrutinized, with the goal of finding the right proportions, the balanced equation, in creating the right mixture between city and country. The first generation of postwar suburbanites emphasized the country side of the equation. Many were antiurban escapists, refugees from the city pulled by the magnetic attraction of home ownership, private lots, green grass, and a vision of family and community life. Herbert Gans's pioneering study, *The Levittowners,* of late 1950s suburbanization found that people moved to Levittown for "the good or comfort-

July 20, 1946 THE Price 15 cents

NEW YORKER

"Dream Houses,"
The New Yorker, (cover), 20 July 1946.

able life for themselves and their families, and the anticipated peacefulness of outdoor living, but mainly they came for a house and not a social environment."[20] Studies such as Gans's suggest that people had few illusions about suburban life as idyllic.

Postwar suburbs generally pleased their residents but displeased the planners. There was an extreme divergence of popular, professional, and intellectual opinion. Critics maligned, while the building industry played the role of booster. Fortunately, in recent years we have gone beyond simple polarities and irrational critiques to examine the suburbs in their full complexity, as both an emergent settlement pattern and as a distinctive way of life. Suburban development often destroyed the landscape that attracted early residents. Belated attention is now directed toward preserving the remnants and in reasserting the role of nature in these most domesticated of landscapes. The pendulum has also now swung in the opposite direction with a new-found attention to the city side, a desire for community connections, and a resurgence of awareness of the significance of public life—ranging from the modest scale of the sidewalk to new civic centers.

SUBURBAN OPEN SPACE

Beyond the bounds of design offices and planning agencies, people do not refer to *open space*. In the vernacular, a simpler word provides its fundamental definition and characteristics. "Where are you going?" "Outside" is the common reply. The out-of-doors, the world outside, is all open space. What is *suburban* open space? There is no simple or commonly accepted definition. Open space is often falsely equated, by landscape architects, planners, architects, and urban designers, with parks and natural landscapes, excluding the equally important spaces of the street and private yard. The question of the distinctive form, character, and function of suburban open space has been given little attention. Perhaps this is because we commonly understand suburbs to be houses in large open spaces. Suburbs are seen as almost all open space—yards, lawns, gardens—as home in a park or garden. Open space is one of the distinctive characteristics of the suburbs, and it also takes on distinguishing *suburban* qualities, experiences, and forms.

Open space is a broad and nebulous concept. It encompasses ideas of the out-of-doors, public access and activity, and the relationship between nature and community. Traditional definitions of designed open space emphasized the role of the public park and park systems. Contemporary open space concepts, much like the modern suburb, find their origins in the nineteenth century. The park movement advocated the creation of green spaces within the city for the physical and mental health of residents and as a compensation for the loss of nature. Parks were democratic places for organized and spontaneous activity. Open space ideology is still indebted to this early formulation, but open space more accurately encompasses all environments. A better definition includes all aspects of the public and private landscape, including streets, sidewalks, yards, and driveways, as well as vacant and natural lands. Suburban open space ranges from the proximate space of home to encompass all outdoor spaces of public concern. These may include places rarely frequented, but part of community identity and character.[21] Stream corridors, wetlands, the distant view of forested ridge lines, or reclaimed railroad corridors can be essential elements in the suburban landscape in maintaining a healthy environment and structuring the physical form and pattern of communities. Toronto landscape architect Michael Hough has promoted the protection of such "borrowed" landscapes, those places that are significant visually and conceptually, even if not a part of the public realm, which help to define a city's form and clarify its natural setting. As much as parks and other intentionally designed landscapes, these landscapes contribute to determining the scale, pace, and satisfactions of community life at all levels.

Open space implies places that are readily available, places to which entry is not restricted. Access, accessibility, and alternative opportunities are critical. Thus, one must look at the location of open spaces to see how, and whether, access is facilitated and encouraged, to examine how "open," or exclusive, any place may be. Access is a social and a pragmatic matter. How do you know of places, how do you get there, how do you move between places? What are the kinds and extent of circulation patterns? How are they organized into formal and informal networks and patterns? Streets are an essential aspect of open space design as places for walking, stopping, talking, play, work, driving, and parking. Proponents of "streets for people" argue for a more equitable design of residential streets, with cars forced to slow down and greater priority given to pedestrian activity.

Planners have yet another twist on open space. In many jurisdictions, the open space element of a general plan will include only natural resources such as creeks, rivers, wetlands, forests, and ridges. Agricultural, forest, and mining lands are also often considered open space because of their nonurban character. Parks and trails may be included as part of the open space fabric, but not necessarily a pivotal part. For example, on Sacramento County's Composite Open Space Resource Map (December 9, 1992), intended to be a holistic view of the county's open space resources, parks are excluded, yet mining resource areas are included. In many jurisdictions, park planning and maintenance are handled by one agency, while natural resource protection is performed by others, leading to a lack of coordination and, sometimes, competition for control over specific sites. Limiting the definition of open space to only natural areas can leave it with the unworthy status of a "formless green residue that is left over when building, parking and setback requirements have been satisfied."[22] "Edge cities," characterized by a complex matrix of property boundaries and governmental jurisdictions, compound the difficulty of defining or categorizing open space. Schools, parks, utility districts, and home owners associations all have jurisdiction over some slice of regional open space. County planning departments have the role of coordinating their activities via general plans and approvals processes, but rarely the funding to do an effective job. Unlike city parks, trails, plazas, and streets, open spaces in suburbs are often semipublic. Greenways, parks, golf courses, trails, tot lots, pools, even streets and plazas, are often owned by corporations or home owners associations. To understand the fabric of open space in the edge cities, it is essential to look at the relationships between a variety of spaces. These range from the very private realm of people's yards to semiprivate spaces, members-only spaces, pay-as-you-go spaces such as malls, and commercial plazas, restaurants, and theme parks, as well as the true public spaces—public parks owned and managed by government. There are tremendous political complexities in the edge cities; however, much of their residential fabric is made up of planned communities with extensive open space reserves. They have the potential to reclaim the natural systems that once kept their landscape healthy.

Design of suburban open spaces can facilitate or inhibit personal and social activities, and symbolically validate or deny meaning to places and experience. They can be designed to contribute to the diversity, interdependence, democracy, and health of a region. They provide alternative forms of stimulation, activity, and challenge.[23] Open spaces can be the spearheads of metropolitan planning—where the natural landscape structure is a primary organizing element of community design.[24]

NOTES

1. William Cronin, *Nature's Metropolis: Chicago and the Great West* (New York: W. W. Norton, 1991).

2. Kenneth Jackson, *Crabgrass Frontier: The Suburbanization of the United States* (New York: Oxford University Press, 1985).

3. Yi-Fu Tuan, *The Good Life* (Madison, WI: University of Wisconsin Press, 1986).

4. Leo Marx, *The Machine in the Garden: Technology and the Pastoral Ideal in America* (New York: Oxford University Press, 1964); and Peter Rowe, *Making a Middle Landscape* (Cambridge, MA: The MIT Press, 1991).

5. "Entice 'Em with Advertising," *Professional Builder* **39,** No. 3 (March 1974):102–107.

6. Reston, Virginia, advertisement c. 1980.

7. Robert Wood, *Suburbia: Its People and Their Politics* (Boston: Houghton Mifflin, 1958).

8. Anne Dingus, "Anyplace but Texas," *Texas Monthly* **21** (August 1983):144–148.

9. Joel Schwartz, "The Evolution of the Suburbs," in Philip Dolce, ed., *Suburbia: The American Dream and Dilemma* (Garden City, NY: Anchor Books, 1976), p. 3.

10. Morton and Lucia White, *The Intellectual Versus the City: From Thomas Jefferson to Frank Lloyd Wright* (Cambridge, MA: Harvard University Press, 1962).

11. Margaret S. Marsh and Samuel Kaplan, "The Lure of the Suburbs," in Philip Dolce, ed., *Suburbia: The American Dream and Dilemma* (Garden City, NY: Anchor Books, 1976), p. 39.

12. Barry Levinson, director, *Avalon* (Tri-Star Pictures, 1990).

13. Robert C. Wood, *Suburbia: Its People and Their Politics,* p. 7.

14. Dolores Hayden, *Redesigning the American Dream* (New York: W. W. Norton, 1984), p. 13.

15. D. W. Meinig, "Symbolic Landscapes: Models of American Community," in D. W. Meinig, ed., *The Interpretation of Ordinary Landscapes* (New York: Oxford, 1979), pp. 164–194.

16. Jackson, *Crabgrass Frontier,* p. 4.

17. Daniel Boorstin, *The Americans: The Democratic Experience* (New York: Random House, 1973), p. 1, p. 307.

18. Robert Fishman, *Bourgeois Utopias: The Rise and Fall of Suburbia* (New York: Basic Books, 1987), p. 17.

19. Joel Garreau, *Edge City: Life on the New Frontier* (New York: Doubleday, 1991).

20. Herbert Gans, *The Levittowners: The Ways of Life and Politics in a New Suburban Community* (New York: Pantheon Books, 1967), p. 34.

21. Kevin Lynch, *Managing the Sense of the Region* (Cambridge, MA: MIT Press, 1976).

22. Daniel Solomon, *ReBuilding* (New York: Princeton Architectural Press, 1992), p. 52.

23. Ibid.

24. August Heckscher, *Open Spaces: The Life of American Cities* (New York: Harper & Row, 1977).

2
MEANINGS
Yard, Street, Park

At the core of the suburb is the residence, the ideal of the single-family house on its own, individual, private lot. The house sits at the center of the property facing, yet set back from, the street. The driveway links street to house, passing through a front yard of green lawn and ornamental plantings. To the rear lies the backyard, often fenced, replete with patio or deck, outdoor furnishings, recreational equipment, and vegetable garden. Collectively, suburbia is the multiplication of this basic module, landscape building blocks strung together along winding streets. Even in higher-density and clustered-housing suburbs, attempts are made to retain the fundamental individualized unit of house and garden.

Murrayhill, Beaverton, Oregon.
C. Girling.

Suburban open space types can be categorized by the configurations of the three basic environments of yard, the private area of each household; street; and park, the collective open space environment. These are broad categories with many subsets and combinations. Their patterns of use and meaning are complex and open-ended, subject to personal, regional, and cultural variation. In addition to these three types we look at aggregates of the types, linkages and connections, and hybrids. Specifically, semi-public front yards coalesce into collective yardscapes, whereas backyards typically retain their individuality. Driveways, linking house to street, constitute a largely unexamined open space. Parks can be orchestrated into park systems, and there are greenway connections as well. Hybrid types of these elements also exist. Some spaces cannot easily be categorized, and we do not even have a vocabulary for them. All of these components are part of open space systems.

Suburban spaces are each given some measure of *suburban* distinction according to how they occupy the middle landscape and how their position straddles the city-country, human-nature polarity. On one side of the equation there is an association with nature. The character of this world is soft, green, and vegetated. On the other side are the hard surfaces of the city and artifice. Materials, sensations, and associations all combine to create distinctive combinations and types of yards, streets, and parks. These types each have a symbolic meaning and an ideological function, but they are experienced at a more personal level as the setting for each individual's environmental autobiography.[1]

House and neighborhood.
Environmental autobiography by Sara Geddes. Collection of Kenneth Helphand.

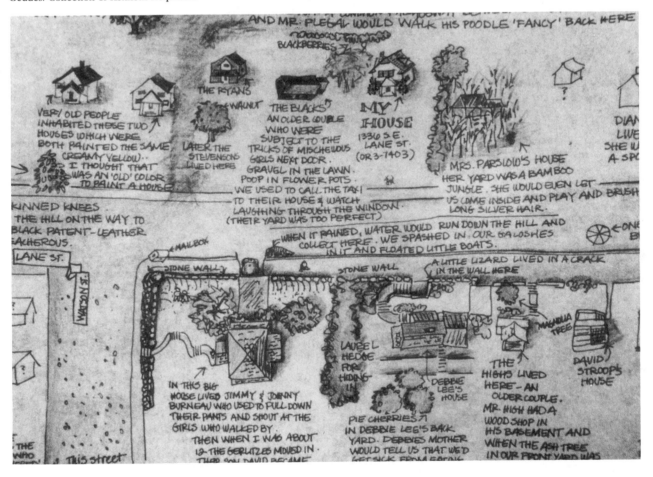

YARD

The garden joined with a house forms a fundamental building block of settled society. In suburbia they are an inseparable pair. At this intimate scale the personal and daily relationship to landscape is defined. It is here that the overwhelming quantity of open-space time is spent. It is also here, where building and outdoors meet, that the professional domains of landscape architecture and architecture overlap. In the European tradition *garden* refers to the whole of the private space around a house, whether it is a modest cottage or a grand estate. In America this land is typically called the yard.

Landscape historian Paul Groth has charted the distinctive meanings of the lot, yard, and garden. The lot is demarcated real estate, the yard an enclosed area for a specific function, and the "garden implies care, commitment and watching as well as enjoyment." The three terms "constitute a hierarchy of care."[2] Groth makes the case that Americans own lots, within which they create yards, which they then in turn adorn with "gardens." Together, the American yard and garden manifest personal care and commitment, albeit not always of a horticultural variety.

Gardens are idealized landscapes, places mediating between the imperatives of nature and culture. Gardens are frames, settings for activity and behavior. They are mirrors, reflections of a culture's values and attitudes. They are places of ideals, aspiration, and life's necessities. The most profound garden idea is that of paradise. Even in the seemingly prosaic suburban yard/garden, Edenic characteristics are present: peacefulness, innocence, an idealized nature, a place where the world is both useful *and* good to look at. The house is a symbol of self, household, and family identity; so too are our yards.[3] The home ground represents desires, ideals, and aspirations.

"Watering" Phillips Ranch, California.
Joe Deal, *Southern California Photographs 1976–1986,* Albuquerque, University of New Mexico Press, 1992.

The word *garden* itself is both a noun and a verb. People respond both to the place and to the process of gardening. We have an affection for the results of labor in our own garden, but for those of others we admire the care, craft, and devotion. In the suburban context there is emphasis on the verb *to garden*. Professional designers make their mark in some, but for the overwhelming proportion of suburban households the garden is the product of amateur design, aided by a nursery and home improvement industry that is quick with advice and assistance. Caring for the yard, particularly the front yard, is often a weekend ritual that takes on community proportions. Half of all American households have vegetable gardens, and nearly everyone does "yard work." Often the division of labor is by gender, reflecting an age-old division between field and garden work.[4] Men do "yard work," mowing lawns and taking pride in their green textured smoothness and weed-free appearance. (In 1990 Americans bought 6.8 million new lawn mowers).[5] They plant and prune trees, rake leaves and shovel snow. Women "garden," with responsibility for vegetable and flower gardens. Both take pride in the products of their landscaping labors, yet not everyone finds pleasure in these practices. Children are pressed into service raking leaves, shoveling snow, mowing and watering the lawn. In the process they are acculturated into suburban landscape mores. The lines between maintenance and play can become indistinct—running through a sprinkler in the summertime and jumping in a pile of leaves are beloved activities in many an American childhood. Each garden offers the benefits and virtues of a personal spectatorship, allowing its owner to watch the home ground go through its daily, seasonal, and annual changes. Many of these transitions are marked by personal memories: we remember when we planted the dogwood, when we buried the bird over there, or when a childhood tree house, now in ruins, was built. Often people are hired to care for the lawn, while other parts of the garden are tended by the owners. Garden work can become tedium, and surely many gardeners are only conforming to community norms. In condominium developments, responsibility for landscape maintenance and design is typically abdicated to an ownership association. Interestingly, in many of these developments garden plots are then set aside for individuals to tend. Lawn care is big business. Turf grass is a $25 billion dollar industry, and lawn care more than $6 billion dollars.[6]

The house and garden represent an investment, both economic and emotional. A house is often sold as a consumer package that comes complete with the latest appliances and "extras," aspired to much like the accompanying suburban automobile. Although the house itself is primary, the package includes the site, the street, and the neighborhood.[7] Trees may be preserved as a selling point, and the lawn seeded or sodded. Unfortunately, more often, to facilitate construction wooded sites are denuded and new trees planted. It is common practice to leave the lot as a blank slate, awaiting the imprint and personalized touches of the owners. Model homes are professionally designed to demonstrate to new home owners how to landscape within the quality and theme of the project. As Claire Cooper Marcus notes in her study of Bay-Area model homes, nature is evoked as a selling point and framed in window vistas, but kept at a distance.[8] Upscale developments market a more pristine nature, but one replete with security and recreational facilities; for lower-priced projects, the single-family home on its independent lot is sufficient enticement.

The conventions of rural farm dwellings persist in suburban landscapes. Farms have historically had three yards. Fronting the road was a ceremonial

"It's Not a Home till it's Planted." From *How to Landscape the Home Grounds,* The Storrs & Harrison Co., 1928, p. 7.

front yard, which led to the porch, front door, and interior parlor. To the side or rear was a workaday dooryard for kitchen and household labor, and farthest from the road stood the barnyard, for animals and equipment.[9] The front remains as the showpiece, seen by the public; the side yard is used for storage, utilities and circulation, and the rear yard is the site for family activity, pets, and vegetable garden. The front yard is like a formal family portrait for which everyone dresses up and shows off, whereas the backyard has the casual demeanor of a snapshot. In addition to shelter and the satisfactions of home life, the yard signifies identity, status, and the pride of ownership. The yard is not just territory, but a means to personalize one's environment *and* to signify participation in the community. In the United States, yards are ideal vehicles for acting out our cultural dialectic between a powerful individualism and an equally strong desire for community. The contrast between the stability of property boundaries, trees, and lawn, and the mutability of smaller-scale plantings, garden furnishings, and ornamentation make our yards an ideal physical forum for this cultural conversation. "Right in your own backyard" implies that fulfillment may be found right before your eyes, that the comforts of home represent the goal of a quest. The front and rear yards, the twin faces of the suburban lot, represent two aspects of the same personality; the public image and the private self. Like the facade, the "face" of the house, the front yard too presents a face to the community. The front yard separates the house from the public thoroughfare of the street, declaring its independence and privatizing the house through distance. It symbolizes proprietorship, a space over which one is lord and master, as well as domesticity, the frame for an idealized familial existence.

The front yard is often characterized as primarily ornamental, the outer skin of the building clothed first by a layer of foundation plantings. Advertising of the 1920s exhorted, "It's not a home till it's planted."[10] In 1927 Massachusetts landscape architect Frank Waugh wrote in *Foundation Planting* that the "ideal American home means a single house for each family, with a little plot of ground about it, said plot of ground to include a front yard between the house and the street with some sort of garden behind the house." He promoted planting as a patriotic duty and noted that in the "Old Country" it was hedges along the street front that gave homes their individuality and that in America these plantings were "pushed back against the foundations of the house." It was an insightful observation, for those same hedges divided the public world from the private one, which in the American suburban home occurs at the front door, not at the street gate.[11] Waugh thought foundation planting to be the most important branch of landscape architecture. Its function was to screen the undesirable and objectionable while dressing up the place, making a cozy and homelike appearance. The effect was much like a gilded picture frame. Peter J. van Melle, in the same book, noted, "This mode of planting implies visibility of the house from the street. It makes for 'open lawns,' which have come to characterize our suburban streets and give them a feeling of spaciousness." He calls this style "a distinctly American school of suburban planting." For most American suburbs, it is still the dominant mode.[12] William Dobriner has spoken of the "visibility principle" as a distinguishing suburban characteristic, whereby the visual openness allows residents to "observe each other's behavior and general life style far more easily than the central city dweller."[13] The suburban landscape *is* typically more open: you can see who is having a party, has bought a new car, or maintains their property. Here the suburbs share a kinship with small-town life.

In the prototypical suburb, beyond foundation plantings lies a layer of lawn, then a line of street trees. The pattern is mirrored across the street. This area is carefully maintained: the walks are edged, plants are pruned, weeds pulled, and everything kept in its proper place. The setting is a miniaturized pastoral. The style is derived from the English landscape garden, which itself had its roots in classical ideals. In the Virgilian picture one sits beneath a grove looking out across a grazed meadow. This is the *locus ameonus,* a beautiful or pleasant spot. The suburban house occupies this same idealized position, set beneath trees with a view to an expanse of finely mown grass. From within, picture windows frame the vista. Until air-conditioning provided interior comfort, television offered home entertainment, and the automobile promised escape, the front porch functioned as outdoor parlor and viewing platform of this prospect.[14] Technology has since facilitated a more privatized household existence. The modest resurrection of porches in new developments represents a desire for a return to a richer community life. However, this may be largely a symbolic gesture, for the countervailing tendencies are strong.

The side yard is a transition space and buffer zone often functioning as a service area, circulation route, and territorial barrier. It sometimes includes remnants from the rural "dooryard." Now it is a place for garbage cans, tanks for oil or gas, air-conditioning units, heat pumps, and storage of bicycles, wood, building materials, recreational equipment, and household ephemera.

The backyard presents a different, more diverse appearance, a scene that is on view only to the household, guests, and sometimes the immediate neighbors. In the past half-century the multipurpose character of the backyard has changed. What once was a working residential landscape is now largely recreational. The backyard was once the primary site for outdoor housework, where clothes dried on lines and, when weather permitted or kitchen heat demanded, food was prepared. Remnants of the barnyard might persist: chicken coops, vegetable gardens, and, at the far end of the yard, the

House and porch. Santa Clara, Oregon, 1993.
Kenneth Helphand.

outhouse. Throughout it all, children played. Most of these activities have since been relocated, as technology has brought them inside or changing community norms have made them illegal.

The backyard is the household world. Yards change their function and pattern as they mirror the cycles of family life. Lot lines and the security of fences, along with parental gaze, define the boundaries and the limits of activity for young children, the primary backyard users. Here they explore and play in a world equipped for their enjoyment, complete with sandboxes, swing sets, inflatable pools, and playhouses. If adequate space and an even modestly rich palette of natural materials are available, this can be a plastic world in which to create tree houses, forts, castles, and imaginary realms. For children, being allowed to play unsupervised in the yard, and then being permitted outside the yard, is a rite of passage as their territorial range expands. When swing sets rust or rot and sandboxes become overgrown, it is a sign that the young family yard has aged into adolescence.

For adults, the backyard is an extension of the kitchen and the family room. The design of the garden as an outdoor room is not exclusively a spatial concept. Outdoor rooms are furnished, even decorated. Several generations ago the front porch was abandoned (most were enclosed) and in its place, in a move to the rear, a patio or deck was built adjacent to the house. The contemporary indoor recreation or family room, with its entertainment wall of television, sound systems, and video recorders, has an outdoor counterpart in the mature family yard complete with barbecue grill, tables,

A family yard, Eugene, Oregon.
C. Girling.

chairs, umbrella, pool, Jacuzzi, and hot tub. Outdoors, like indoors, has become a place for relaxation and a display of conspicuous consumption. Backyards can become "overequipped" with adult toys, each lot attempting to be an inclusive recreational domain offering the opportunities previously found only in community spaces. The consequences of this trend are significant. If a private swing, sandbox, or pool is available, there is less desire and little need to frequent a public open space. For more than a century the American yard has defined "a self-contained unit, a private wonderland walled off from the rest of the world."[15]

Yards also have other inhabitants. They are home to wildlife—birds and small mammals. At urban fringes residents find themselves in a zone where their yards may provide nourishment for deer or coyotes. There are also pets. The numbers are staggering; more than half of all American households have a dog, a cat, or both.[16] Free-ranging cats sit astride fences, languish in the grass, or curl up on doormats. In most communities dogs are not permitted to run free. Millions of yards have dog houses and are fenced to keep the dogs in. The dogs' barks signal the approach of strangers as they mark and defend their territory.

Although sharing some common characteristics, suburban residential yards vary by social class and income. With increased affluence, privatization increases, lots are larger—with boundaries carefully demarcated and "hardened"—and security is increased. The yard becomes more specialized, less multipurpose, as zones are defined for single uses. Thus work, play, circulation, and storage are each given its place. The yard as a workplace for agriculture, automobile, or household disappears in favor of the ornamental and the recreational. The scale of areas and facilities expands to accommodate a swimming pool or tennis court. A makeshift character gives way to a consciousness and pretension in design. Some elite and exclusive communities even forbid individuals from working on their cars at certain times, or forbid play or the storage of goods or vehicles in driveways. At a certain level, professional assistance becomes essential. In many neighborhoods

RESIDENTIAL YARD TYPOLOGY

Social Class	Planting	Work	Household Activity	Social Activity	Symbols, Artifacts	Car	Boundary
Lower Income Lot Multi-purpose areas	• Subsistence • Farming • Farmyard • Utilitarian	• Landscape as a work place • Agricultural work • Automotive work	• Functional • Outdoor housework, e.g., clothes drying	• Informal, unstructured activity • Play all over • Makeshift equipment • Inflatable pool • Dropping in	• Unconscious, not "designed" • Vernacular expression • "Designed" by individual	• Ubiquitous • Worked on, yard as supply area • Designated area • carport, driveway	• Functional fencing • Chain link • > visibility
Middle Income Suburban Lot Developments Designated areas	• Backyard vegetable garden • Front yard public garden	• "Home" work not essential • "Work" as recreation • Household work inside • Do-it-yourself • Hobbies	• Indoor housework • Garden "work"	• Play areas structured • Purchased play equipment "sets" • Outdoor furniture/party equipment • Above-ground pool	• Conscious symbolism • Status symbols • User designed • No gardener, cut your own grass	• 1-car garage • Multi-purpose driveway • 2-car garage, electric garage-door opener • Single-purpose driveway	• Wooden fences • Hedges
Upper Income Single-purpose areas Estate	• Specialized gardens (flower gardens, rose gardens) • Gardener's aesthetic • Greenhouse • Gentleman farmer • "Hobby farm"	• Little work by owner • Garden staff	• Visual predominates • Supervision of others	• Formal, structured activity • Segregated "courts," "fields" • Pools • Garden buildings • Invitations	• Professional design • Professional maintenance • Gardener	• 3-car garage • Heated garage • Garage building • Entry drive • Chauffeur	• Security system • House hidden from street • < visibility

Residential yards: social class and function.
Kenneth Helphand.

teams of trucks descend on the scene during the day. Gardeners unload their equipment, pools are cleaned and monitored, and cleaning persons attend to their various tasks.

The yard provides a sense of proprietorship and ownership, as seen through the window or in surveying the bounds of one's modest estate in a walk around the house. The yard affords some measure of psychological security and a sense of privacy from both intrusion and observation. From the house, access to the yard is through front, rear, side, and garage doors. The front is the ceremonial entry and is often used only for formal guests, whereas residents typically use a kitchen or side door. These entryways become repositories for toys, tools, bicycles, clothes, shoes, boots, recycl-ables, and household ephemera. The important linkages to the wider world cut across the front yard.

Yards coalesce into collections of front yards and backyards—yardscapes. In the aggregate, the front yard joins the street and creates a collective open space that is both personal and collective. To the rear, the more privatized backyard *may* form part of a common park system or at least serve as access to one, but rarely does. However, there is sometimes a linkage to an alley network. Yardscapes are part of the community open space system. Part of the front yard is subject to civic regulation in the form of easements. When we speak of living along a street, we mean not just the road, but also these yardscapes.

Yardscape, Denver, Colorado.
Kenneth Helphand.

DRIVEWAY

There is an autonomy to each house and yard entity, yet each is connected
to a larger network. Front walks once provided direct access to sidewalk and
street; they now lead to a driveway, one of the American landscape's most
ubiquitous, yet neglected, spaces. The driveway may be among the most
representative of American open spaces, performing both pragmatic and
symbolic functions. The driveway sits at that juncture between the equally
assertive imperatives of the traditional stability of home, neighborhood, and
community, and the modern mobility of the automobile, speed, and travel.
At a deeper level, driveways link the symbolic rootedness of place, the
comforts of family, and the security of individual plots of land with the
street, dreams of movement, the freedom of the road, and the release of
speed. Driveways link the hard surface of the technologically engineered
roadway with the soft domain of lawn, carpet, and sofa.

Driveways originated with the advent of cars, which had to drive across
the yard to a garage in the rear. Both garage and driveway progressively
moved closer to the house. What were once the outbuildings to a main
house gradually became absorbed into a single structure encompassing all
functions. Plumbing, housework such as laundry, and storage—all once
outdoor or outbuilding functions—are now subsumed under a single all-

encompassing roof. So too with the automobile, presenting an interesting historical parallel. In the late Middle Ages, people and animals, previously housed under a single roof, were segregated into separate buildings. The car, once kept outside in a barn or separate garage, now often shares a common roof. It has become part of the family.

Early driveways were just ruts, with strips of intervening grass, leading to the garage at the rear of the lot, often located off a service alley. At first, the car was a modest intruder into the yard. As the garage moved in proximity to the house, so too did the driveway. Driveway materials have changed in corresponding fashion as its importance and role have increased. The driveway was surfaced, first compacted by tires—then gravel was added, then asphalt or concrete—now displaying the occasional opulence of pavers or brick. So too its location became progressively more important, its scale increased, and its role expanded. A typical driveway for a two-car garage is 800 to 1,000 square feet. By comparison, the average new suburban home is almost 2,000 square feet. The modern driveway has joined the ensemble of house and garage in a unified structure, assuming the role of primary vehicular and pedestrian entry to the house. The front walk from street to house is gone or replaced by a walkway from driveway to front door. Our homes are now made up roughly of one-third family space of living room, dining room, kitchen, and family room, one-third the private realm of bedrooms, and one-third automobile space.

Home, Muncie, Indiana.
Kenneth Helphand.

Driveway, Springfield, Oregon.
Kenneth Helphand.

Driveways are one of many American "hybrid" spaces, places designed primarily for a single function, but which garner myriad secondary functions. In many ways driveways are actually paved portions of front yards that act as personal plazas and courtyards enclosed only at one end—a kind of front yard patio. They have assumed many traditional front yard functions. They are part of the symbolic field upon which the dwelling resides, indicators of social class and identity, and informal recreation spaces. Driveways are visible to passersby. As extensions of the road they are accessible to other vehicles, for service and turning around, yet they are in private ownership and used for family functions. As the primary, or even the exclusive, pedestrian and vehicular entrance to the home, the driveway is, for those looking in the other direction, toward the street, a gateway to an almost infinite national network. One indicator of its significance is that when it snows, it is the driveway that is the first place to be plowed, so one "can get out." Driveways are also parking places, workplaces, and storage places, where cars and other large mobile possessions, vehicles of leisure and affluence, are stored, tuned, displayed, and groomed. It is here that recreational vehicles, trailers, and boats hibernate for the winter, lying dormant awaiting their warm-weather lives of mobility.

Driveways are social spaces for meeting neighbors, commercial grounds for garage sales, recreational areas for children, and the places where building projects spill out of basements and garages. They are miniature fields for soccer, hockey, or baseball. Garage doors are strike zones for pitchers and surrogate partners for tennis practice, (perhaps one reason glass windows are now rarely used). The pole supporting a basketball hoop or a backboard above the garage is so common that it is an almost standard issue item for the American home. In the city, basketball is a playground game and a public event, but in the suburbs it is a driveway game and largely a private affair.

The driveway is itself a middle landscape, where our urge to be on the move, our infatuation with mobility and technology, coexists with our desires for stability and the modest pleasures of personal and community life. Driveways have begun to assert their own identity as distinctive units in the domestic and community landscape. They increasingly dominate streetscapes as front yards diminish to vestigial landscape relics and the street floods over its levee of curb and gutter toward the house. The trends are revealing. There is an ever-increasing frequency of looped driveways, and not only in upper-class developments. Here the driveway becomes the main element of the front yard, and the automobile's position as icon and status symbol is displayed to an even greater degree than in the conventional arrangement. The driveway itself becomes a status symbol. Many homes are now built with three-car garages and huge accompanying driveways. Others have storage slabs to one side for wheeled or marine vehicle storage. Gradually, the front yard is becoming paved. In the battle between street and house, the street is winning. Automatic garage door openers make it convenient to enter the house directly from the road, never going outside, forgoing even the most modest chance encounter with neighbors as one exits the cocoon of the automobile.

A central distinction regarding open space is that between public and private domains and the subtle gradients between them. These distinctions occur primarily in the transitions between house, yard, and street; between households, neighbors, and the public. Legal (de jure) and informal (de facto) mechanisms of physical design and cultural habit articulate a broad spectrum of public to private relationships. There are explicit messages: Keep Out, No Trespassing, Armed Response, Beware of Dog, or Welcome.[17] There are also subtler messages, where physical form acts as the clue that signal divisions through the spatial positioning of hedges, fences, gates and the sheer length of the walk to the front door. Visibility is legally regulated.

Riverpointe, Eugene, Oregon.
Kate Van Rooy.

Standards typically allow fences up to 6 feet in rear yards and only 2½ feet in front yards. Children's play behavior acts as a major indicator of the differences between semipublic, semiprivate, and private spaces. If one is playing ball in the street or on the sidewalk or chasing someone, it is permitted to go across another person's front yard and driveway to retrieve an errant ball or tag another child. But if that same ball lands in a backyard, a private space, only the brave volunteer for a retrieval mission, *or* permission is asked, *or* the ball is sacrificed to the unspoken god of property rights. An invitation is required to enter a backyard, where friends and family gather.

STREET

J.B. Jackson has noted that the unity of house and garden, which evolved a millennia ago, has undergone a revision.[18] The car, an individualized unit of mobility, technology, and communication, has been added to the configuration. Nowhere is this more apparent than in the suburban landscape, itself made possible by mass automobile ownership, the proliferation of roads, and a culture built around the car. To the traditional interplay of city and country, dwelling and nature, has been added mobility and the street. The dialectic of culture-nature is now a triad of culture-nature-mobility. To be truer to contemporary circumstance, the best-selling magazine should be titled *Better Homes and Gardens* and *Streets*.

Houses and yards face the street. Driveways link the house to the street, and through it, to the rest of the world. Streets are circulation corridors for vehicles ranging from trikes to trucks, but they are conceived and created almost exclusively from the perspective of automobile travel. They are also conduits for services, territorial divisions, and storage spaces. Streets are places to walk, social spaces, and primary open spaces for recreation. Streets are places of danger, even terror, especially for young children playing, dashing across traffic to fetch wayward balls or charging out of driveways on bicycles. The street is a place of identification; it is where you live. Addresses signify a building's position on the street, and directions are given in street terms. Streets are public thoroughfares, yet they are also possessed by those who live alongside them. Most suburbanites retain a proprietary relationship to the street in front of their house. Streets have personalities. They form the primary web that physically structures and binds a community, and they are persistent. Photographs of neighborhoods devastated by hurricane or flood show flattened houses and yards of debris, all needing total rebuilding. The streets, on the other hand, are largely intact and form the framework for rebuilding.

During the past century of the automobile's ascendancy, the street has been hardened, progressively widened, smoothed, increased in status, expanded in scale, and has assumed a multiplicity of functions. At the extreme, streets are highways, virtually autonomous environments, as seen most dramatically in America's interstate system. Even at the modest level of the residential suburban street, they are formidable artifacts. Streets are not only paved routes for vehicles, they are complex corridors of space. A cross section through a street finds below, above, and at the margins of pavement, an infrastructure of sewers, tunnels, ditches, catch basins, manholes, hydrants, poles, signs, and wires. Each suburban residential street has a center line at the crown of the roadway marking a rough symmetry of traffic lanes:

parking lanes, gutter, curb, planting strip, sidewalk, front yard, driveway, house. The roadway runs down the center of this space, but the "street" stretches from building to building. (Legal street and road definitions include all land within a right-of-way, paved and unpaved.) Not all of these components are always present, and each component of the section can be modified. With each variation, different suburban inhabitants may be favored: drivers, children playing, cyclists, pedestrians, or babies in carriages.

Suburban streetscapes differ substantially from their urban counterparts. How do form and function distinguish the *suburban* street? Suburban residential streets are flanked by fewer structures and have lower traffic volumes, as well as fewer intersections, lights, and crosswalks, than their urban counterparts. Engineered for maximum use and the smooth, steady flow of traffic, they are much wider than necessary for their traffic volume. They appear neat and uncluttered. Paradoxically, many suburban streets are often absent of cars, or have just a scattering of temporary parking. Virtually all suburban zoning mandates *off-street* parking; typically, two parking spaces per dwelling unit are required. In some communities on-street parking is forbidden.

The volume of street space may be measured in width from curb to curb, trees to trees, or building to building; in length from block to block, or corner to corner; and overhead by a canopy of trees, signs, telephone poles, and lights. This volume of street space influences the street experience and the behavior of people who use it. In most suburbs the balance between traffic and street life has been decided, by design, in favor of the automobile. However, low traffic volumes allow other possibilities. Modest traffic enlivens street life, while still permitting necessary movement for residents and facilitating the servicing of homes, allowing garbage to be collected, plumbers to call, and other necessary maintenance to be provided. There is a subtle distinction between the street's role as a traffic artery and the street as open space. The automobile has surely diminished the role of the street as a recreational open space, both by taking people to other locales and as an impediment to activity. Street social life is in decline, as people spend

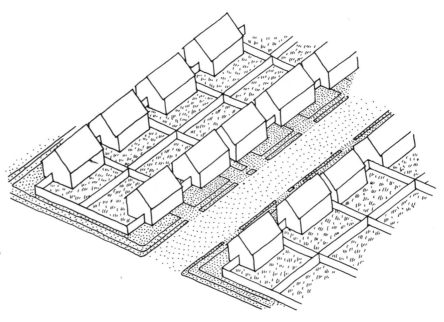

Street showing the gradation and overlap of streetscape and yardscape. Note the porous front yard territory versus the privatized back yards.
Kate van Rooy.

more time indoors, in backyards, and in locales beyond their neighborhoods. The most common street activities are informal interactions and conversations along the sidewalk. However, in many places the predominant pedestrians are dog walkers, exercise walkers, and joggers. Some streets are more spirited, their residents organizing formal events with annual or seasonal block parties. Municipalities grant permits for temporary street closure, allowing the roadbed to become a large community patio for tables, food, music, and dancing.

In the suburbs, children are the primary street dwellers. The street has stubbornly remained a place where games are played, with rules modified to fit the physical and social circumstances. Yardscapes lead directly to the street, and play activities flow from one into the other. For children, the hard, continuous surface of the street is as ideal for some games as the continuous lawns of yards and parks are for others. Although there has been ample study of children's urban street games, there has been little work on the suburban realm. Steven Spielberg's film *ET: The Extra Terrestrial* portrayed a glorified world of preadolescent and adolescent children (boys especially) in the suburban landscape. In this fringe environment—it is a new subdivision encroaching on a forest—the woods hold secrets; but in the world of the streets and a subdivision under construction, it is the children who know the shortcuts, who move seamlessly on dirt bikes across streets, yards, driveways, and constructions sites, leaving the adult world befuddled. This is their territory, and there is a magic in it.[19] Children are adept at environmental adaptation, but there can be no doubt that a street conceived to serve multiple functions will be more likely to do so. At a certain point it is clear that traffic overwhelms any possibility of using the street for anything other than driving.

Aerial photographs of most American communities show a break at the edge of a regular gridiron pattern located at the core of settlement. Inevitably there are divisions, where on one side of a street there is a grid pattern and on the other, the curvilinear pattern of subdivisions. Found across the nation, this hiatus in geometry marks a specific period, circa World War II. Even in small towns, the "suburbs" start at the curves. The simple, readily identifiable pattern of grids and curves has pragmatic differences, but also powerful symbolic overtones. The gridiron street pattern has its sources in classical antiquity, whereas the curvilinear pattern represents a countertradition, an association with rural paths and roads codified in the form of the nineteenth-century Anglo-American Romantic suburb.[20] At a fundamental level the forms are surrogates for the constellation of ideology, values, and experiences that are city and nature/country. The orthogonal regularity of the grid and its accompanying organizational system of a street-oriented building pattern (at least for residential streets) has been the standard American urban formula. It connotes "city." The grid is clear, comprehensible, classic, and has often been accused of being boring. However, on closer inspection, grid does not mean regular, for block sizes and configurations vary. Most communities were platted by incremental residential additions that introduced small but significant deviations in what is theoretically an infinitely extendible pattern.

By contrast, the curvilinear suburban street has multiple origins and ideological associations. Despite its careful contrivance, the curvilinear pattern is associated with "nature." The perception is that rural roads conform to the contours of topography, although, in fact, for most of the American landscape they are aligned toward the cardinal directions, following the

Subdivisions (aerial), Miami, Florida.
Kenneth Helphand.

survey system of township, section, and range. Curves also conform to a picturesque aesthetic ideal harking back to an eighteenth-century aesthetic and Hogarth's serpentine line of beauty. They are also evocative of entry "drives," adding an elitist and aristocratic pretension associated with the Romantic suburb. As Lois Craig has noted, "In America the grid is the more public pattern than the curvilinear . . . the curved line reads as opposition, as defiance, as signifying domains of leisure and privacy."[21] Thus, new designs that combine these shapes are not just formal exercises, they are also seeking to combine the suburb's ideological polarities. Not surprisingly in the 1980s and 1990s, as the urban aspect of suburban life is asserting its imperative, the grid has returned. Charles Wolfe urges planners to "utilize the street as a legal and planning tool to structure neighborhood form and appearance. Yet [it] must assure a functional, continuous layout that integrates vehicles and pedestrians and must avoid neighborhoods that turn inwards on themselves. Given these considerations, the gridiron, so maligned in the recent past, may have a new life."[22]

Each street is part of a road hierarchy stretching from housing unit to local street, to collector, to arterial, to highway. The suburban neighborhood ideal has been to create streets that provide access but minimize through traffic. This may be the aspiration, yet as street scholar Donald Appleyard noted, the hierarchical arterial concept intended to minimize traffic on residential streets often fails, and sometimes half of a subdivision's homes are located on high-speed streets.[23] The traffic hierarchy implies a differentiation of use. All aspects of the system favor automobile traffic, yet local streets need also to accommodate comfortably pedestrians and cyclists. A key problem is how the connections are made within systems, specifically, how streets can be crossed by those not in cars. The alternative has been to create parallel systems—sidewalks are just that—or independent pedestrian and bike trails. In recent years renewed attention has been directed toward the alley, the midblock service street—often an unpaved rural remnant—as a way of taking traffic pressure off main streets. Alleys also alter the geography of household comings and goings and further shift the dynamics of the yard from front to back.

In the early era of mass automobile ownership, planners struggled with finding an accommodation with the car. Clarence Perry's 1929 pioneering schemes for neighborhood units offered a hierarchical network of curvilinear local roads serving single-family homes, typically feeding to higher-density dwellings, apartments, and commercial areas and then connecting to arterial roads. Often an entire neighborhood was set within a larger grid. Perry's plan, as adapted by the FHA (Federal Housing Administration) in modified form, did in fact become a common pattern of subdivision development. The intention was that neighborhood identity and cohesiveness would be structured by the arrangement of streets and parks. The scheme minimized street coverage, and the space "saved" was intended to be offered as public open space and deeper yards. In practice it often meant that more housing units were constructed without the amenity of more open space.[24]

The dichotomy between city, technology, and modernity and nature, country, and pastoral retreat is nowhere more clearly exemplified than by a car winding its way down a paved surface containing conduits of services and energy, all flanked by a green verge and columns of street trees. The street is engineered, geometric, and surfaced, whereas the yards and street trees that frame it are soft, green, and quiet, a counterpoint to the mechanization of the street and its vehicles. In new subdivisions the machined street is at first dominant, but plantings eventually mature. Within a generation raw, bare landscapes are transformed into streets where houses are framed by gardens and set within parks.

PARK

The American suburb has an English pedigree in the "bourgeois utopias" created by eighteenth-century English merchants for whom the suburb was conceived as an ideal community, mediating between the demands and pleasures of country and city. One such early suburb was Clapham, where, beginning in the 1790s, London merchants could be "aristocrats on weekends," living in suburban villas constructed around the village's green common. These homes had been grafted onto the traditional landscape form of the common, and out of this rootstock something quite new emerged. "The true suburban landscape as seen at Clapham, is a balance of the public and the private. Each property is private, but each contributes to the total landscape of *houses in a park*" [author's emphasis].[25] At Clapham the title to the archaic common land was not legally changed, but the territory was appropriated by the encircling suburban villas. The common was "owned" visually and by the proprietorship of proximity. In the nineteenth century another model emerged, first in Britain and then in the United States. The Romantic suburb placed homes in a designed picturesque landscape, with the addition of small naturalistic parks for local enjoyment.

In subsequently designed suburbs, common areas and picturesque parks were created, but often in a much truncated fashion, initiating a trend in suburban history of favoring private pleasures over community opportunities. A neoclassic formalism of circles and crescents replaced the grand scale of the common, and the public green space progressively diminished under pressures to build more houses. Most suburbs were created without any communal open spaces. However, desire for open space persisted, and parklike areas kept recurring in small leftover green areas, planted boulevards, central greens, and school yards. Occasionally, land ill suited for development was deeded to a community as a philanthropic act. Appropriating private open space as common land became a suburban convention, although the land might be a golf course or the ephemeral edge of suburbanization, which would soon be ceded to more housing.

In a certain sense the design of suburban open space, and especially of suburban parks, has involved the struggle to return to the comforts of the village ideal with its green center, offering connections to a traditional way of life and the comforts of a middle landscape. Although elements of the village often appear in debased form in the suburb, there is an equally powerful desire to provide a romantic attachment to nature. Suburb scholar Robert Fishman notes, "The distinguishing feature of . . . classic suburbs, however, was not such common institutions as churches or country clubs but the landscape. The pattern of tree shaded streets, broad open lawns, substantial houses set back from the sidewalk was a pattern of propriety, family life, and union with nature that represents the culmination of suburban style." This physical ideal had to wait for the growth of plants to mature. It was "a genuine communal creation, a style created by the bourgeoisie for itself. The suburban landscape, not the individual house, is the true monument."[26]

The origins of the common, or green, lie in the European tradition of shared rights to certain forests, pastures, and bodies of water.[27] Transplanted to the New World, the common was a grazing area, market, and parade ground, which evolved into a community hub flanked by church, meeting house, and then hotel and inns. Subsequently, it often became a crossroads and the center for business. Although its roots were utilitarian, the common's role changed, and it was beautified and planted.[28] The resurgence of "commons" and "greens" in recent "traditional" developments is partly advertising hype, but also reflects a genuine desire for a return to a shared central place in a time of weakened community ties and association. The square is the urban relative of the common. It is a unifying element, a place of assembly, commerce, and civic display. The square has not typically been associated with the suburb, but in its early forms the suburb often grafted itself upon a preexisting settlement and assimilated the square, commons, or Main Street within its domain. Like the common, the square too is reestablishing its importance as urbanity reasserts its place in the suburban equation.

The public park, a product of nineteenth-century urbanization and industrialization, was intended as a *rus en urb,* a piece of country in the city. The park was to act as a palliative to the urban landscape: soothing, healing, and allowing breathing space in the crowded, growing metropolis—thus parks were known as "green lungs." The motivation for the creation of parks was reformist, and their role was physical, social, and moral, built on an expectation of improving the environment, social conditions, and the human spirit. The first parks were "people's gardens," a democratization of the landscape spaces of the elite and powerful. Parks represented a social ideal of public open space as a meeting ground for persons of different social classes. They were an urban response to the Industrial Revolution and the modern world, an environmental answer to a society increasingly alienated from nature. Public parks inherited the garden's positive associations. In the park one was in direct contact with nature, which was physically and emotionally healthful and, as part of the prevailing transcendental and romantic ideology, an uplifting moral force. Here the world was less structured, one felt freer, and beauty resided in nature's forms. In contemporary America we retain, in muted fashion, aspects of all these values.

Frederick Law Olmsted, in an article on "Park" in the *New American Cyclopedia* of 1861,[29] commented on the diverse origins of the public park and its "relatives," the pleasure ground, arboretum, promenade, common, green, cricket ground, botanical garden, zoo, and informal recreation spaces found at the edges of urbanization.[30] The formal origins of the public park derive from a democratized version of English country estates. These "parks" took the form of an idealized pastoral of open meadow, browsed trees, and sculpted topography. We now take it for granted, but it is only in the last century that public parks became units of city design and subsequently expanded into the hinterlands. The nineteenth-century picturesque pleasure ground was succeeded by the reformist civic park of the early twentieth century and then by parks dominated by recreational facilities. More recently the park system idea, which has nineteenth-century origins, has again returned to favor.[31] Each of these eras of American park development has had its suburban counterpart.

What is the role of parks for people dwelling in the suburban landscape? What kind of park do you have when you already live in *houses in a park?* What might be the characteristics of the *suburban* park, when each yard is a micro or miniature park with facilities for passive and active recreation complete with swing set and sandbox, patio, backboard, trees, grass, or pool, with everything conveniently adjacent to kitchen, refrigerator, music, and television? Even modest-sized backyards, lawns, and driveways can become surrogate courts and miniature playing fields. In this personal micro-park nothing need be packed in a picnic basket, for eating on the lawn can be a daily occurrence. Suburban parks do perform traditional park functions as places of nature, recreation, and civic symbolism. However, in certain ways suburban parks are less crucial, inasmuch as the yardscape assumes many park functions. Moreover, as the automobile is the primary mode of suburban transportation, the suburban park must accommodate it with road and parking area.

The distinctiveness of the pastoral and picturesque, the Olmstedian vocabulary of most park design, has a different meaning in suburbia, for here these forms are not a break in the pattern but part of the continuum. In the suburbs the line between yardscapes and parkscapes is not sharply drawn. "The lawn is the owner's principal contribution to the suburban landscape—the piece of the 'park' he keeps up himself."[32] On the other hand, although the yard may have a parklike aspect and has assumed some of its functions, it cannot, except for the extremely affluent, offer the appeal of vast space, unimpeded vistas, or the opportunity to experience the complexities of nature. These benefits do not appeal to everyone, nor should they be expected to, but for many they are essential experiences. Yards cannot offer a communal landscape, the experience of chance encounters, the paradoxical pleasures of being a stranger or alone in a public place, nor do they provide space for community events, large-scale recreational activities, or public and civic celebrations.

In the child- and family-centered suburb it is the school yard that is the primary, and often largest, public open space and neighborhood park. In most subdivisions the park stops here. Perry's neighborhood unit scheme of 4,000 to 7,000 people was predicated on a population sufficient to support an elementary school with a park at the center, with neighborhoods defined by their radial walking distance from the school and its grounds. The typical one-story school building conformed to the residential pattern. The school's front yard was the formal entry and lawn, and to the rear lay the recreational yard. For elementary schools a playground and modest fields were included. These often constitute the primary local community open space, equipped with swings, slides, jungle gym, and wading pool, where mothers and children gather. For junior and senior high schools there are grander recreational complexes of pools, tracks, basketball, baseball, and football fields, largely used for organized team sports.

The public park has not been a fundamental part of the suburban image, where the privatized world dominates and the collective landscape has been dominated by other forms of community and commercial life: school, shopping mall, roadside strip, and office park. "Park" is a powerful metaphor that is applied to a variety of situations. The park nomenclature implies an association with outdoor recreation, a general enjoyment of nature, and an embodiment of the American middle landscape. However, when used to name business, corporate, industrial, or educational "parks," the term often offers only the image, not the substance. If the public park is to be a meeting place of persons of different social classes, how is that desire fulfilled within suburban communities of class homogeneity? The country club and golf course have been called "the suburban equivalent of the urban park," but whereas golf courses and their acres of pastoral space may provide the visual relief of the urban park, their social significance is dramatically differ-

Suburban Park, Columbia, Maryland.
Kenneth Helphand.

ent. Golf courses are not nature in the city, but contoured, sculpted recreational creations. Most often they are private enclaves, where it is forbidden to do something as simple as walk, run, walk a dog, or throw a ball. The traditional country club was a great house on lavish grounds with facilities for golf, tennis, and swimming. The country club was the suburban privatized park, open only to members, in a community where permits displayed on windshields and bumpers signified the privileges of residency. Golf is less an elitist country club habit, and in affluent developments courses have become the armatures around which communities are built.

Parks are the product of deliberate design, but there are also ample open spaces that are ignored, yet worthy of our attention. These are unnamed open spaces, neglected and devalued landscapes, treated in the most minimal functional fashion. They are leftovers. Many of these sites are products of linking the suburban residential environment with its surroundings. They are the inaccessible greens in the hearts of cloverleaves, shadowed spaces beneath off-ramps, and immense unused paved areas of parking lots. They are the remnants of earlier eras in railway corridors, derelict industrial sites, and cracks between developments. They are the vacant lots awaiting the inevitability of their transformation. Such sites are ripe for reclamation and imaginative possibilities. One type of leftover landscape has been highly prized. As suburbs grew, they were an advancing front of development, an unstable frontier, moving across or leapfrogging over a landscape.[33] As suburbs developed, the adjacent woods, field, or hillside was for a time a place to play in, a buffer from the next development. Although many of these leftover areas appeared to be wasted, they were not. The small cracks, the rough edges, the ravines, gullies, sloughs, and remnant alleys were places for children to play and wildlife to forage and nest. These areas are often the most remembered landscapes of those growing up in the suburbs. This edge condition, while transitory, was desired. The preferred suburban lot is one that faces the communal street to the front and has a rear yard that backs up into woods, common land, or golf course. Housing prices bear out the fact that these are the most prized situations. Part of the struggle in suburban open space design is how to stabilize this landscape of circumstance into a landscape of design.

SYSTEM AND NETWORK

Beyond the scale of subdivision, open space networks, largely in the form of park systems, also bear examination. Parks systems may be at any scale from local to national, and the components of all systems may impact on given suburban communities. All systems deal with the connectedness of open spaces. They appear in diverse patterns and configurations. They may be fingers, corridors, ways, belts, or matrices. Park systems can act as more than integrated systems of green spaces, as significant as these may be. They can also function as an armature, a framework and skeleton for community development. Olmsted's Emerald Necklace, the first major park system in the United States, functioned in such manner, structuring community development along its course ringing the city of Boston, as did George Kessler's scheme for Kansas City and numerous park planning projects. The plan by Charles Eliot a century ago for a metropolitan park system for the Boston area is still relevant in its sensitivity to both landscape and the pragmatics of politics. Eliot surveyed the landscape of the metropolitan region, recognized its distinctive resources, places in jeopardy, and potential linkages. He sought logical connections in water corridors, valleys, and ridges and where none existed, proposed boulevards and parkways to bridge the gaps. The basic concepts were clear and a direct response to a metropolitan region that was rapidly urbanizing and suburbanizing in burgeoning railroad suburbs. His plan was directed at preserving the integrity and quality of the landscape, especially its water system, to link the region together, to ameliorate damaged lands, and to make the component elements in the system accessible to residents throughout the area. Eliot's system and its extensions became the framework for the park systems of all of suburban Boston, and a national model as well. In suburbs, larger community and regional parks are often part of metropolitan park systems, which in their total acreage attempt to offer a wide variety of outdoor amenities, everything from cactus, rose, or Japanese gardens, to outdoor theaters or specialized sports facilities. Unfortunately, linear open spaces, the essential connective tissue of park systems, are lacking in most suburbs, where streets were designed to be the primary conduits. However, as noted earlier, redesigned streets can serve as an integral part of the suburban open space network.

Twenty-five years ago even an observer as perceptive as Herbert Gans could minimize the environmental impact of urban sprawl. In 1967 he wrote, "The disappearance of farmland near big cities is irrelevant now that food is produced on huge industrialized farms, and the destruction of raw land and private upper class golf courses seems a small price to pay for extending the benefits of suburban life to more people." In debates over conservation and wilderness lands Gans sided with the forces of development: "Making inexpensive and efficient transportation available to distant wildernesses would be more sensible than preventing many people from living in the suburbs in order to retain a wilderness nearby. . . . Although land should be saved for the requirements of ecological balance and for the use of future generations if current needs are not urgent, I believe that restricting current development for an unpredictable future is undesirable."[34] That this sentiment appears so strikingly out of date is a testament to the development of environmental thought that has occurred within a generation.

The environmental movement, a concern for personal fitness and health, and a desire to retain a sense of suburban place have made the maintenance and creation of open space systems a central suburban concern for residents, developers, and policymakers. The periphery has been built up, and most of the vacant lands have been filled in. Thus the need for deliberately planned open space systems is all the more urgent. The multi-faceted greenway movement encompasses a diversity of these concerns. Greenways are linear landscape threads. They take many forms, but are often created on lands reclaimed for recreational purposes. Their purpose is to provide open space possibilities near homes, ideally "right in one's backyard," and at the same time afford the possibility of easy connection to more distant places and other open space opportunities. It is important to note that the connection itself is not exclusively a transportation route, but also recreational and even educational in purpose, through walkways, bike trails, scenic drives, or water corridors. Moreover, greenways have the potential to organize and structure the pattern of development by defining boundaries, orchestrating the hierarchy of land uses, and providing buffers between differing land uses. This is especially true if they are conceived from the inception of a plan as an integral part of the community design.

Greenway, Columbia, Maryland.
Kenneth Helphand.

Within a landscape there are natural connections, the continuity of corridors in rivers, streams, canyons, and valleys. The studies of landscape ecologists are confirming what is apparent to our senses, that the maintenance of the integrity and quality of these corridors is essential for water and air quality and in providing viable habitats for plants and animals. The intuitive organization of park systems is now reinforced by the science of landscape ecology, which is investigating the forms of patch, corridor, and matrix.[35] At the level of personal experience, these green spaces bring nature into the community or, in reverse fashion, allow the community to enter nature in as modest a manner as possible.

In planned communities, open space networks bring the park system idea down to the local level. However, regional coordination and regulatory intervention are essential. It is commonplace to see an individual community, neighborhood, or development designed with an attentiveness to the connection of elements in the natural and cultural landscape, but with potential linkages truncated and amputated by the subsequent and adjacent development. Planning can enforce the necessities and parameters of connection, ideally before the fact, and can still be effective after development has taken place. Even golf courses, often the only networks of green space in planned communities, offer added dimensions. They can be designed to moderate their impact on water, soil, and plant resources. In their paved paths for carts they offer an infrastructure for bikes and pedestrians, although this use may require some modification to the etiquette of the game or to local rules. In northern climates they are already used as cross-country ski trails.

Suburban development has emphasized the paradox of development, the "tragedy of the commons," as it has often destroyed what was most desired.[36] Part of the suburban attraction has been a desire for the best of both worlds. Many of the satisfying open space experiences of the suburbs are at the undeveloped fringes, which last for only a brief historical moment, but perhaps an entire childhood, before they are destroyed by the seeming inevitability of development. A key question is how to retain elements of that accidental character and make it part of the official suburban program. As we examine suburban open space, it is imperative that the look is inclusive, that *all* scales of open space are considered, from yardscape to streetscape to parkscape, and that we not lose sight of the spaces in between, for it may be the systems of open space connections that are the key.

NOTES

1. Kenneth Helphand, "Environmental Autobiography," *Childhood–City Newsletter* **14** (December 1978):8–17.
2. Paul Groth, "Lot, Yard, and Garden: American Distinctions," *Landscape* **30**, No. 3 (1990):29–35.
3. Claire Cooper Marcus, *The House as Symbol of Self* (Berkeley: Institute of Urban and Regional Development, University of California, 1971).
4. J. B. Jackson, "Nearer than Eden," in *The Necessity of Ruins* (Amherst, MA: University of Massachusetts, 1980), p. 27.
5. Robert Samuelson, "The Joys of Mowing," *Newsweek* **117**, No. 17 (April 29, 1991):49.
6. Samuelson, "The Joys of Mowing," p. 49, and F. Herbert Bormann, Diana Balmori, and Gordon T. Beballe, *Redesigning the American Lawn* (New Haven, CT: Yale University Press, 1993), p. 62.
7. Kenneth Jackson, *Crabgrass Frontier: The Suburbanization of the United States* (New York: Oxford University Press, 1985), p. 262.
8. Claire Cooper Marcus, Carolyn Francis, and Colette Meunier, "Mixed Messages in Suburbia: Reading the Suburban Model Home," *Places* **4**, No. 1 (1978):24–37.
9. Thomas C. Hubka, *Big House, Little House, Back House, Barn: The Connected Farm Buildings of New England* (Hanover, NH: University Press of New England, 1984), p. 9.
10. *How to Landscape the Home Grounds* (Painesville, OH: The Storrs & Harrison Co., 1928).
11. Amos Rapoport, *House Farm and Culture* (Englewood Cliffs, NJ: Prentice-Hall, 1969), p. 80.
12. Frank Waugh and Peter J. van Melle, in Leonard H. Johnson, ed., *Foundation Planting* (New York: A.T. De La Mare, 1927), pp. x–xvii.
13. William Dobriner, *Class in Suburbia* (Englewood Cliffs, NJ: Prentice-Hall, 1963), p. 63.
14. David Rochlin, "The Front Porch," in Charles W. Moore, Kathryn Smith and Peter Becker, eds., *Home Sweet Home: American Domestic Vernacular Architecture* (New York: Rizzoli, 1983), pp. 24–29. A superb porch typology is included.
15. Jackson, *Crabgrass Frontier*, p. 58, p. 279.
16. Yi-fu Tuan, *Dominance and Affection: The Making of Pets* (New Haven, CT: Yale University Press, 1984), p. 88.
17. Lois Craig, "Suburbs," *Design Quarterly* **132** (1986):23.
18. J.B. Jackson, "The Vernacular Landscape Is on the Move . . . Again," *Places* **7**, No. 3 (1991):24–35.
19. Steven Spielberg, director, *ET: The Extra Terrestrial* (University City Studios, 1982).
20. Donald Appleyard, *Livable Streets* (Berkeley: University of California Press, 1981), p. 150.
21. Craig, "Suburbs," p. 23.

22. Charles R. Wolfe, "Streets Regulating Neighborhood Form: A Selective History," in Anne Vernez Moudon, ed., *Public Streets for Public Use* (New York: Columbia University Press, 1991), p. 121.

23. Appleyard, *Livable Streets,* p. 150.

24. Wolfe, "Streets Regulating Neighborhood Form," p. 110.

25. Robert Fishman, *Bourgeois Utopias: The Rise and Fall of Suburbia* (New York: Basic Books, 1987), p. 71.

26. Fishman, *Bourgeois Utopias,* p. 146.

27. Paul Oliver, *The Village Green.* (Arts Council of Britain, n.d.). In Great Britain the common is larger, rural, utilitarian land, whereas the green is the symbolic nucleus of the community. In American usage the terms are synonymous.

28. John Stilgoe, "Town Common and Village Green in New England: 1620 to 1981," in Ronald Lee Fleming, ed., *Common Ground* (Cambridge, MA: Townscape Institute, 1982).

29. Frederick Law Olmsted, "Park" from the *New American Cyclopedia 1861,* in Charles E. Beveridge and David Schuyler, eds., *The Papers of Frederic Law Olmsted,* vol. 3, *Creating Central Park: 1857–1861* (Baltimore: Johns Hopkins University Press, 1983), pp. 346–367.

30. Lance Neckar, "The Park: Prospect and Refuge," *Reflections* 6 (Spring 1989):4–13.

31. Galen Granz, *The Politics of Park Design* (Cambridge, MA: MIT Press, 1982); and Kenneth Helphand, "The Western City Park," *Parks in the West and American Culture* (Sun Valley, ID: Institute of the American West, 1984).

32. Fishman, *Bourgeois Utopias,* p. 147.

33. Patricia Leigh Brown, "A House for a Life That Used to Be," *New York Times* (September 3, 1992):B4.

34. Herbert Gans, *The Levittowners: The Ways of Life and Politics in a New Suburban Community* (New York: Pantheon Books, 1967), p. 423.

35. Richard T.T. Forman & Michel Godron, *Landscape Ecology* (New York: John Wiley & Sons, 1986).

36. Garett Hardin, "The Tragedy of the Commons," *Science* **162** (December 13, 1968).

3
ORIGINS
The Early Models

Many of America's most renowned designers have struggled with designing suburbs. Throughout suburban history there are models worthy of attention. They offer a precedent, an extant model for study. Three landmark American suburban developments, Riverside, Illinois, designed by Frederick Law Olmsted and Calvert Vaux in 1869; Radburn, New Jersey, by Clarence Stein and Henry Wright in 1929; and Broadacre City by Frank Lloyd Wright in 1935, are of particular significance. The greater portion of Riverside was developed, Radburn was only partially realized, and Broadacre remained an aspiration. Each was publicized, discussed, and critiqued at its inception and in subsequent years. Each was a compromise between ideals and the pragmatics of its situation, site, and circumstances. Each of these developments manipulated basic suburban symbology and imagery, while adding their stamp to suburban iconography, as they dealt with the triads of city, country, and road. Each offered a distinctive composition of yard, street, and park. These community designs were about the struggle to define a new morphology of settlement. The new inhabitations and their ways of living were, on the one hand, nostalgic and pastoral in reflecting a desire for country living and contact with nature, and, on the other hand, profoundly modern in their dependency on the technologies of transportation, electricity, and communications that enabled the new patterns and ways of life to emerge. Collectively, the open space legacy of these communities forms a framework to begin a discussion of the postwar suburban landscape.

FREDERICK LAW OLMSTED: RIVERSIDE

The suburb emerged in the nineteenth century as a product of, and reaction to, the mechanization, urbanization, and alienation of the Industrial Revolution. The railroad, the century's symbol of the "machine," entered the tranquil "garden" of preindustrial rural life.[1] It was equally the vehicle that provided access to the new suburban garden. The railroad enabled one to live in a countrified setting with easy access to the city. Best known of the railroad suburbs was Riverside, designed by landscape architects Frederick Law Olmsted and Calvert Vaux in 1869. Having created the prototype for urban park design at New York's Central Park, these collaborators similarly set the standard for the preautomobile suburban community at Riverside, Illinois.

Riverside. House and yard c. 1870.
Kate Van Rooy.

The Riverside plan was a crystallization of decades of discussion about the ideology, character, and design of suburban homes, landscape, and communities. The primary precedents for the design and ideology of these new developments were English.[2] Andrew Jackson Downing's theoretical and pragmatic publications, such as his seminal *Treatise on the Theory and Practice of Landscape Gardening* of 1841, popularized elements of English landscape design and style in the United States. Significantly, this work was subtitled *Adapted to North America,* and Downing was dedicated to creating a discrete American landscape style. Suburbs, which had an English pedigree, took on a distinct stamp in nineteenth-century America. In a different culture and a new landscape the same forms acquired new meanings, grander scale, and an enriched language.

Downing, whose writings would so influence the character of American domestic architecture, offered his own suggestions on suburban design. "Our Country Village," an 1850 essay in his magazine *The Horticulturist,* described the landscape character of a planned rural village "in the suburbs of a great city." He imagined this new Hudson River Valley settlement as "combining the advantages of the country with early railroad access." People could live in "a neighborhood where, without losing society, they can see the horizon, breath the fresh air, and walk upon elastic greensward." Downing's advice focused on the specifics of streetscape and park planning. He offered two commandments: First, "Thou shalt plant trees, to hide the nakedness of the streets." Most any community, he noted, would be improved by "shade trees in the streets, and a little shrubbery in the front yards." The second was "Thou shalt not keep pigs—except in the back yard!" indicative that for Downing, design should reflect the outward signs of a "refined civilization" and shed the ruddiest qualities of the rural landscape. The "indispensable desiderata" of these prospective communities were "a large open space, common, or park, situated in the middle of the village—not less than twenty acres, and better if fifty or more in extant. This should be well planted with groups of trees and kept as a lawn. . . . This park would be the nucleus or *heart of the village,* and would give it an essentially rural character." In Downing's scheme the best residences would surround the park, and wide streets planted with elms or maples would lead out from it. This suburban park built on the heritage of the village green, with the purpose of preserving a "permanent rural character" at the core of the settlement. In this "common ground of entertainment," park and pleasure ground, one could enjoy the private pleasures of the garden in a public setting. Downing, like other nineteenth-century park reformers, was intent on the moral improvement of the citizenry. This would be a setting "more healthful than the ordinary life of cities, and more refined and elevating than the common gossip of country villages."[3]

Downing died in 1852, but others would soon begin to construct these new villages. Outside Cincinnati, the village of Glendale was planned in 1851 and may rightfully be called the first romantically planned suburb in the United States, with its curved streets, small greens, and rich plantings. At Llewellyn Park, 12 miles outside New York City in northern New Jersey and designed by architect Alexander Jackson Davis in 1854, the suburban dialectic was explicit. The suburb had been advertised as "Country Homes for City People."[4] The 350-acre site, illustrated in later editions of Downing's work, had 50 villa properties of 3 to 10 acres. All those who lived in the community also had the benefit of access to 60 acres of park, a road circumnavigating the development, internal carriage roads, and, "by common consent," no fences dividing property. The main park, called the Ramble, had carriageways and walks along its dramatic ravine, taking visitors and residents through carefully composed picturesque scenes. Residents were assessed annually for park upkeep. "The Park itself and all the private places, seem like one large estate," wrote Henry Winthrop Sargeant.[5] Robert Fishman perceptively noted that Llewellyn Park, although derived from English suburban prototypes, "embodies a relationship to the landscape that does seem distinctly American. Its dramatic mountainside site, with views extending down to Manhattan some twelve miles away . . . the large villas of Llewellyn Park seem almost swallowed up in nature."[6]

In February 1868, shortly before beginning work at Riverside, Frederick Law Olmsted did a plan for Shady Hill, the Cambridge, Massachusetts estate of Charles Eliot Norton, bordering the Harvard University campus. Olmsted described his plan as an attractive neighborhood with "the more agreeable rural characteristics of a New England Village," while introducing "all the street conveniences of a crowded town." He suggested providing "a small public green or lawn suitable to be used as playground by children of the Neighborhood." A key proposal was to open closed streets and walks in order to create linkages to adjacent properties. This was not to be a self-contained urban addition. The 1868 plan of the 35-acre estate shows a parkway snaking through the site, joining an old railway bed leading to the Cambridge Common and almost connecting to Harvard Yard.[7] The desire to combine rural and village character with urban amenity was clear, as expressed in the open space mechanisms, a modest parkway connector to the city located only a few hundred yards away, and streets and walks tying into the surrounding city. The estate was subdivided but not developed until a later design, without the internal parkway, was completed by Olmsted's protégé Charles Eliot in 1887.[8]

In an August 29, 1868, letter to his partner Calvert Vaux, who was traveling in Europe, Olmsted wrote enthusiastically about the prospects of their new Riverside project: "The Chicago operation is to make a suburban village out of the whole cloth on the prairie & connect by parkway with the town."[9] With Vaux away, the Riverside plan was Olmsted's alone. His report for the *Proposed Suburban Village at Riverside* would summarize his suburban ideology and, at a very early stage, fix the elements of subsequent suburban design. In "true suburbs," wrote Olmsted, "urban and rural advantages are agreeably combined," to create "the most refined and most soundly wholesome forms of domestic life, and the best application of the arts of civilization to which mankind has yet attained." The ideal suburb was "an advance upon" town life. The goal was "not a sacrifice of urban conveniences, but their combination with the special charms and substantial advantages of rural conditions of life." He desired the "greatest possible contrast" in terms of town and country, as long as it was "compatible with convenient communication and pleasant abode of a community."[10] Here a family could live in proximity to the city, among members of its social class, in a home set in a domesticated nature, the ever-ready American elixir.[11]

The 1,600-acre community of Riverside is located on a bend of the Des Plaines River and linked by railroad to Chicago, nine miles to the east. The area east of the river was laid out according to Olmsted's plan, whereas the west segment was not completed by 1870, when Olmsted and Vaux ended their association with developer Emery E. Childs and the Riverside Improvement Company. The provision of progressive urban services was an essential part of early suburban development, with the new technological amenities, the service umbilicals, brought directly to a home owner's lot. The company offered the "most innovative and comprehensive" range of urban services, including "water and sewer mains, individual gas hookups, paved roads, street lamps, sidewalks, parks, and a railroad depot," all in place before one bought a property.[12] Riverside had financial difficulties and was not an initial success, yet it grew modestly to a population of 450 in 1880, and to 1,551 by 1900. Six years after its founding it was incorporated as a village.

The straight line of the railroad ran west from downtown Chicago. Before crossing the Des Plaines River and continuing out into the prairie, it stopped at Riverside's railroad station, the community core, complete with

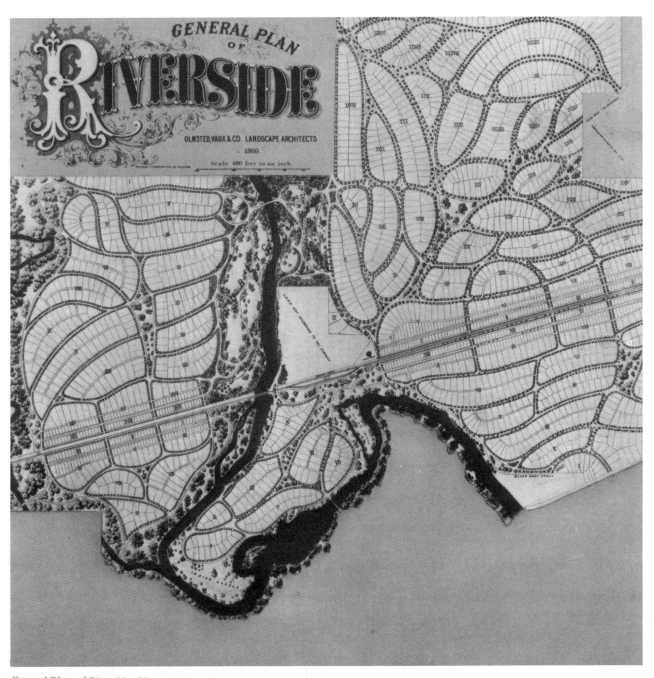

General Plan of Riverside; Olmsted, Vaux & Co., 1869.

From Julius Gy. Fabos, Gordan T. Milde, & V. Michael Weinmayr, *Frederick Law Olmsted, Sr.* Amherst: University of Massachusetts Press, 1968, p. 51.

hotel and a modest commercial center, and adjacent to the Riverside park. From this center curved parkways led to tree-lined streets and individual lots. For Olmsted, "the essential qualification" of suburban life was domesticity balanced with community life.[13] Each needed to be addressed in the design; however, given the limits of physical design, these relationships could only be "suggested through the arrangement of the means of division, and the passage between private and public ground." Although house design, Olmsted noted, could not be controlled, homes could be kept back from the street to help preserve a "general rural effect and domestic seclusion." Riverside's restrictive covenants mandated 30-foot minimum setbacks with no fences allowed, and each 100- by 200-foot lot had a space for a barn, stables, and gardens—a rural landscape in miniature.[14] Olmsted added, "We can insist that each house-holder shall maintain one or two living trees between his house and the highway-line. A few simple precautions of this kind, added to a tasteful and convenient disposition of shade trees, and other planting along the road-sides and public places, will, in a few years, cause the whole locality, no matter how far the plan may be extended, to possess . . . the attraction of neatness and convenience . . . the charm of refined sylvan beauty and grateful umbrageousness . . . and aspect of secluded peacefulness and tranquility." The suburban polarities were clear. Olmsted's objective was a character that was "informal . . . and positively picturesque, and when contrasted with the constantly repeated right angles, straight lines, and flat surfaces which characterize our large modern towns, thoroughly refreshing."[15]

Olmsted's planning at Central Park had demonstrated his genius in the design of circulation and transportation systems. The walking city had given way to the nineteenth-century city of streetcars and railroads. The urban fringe location of Riverside was made possible by its rail connection, while within the community roads defined its structure. In addition, Olmsted's emerging concern for interconnected open space systems would be expressed in plans for a parkway linking Riverside to Chicago. Well aware of the symbolism of form, he said that town streets, "with their ordinary directness of line . . . suggest an eagerness to press forward." He recommended "gracefully curved lines, generous spaces, and the absence of sharp corners, the idea being to suggest and imply leisure, contemplativeness and happy tranquility."[16] The road was a community skeleton, and care was directed toward its scale, surface, drainage, frontage, form, and adjacent land uses. Roadways were depressed two to three feet, thus minimizing their visual impact. The curved, tree-planted streets broadened, especially at intersections, into modest-sized open areas, minigreens, and play areas, following the recommendation that "at frequent intervals in every road, an opening large enough for a natural group of trees, and places for croquet for ball grounds, sheltered seats, drinking fountains" should be provided.[17] Thus, the boundaries between roadway and park were mooted.

At Riverside, Olmsted proposed a true parkway combining open space amenity and mobility, an "approach road" to and from Chicago, two to six hundred feet wide. It was to be a promenade, roadway, and "open-air gathering" place with distinct routes for carriages, commercial traffic, pedestrians, and horses. Olmsted foresaw "lines of villas and gardens" adjoining it.[18] For him, "a road suitable for pleasure-driving" was "one of the greatest common luxuries a civilized community can possess."[19] The nationwide depression of 1873, however, halted construction.[20]

Forty-four percent of Riverside's 1,600 acres was for public use, and three miles of river were preserved in park, along with smaller parks in the village and the streetscape. In a letter to his wife, Mary, Olmsted wrote that he proposed to make the "groves & river bank mainly public ground, by carrying walks along it & to plan village streets and "parks" & little openings."[21] The Des Plaines River is Riverside's natural armature, the streets the cultural. Roads brought people to the river, and drives paralleled its banks. "The chief advantages which a suburb can posses over a town on the one hand and a wilderness on the other, will consist in those which favor open-air recreation beyond the limits which economy and convenience prescribe for private grounds and gardens. The main artificial requirements of a sub-

Riverside. Homes fronting internal parkway.
Kenneth Helphand.

urb then, are good roads and walks, pleasant to the eye within themselves, and having at intervals pleasant openings and outlooks, with suggestions of refined domestic life, secluded, but not far removed from the life of the community," wrote Olmsted.[22]

At Riverside, his first completed community design, the Olmstedian essentials of suburban landscape principles of community design were apparent. There was a systematic hierarchy of open space types, from the

Riverside. Park along the Des Plaines River.
From Julius Gy. Fabos, Gordan T. Milde, & V. Michael Weinmayr, *Frederick Law Olmsted, Sr.* Amherst: University of Massachusetts Press, 1968, p. 52.

private realm of home, to the local realm of the street, to the community with its shopping center and train station, to connections to the metropolitan region. Home was a large sylvan suburban lot, a place of domesticity and private pleasures, with provision made for the most up-to-date urban services. Connections were designed throughout the community, through tree-lined streets and small local park spaces, creating parkland and linkages where no natural corridors existed. A significant landscape amenity was recognized—the natural landscape of the river and its corridor was protected as public parkland and joined to the community. From the railroad station Chicago was both close and a world away, as the world of work, industry, and commerce was kept at bay.

The Olmsted office would apply these principles in numerous developments over the succeeding decades in diverse settings, some in more urban settings and others in commuter suburbs and resort communities, those that aspired to be self-contained versus those that integrated into broader communities. The principles persisted and proved to be remarkably flexible. Perhaps most significant is that although they were conceptualized before the advent of the automobile, they proved to be adaptable to the dramatic imperatives of that vehicle.

In 1923 *Landscape Architecture* magazine featured a chart of 29 selected Olmsted Brothers projects from 1883 to 1923 complied by Henry Hubbard, Harvard educator and sometime member of the firm.[23] The chart enumerated the elusive boundaries between private desires and public responsibility codified into the covenants of restricted communities. A careful reading reveals both exclusions and expectations. Concerns and restrictions changed with the times, as domestic animals were excluded and stables gave way to garages. The subtleties of neighborliness defined as fences or hedges were sometimes allowed, but height limits were established and setbacks from 10 to 100 feet required. The suburban dream was not open to all. Exclusion was explicit in racially limiting covenants or implied by the economic prohibition of a minimum house cost. Generally, there were limitations on most nonresidential uses. The chart was an abstraction of an image, one that was to be carefully maintained to keep the suburban balance.

CLARENCE STEIN AND HENRY WRIGHT: RADBURN

In the 1920s a small group of individuals, including Lewis Mumford, Benton Mackaye, Clarence Stein, Henry Wright, Stuart Chase, and Charles Whitaker, formed the Regional Plan Association of America (RPAA). They were architects, planners, foresters, authors, critics, economists. We might now describe the group as a think tank. The RPAA put forth a vision of planning for twentieth-century America that went from the scale of house, to town, to metropolis, region, and nation. In 1925, Mumford, the intellectual leader of the group, succinctly summarized the technological changes that were transforming the basis for community development and organization. The transportation revolution, attributable to the automobile; the communications revolution, occasioned by the invention of the telephone; and access to electricity were changing the historical basis of settlement.[24] New ways of life were possible. The design of new communities and suburbs was one arena in which progressive reformers were seeking a response to these changes. The aspirations of the RPAA were ambitious; its members were

Radburn. House and yard.
Kate Van Rooy.

exploring models for the twentieth century. The organization's legacy is largely ideological, but it also exists in the reality of the Appalachian Trail and other national trails it spawned, and in the community design and planning of Clarence Stein and Henry Wright, most notably at Radburn, New Jersey.

Mumford and his colleagues were much influenced by the work of Britain's Garden City experiments and the ideas of Ebenezer Howard and Patrick Geddes. Reacting to the extremes of wealth and poverty in Britain's nineteenth-century industrialized cities, especially in the deplorable industrial slums, Howard conceived of an alternative, egalitarian urban form—the Garden City. New, planned cities, argued Howard, would offer ordinary people a third alternative to the town-or-country quandary—the "town-country magnet" would provide "all the advantages of the most energetic and active town, all the beauty and delight of the country"—in short, a healthy and balanced existence.[25] Garden cities were to be organic wholes, ancestors to today's sustainable communities. Each city, composed of interdependent systems, would be limited in size by its ability to supply all the basic services while still maintaining accessibility of people to commerce, work and recreation, as well as communication between people. When individuals could no longer envision their whole community, it had become too large.

In the prototypical scheme, the community of 32,000 occupied the central 1,000 acres of a 6,000-acre landholding. At the center of the circular plan was a 5-acre garden surrounded by civic, cultural, and medical buildings, encircled by a 145-acre park. The crystal palace, a glass gallery of shops and gardens—a shopping mall—created the link between the public park and the residential areas. Housing was in six wards located between the open space center and the factory perimeter. No house was more than 600

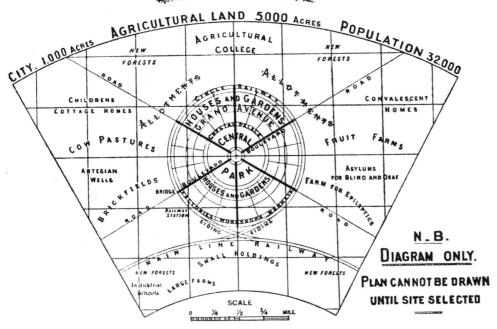

Garden City Diagram.
Ebenezer Howard, 1902. From F. J. Osborn,
ed., *Garden Cities of To-Morrow,*
Cambridge: MIT Press, 1965, p. 52.

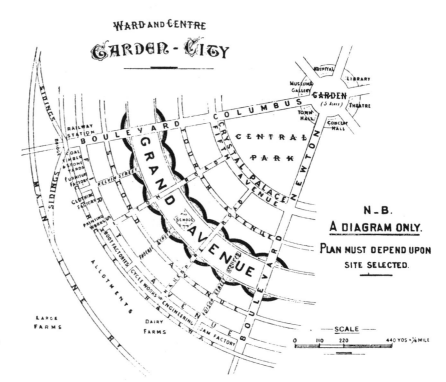

Ward and Centre, Garden City Diagram.
Ebenezer Howard, 1902. From F. J. Osborn,
ed., *Garden Cities of To-Morrow,*
Cambridge: MIT Press, 1965, p. 53.

yards from the community's center—Howard was mandating a pedestrian community. An apron of open land around the community was a permanent greenbelt of agriculture and forestry. The new city would be connected to other similar communities in the region by a high-speed railroad that encircled its industrial perimeter. Simplistic and diagrammatic, the plan itself never received much acceptance; however, the principles for new town planning espoused by Howard did. He proposed that new towns be regionally dispersed, living, working, and recreating communities, limited in size and population. Convinced that such communities needed physical and economic autonomy, he suggested that they be located at safe distances from urban centers. For economic prosperity, they needed a variety and sufficiency of commerce. They were to be self-governing, with urban lands under public control, planned and developed in an orderly manner, and not subject to speculation. In addition to having private yards, urban people had to have free and easy pedestrian access to many kinds of public spaces: public gardens, parks, boulevards, *indoor* shopping, allotment gardens, farms, and forests. The goal was not complete self-sufficiency, for isolation did not ensure success. Howard advocated a regional network of small communities which he called "social cities." This larger network, connected by train, of perhaps 10 such cities including a central city, would have the mass and economic base to balance employment with people. Social cities would dispense with the traditional urban hierarchy in favor of a more democratic distribution of wealth, culture, and industry.

Howard's radical attitudes toward land and townscape became fundamental principles of British new town planning. Along with his Garden City Association, he shepherded the planning and construction of two new towns, Letchworth, begun in 1903, and Welwyn Garden City, in 1919. Both of these garden city experiments were private ventures undertaken by Howard and his associates with funding obtained from a wider group of investors. Both were located in rural areas—Letchworth 35 miles, and Welwyn 20 miles north of London. Letchworth grew slowly; nonetheless, it contributed significantly to British town planning, notably through its well-designed low-rent housing for factory workers and ample public open space. Commonly cited for its innovations in landscape design, Letchworth had, in addition to its protective greenbelt perimeter, several very large parks located within a half-mile of most residents. But that was not all. Each residential block had a small common yard to the rear of the houses, connected via walkways to the street. Except in the highest-density worker housing, most residents had their own gardens as well, lots commonly being 20 by 100 feet. A variety of trees and shrubs lined the streets and enlivened the parks—Letchworth had achieved a lush, gardenlike quality, and it was this dramatically different townscape that attracted worldwide attention.

Welwyn Garden City, Howard's second garden city experiment, built on the experiences at Letchworth. Howard and a new group of associates again established a private town corporation to purchase and dispense the lands. However, they were more determined than the preceding group to control the inflation of land values, a condition that plagued Letchworth. The town plan was designed by Louis de Soissons, who, along with Howard and other directors, lived in the town as it developed. Rail lines divided the town into four quadrants. A large industrial area and a very compact town center were located near the crossing of these lines. The quadrants were then further subdivided into "units," each of which had a center of its own including shops, "public hall," and playground. Welwyn's open space plan was even

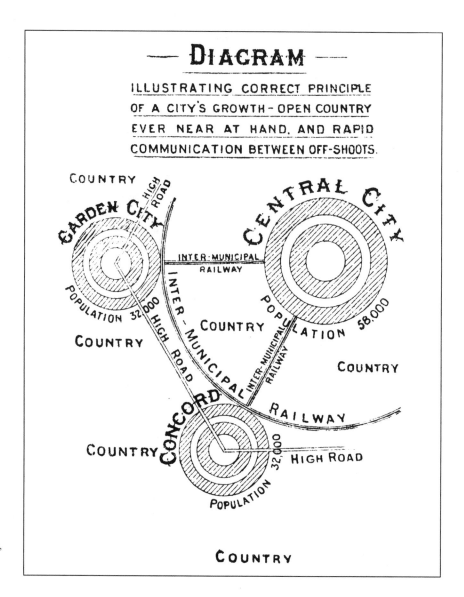

Social Cities.
Ebenezer Howard, 1902. From F. J. Osborn, ed., *Garden Cities of To-Morrow,* Cambridge: MIT Press, 1965, p. 143.

more sophisticated than Letchworth's. It was spacious in layout and characterized by curving tree-lined streets, which gave it a visual quality similar to London's garden suburbs. More than one-third of the town's legal area was designated as open space. Generous fingers of open space reached into the town's interior, and each quadrant had a large park connected via open space to the perimeter greenbelt. At Welwyn, blocks of high-density housing had shared yards, and a large proportion of the homes had large private gardens.

Architect and planner Clarence Stein described himself as a disciple of Howard and Raymond Unwin, the architect of Letchworth and Welwyn Garden Cities and Hampstead garden suburb. Henry Wright, Stein's collaborator, was an architect, but he had also worked in Kansas City for landscape architect George Kessler, the designer of one the nation's premier park systems. Their first experiment was at Sunnyside, within New York City, essentially a subway community. Sunnyside was notable for its interior block development, where houses surrounded central courts composed of private gardens and shared common space. Radburn, their next endeavor,

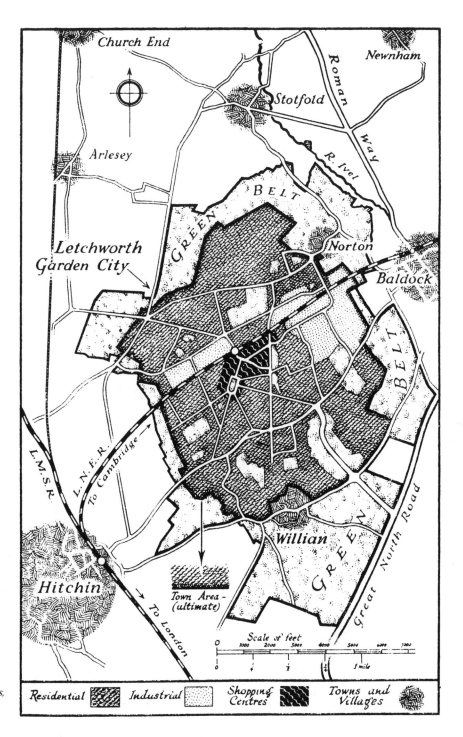

Plan of Letchworth.
Raymond Unwin, 1909. From Frederic J.
Osborn & Arnold Whittick, *The New Towns,*
London: Leonard Hill Books Ltd., 1963.

aspired to be an American garden city, following Howard's dictum that
"town and country must be married." Radburn added a third component; it
was "A Town Planned for the Motor Age." Only a few other designs, notably
John Nolan's 1918 plans for Mariemont, outside Cincinnati, had been
planned explicitly for the automobile.

At Radburn the aspiration to build an autonomous new town was
thwarted by geography and economics. The site, in northern New Jersey,
would soon be surrounded by other developments. It was destined to be a

commuter suburb, not a garden city, and it would develop without the desired greenbelt or economic base and never grow to its envisioned size. The first homes were occupied only six months before the October 1929 crash that marked the onset of the Great Depression. Originally planned for a population of 25,000 to 30,000 on a square mile, only two of its super-blocks were constructed. The core area is only 100 acres with about 500 dwelling units.[26] Despite this modest scale, the Radburn plan would exercise a remarkable impact on subsequent suburban design. Sometimes its design principles were followed, but more often work was done that echoed Radburn in name only, without its substance, truncating its comprehensive vision.

Radburn was promoted as "A Town for the Motor Age" and as "A Town for children." To achieve such goals, both physical and social planning were crucial. Spatial patterns were intended to foster a rich family life, focused on children, with a community design that fostered social interaction. The design mechanism to achieve these ends was the Radburn plan. Its five essential components were outlined by Stein in his 1957 book, *Toward New Towns for America:*[27]

1. The Superblock
2. Specialized Roads Planned and Built for One use Instead of all Uses
3. Complete Separation of Pedestrian and Automobile
4. Houses Turned Around
5. Park as Backbone

These five components were not autonomous, but interdependent, reinforcing each other in an integrated scheme. Radburn was to be a "town turned outside-in—without any backdoors . . . where roads and parks fit together like fingers of your right and left hands."[28] Each house fronted both a pedestrian walkway and a cul-de-sac street of 15 to 20 houses. These culs-de-sac wrapped around a green park spine to create a superblock of 35 to 50 acres served by arterial roads. The concept of a neighborhood unit, developed by Clarence Perry, was an essential component in the scheme. Perry's ideal neighborhoods included 4,000 to 7,000 people, the population needed to support an elementary school, the institution at the core of Radburn's neighborhoods and of most suburbs ever since. Overlapping Radburn's superblocks were neighborhoods of a half-mile radius with an elementary school at the center of the circle. Each neighborhood was also to be serviced by a local shopping center. The overlapping circles converged at the site's highest point, where the high school was to be located. Each neighborhood was to have 7,500 to 10,000 inhabitants; however, none was ever completed. The goal of each of these progressive social units—the cul-de-sac, the walkways, the superblock, the park, and the neighborhood unit itself, was a traditional one, to have a face-to-face community, versus the collection of strangers so characteristic of urban life.[29]

Each Radburn house, single family or attached, had two faces. The houses were "turned around," and the relationship between back door and front was mooted. The living room area faced inward toward pedestrian walkways and the central green park, and the kitchen faced the cul-de-sac, the street, and the connection to the highway. At its core, the two faces of the Radburn house attempted to combine city and country, to reconcile the suburban polarities. Stein and Wright were very clear in identifying several realms of private and public space in the community: the house and a small

Plan of Radburn, New Jersey.
Clarence Stein and Henry Wright, 1929.
From Clarence S. Stein, *Towards New Towns
for America,* Cambridge: MIT Press, 1966,
p. 43.

Cul-de-sac, Radburn, New Jersey.
Clarence Stein and Henry Wright, 1929.
From Clarence S. Stein, *Towards New Towns
for America,* Cambridge: MIT Press, 1966,
p. 42.

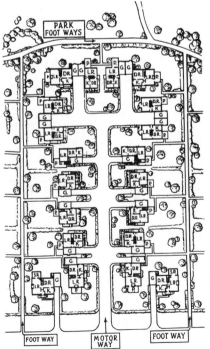

private yard would provide space for intimate family activities; casual inter-action, recreation, and children's activities would occur on public walks or at tot lots, parks, playfields, school yards, and community pools; and the culs-de-sac would provide functional access for the family and socialization opportunities on the streets. Stein wrote about trying to decide where to hang the wash, for the location was not immediately apparent. It was finally relegated to the cul-de-sac side of the houses. The opposite "public" side was where visitors and prospective buyers were taken.[30] Originally, each house had three doors: one on the kitchen/car side, which was more utilitar-ian and heavily used; one on the garden side, opening onto a porch; and a rarely used more "formal" side entry to the living room. These were soon simplified to two. Houses were linked by garages, and half of the dwellings were multifamily. As the site plan changed, the house plan varied and was adapted to fit its particular situation in the community scheme. Each was site specific, thus houses at the end or middle of a cul-de-sac were distinct, on lots averaging 4,500 square feet.

Central to the Radburn idea was how to create "a town in which people could live peacefully with the automobile—or rather in spite of it."[31] The importance of the Radburn plan's response to the automobile cannot be overestimated. Although Stein and Wright desired to build a true American garden city, they were well aware that in such proximity to New York, this would be a commuting suburb. The response to the car was pivotal, espe-cially in the still-formative period of automobile development. The de-signers and the home buyers of Radburn had grown up with the automobile and had personally witnessed its formidable and often devastating impact on society and the city. New patterns were needed. Stein believed the automobile made the urban grid "as obsolete as a fortified town wall." The reality that "the roadbed was the children's main play space" was contrasted with the fact that "parked cars, hard gray roads and garages replaced gar-dens."[32] At the most personal level he noted the thousands killed or injured, the noise, and the loss of community. In many ways Radburn represented a desire to return those lost gardens to the landscape.

Radburn, 1980. Patio along the cul-de-sac "street" side.
Kenneth Helphand.

One community design mechanism included a refined hierarchy of roads and circulation from footways to service ways to arterials to highway. The road was to serve, not dominate, the community. The character and scale of each road in the hierarchy varied. Inspired by Frederick Law Olmsted's innovative scheme for Central Park, which has four separate circulation networks, Radburn's plan offered separate car and pedestrian networks. The system of spatial arrangement, overpasses, and underpasses meant that to traverse the community on foot, streets need not be crossed. There are more than four miles of walkway in Radburn's original built area, connected to another four in later additions.[33] An additional advantage of the plan was that only 21% of land area was road, versus the conventional 35% at the time. The saving in cost was substantial, and the money was largely used to finance the generous open space system. The other key mechanism was the superblock 1,200 to 1,800 feet long, versus the conventional 200- to 600-foot urban block. Each superblock was ringed by arterial roads and penetrated by shorter, narrower culs-de-sac, with traffic diminishing to zero at the core, the park. The Radburn superblock plan was first sketched by Herbert Emmerich during one of the planning discussions. A manager, not a designer, he later became head of the Federal Public Housing Authority.[34] No Radburn home was more than 400 feet from parkland *or* roadway. The superblock invention with its signature culs-de-sac became a template for suburban layout, only recently challenged by planners favoring traditional grid layouts.

Stein's sensitivity to the actual lives of children and their families was remarkable. Observing the built landscape, he saw that the paved lanes and the culs-de-sac were used for play. The hard surfaces were essential for wheeled toys.[35] Despite his profound concern for safety, he did not think children and autos should be completely separated, because, he said, "the spirit of adventure should not be extinguished." The walkways, cul-de-sac, and superblock provide the practical dimensions for monitoring children by giving geographical limits to behavior and parental knowledge of the safety of the path system. Surely children cannot be forbidden to cross streets, but

Radburn, 1980. Houses along walkway connecting street to interior park.
Kenneth Helphand.

Radburn at least afforded the possibility for segregated travel. For adults the incentive and pleasure were provided as well. No one walked to work, but the local shopping area had off-street parking and was one of the first, along with Kansas City's Country Club District, to provide pedestrian linkages into the neighborhood. A 1970 study noted that 47% of Radburn residents shopped for groceries on foot, versus 23% at the new town of Reston and 8% in an unplanned community.[36]

Each pedestrian walkway led to the park. Bordered by wide paths on all sides, it was a pastoral linear meadow expanding into recreational fields, with benches, shelters, and play areas along the way. The land was held in trust and protected, the restrictive deeds of earlier suburbs acting as the legal precedent.[37] The emphasis was on recreation, leisure, and provision of a safe, stimulating environment for kids, with all the most modern conveniences. Developed during a time when recreation was the dominant ideology for park planners, there were 20 acres of park, two pools (which were the de facto community centers in the summer), four tennis courts, four ball fields, three playgrounds, an archery plaza, and two summer-houses, along with recreation directors, a summer day camp, and, during the rest of the year, an after-school program. There was also an extensive program of adult education.[38]

Radburn. Community Pool.
Kenneth Helphand.

Radburn. Interior park within superblock.
Kenneth Helphand.

Landscape architect Marjorie Sewell Cautley, who was responsible for the planting scheme, said one could understand the Radburn plan only by walking. "In the first place there are no backyards," for front and rear yard definitions were mooted. The scene was a rich one. Densely planted, it soon filled in, affording views to small lawns and gardens, walkways, hedges, and the park. Careful attention was paid to each situation. Houses "shut in" at the ends of streets had the most extensive views "up and down the parks." In the home areas planting was originally done as "garden groups," and there were distinctive plantings for each street as well. For example, one street was planted as an orchard garden, another a walk of mock orange and dogwood, another of honey locust, mountain ash, rose vines, and spirea.[39] There were no restrictions on individuals' changing plantings on their lots. The overall effect was one of houses set within an overgrown garden. At the clearings, the superblock core, were found the parks.

In 1930, Cautley wrote, "One year ago these parks were spinach fields . . . it is the desire of the landscape designer to preserve for Radburn a part of the beautiful natural growth that is being destroyed so rapidly throughout northern New Jersey." Her planting plan included native cedars, junipers, and wild roses so that "there will still be an echo of the woods and meadows upon which it was built." In a 1921 article, "Shall We Community Plan?" Henry Wright spoke of the desire for "strands of open territory in close relation to the residential groups. . . . These areas would preserve, as far as possible, the natural landscape."[40] Wright's statement is a prescient one. As originally conceived, the complete Radburn plan was to have connected to the Saddle River, whose riverbank was to be preserved as parkland. Unfortunately, this phase was never completed. He also wrote of areas of "natural subdivisions," presumably determined by topographic relationships, and Stein thought it important to hold lands in reserve for unforeseen community needs.[41] Landscape amenity was not a frivolous expense but a fundamental aspect of community life. "Like Olmsted, Stein and Wright dared put beauty as one of the imperative needs of a planned environment: the beauty of ordered buildings, measured to the human scale, of trees and flowering plants, and of open greens surrounded by buildings of low density, so that children may scamper over them, to add to both their use and their aesthetic loveliness . . . these planners insisted on including open spaces and generous plantings as part of the essential first costs of housing," wrote Mumford.[42]

Was Radburn a success? The community progressed slowly. In the Depression economy, 80% of Radburn homes were repossessed. Yet in 1936 *Architectural Forum* lauded the design. For $8,900, a buyer was able to purchase a six-room house along with a "garage, concrete walks, water, a complete park and playground system and landscaping that reminds you of parks and not of sticks on the sand. It gave your acres a caretaker in the form of the Radburn Association, and it gave your house individuality with cul-de-sac streets. But more than all that, it gave you and your neighbors continuing attention in an integrated community."[43] Although the aspiration was for a town that would have housing for diverse social classes, Radburn would be thoroughly middle-class. The initial house prices of $7,900 to 18,200 were about double the American average at the time.[44] Radburn offered the amenities of a country club within a residential landscape. The character was campuslike, and, in fact, 87% of Radburn men and 74% of the women had gone to college, in 1934 when fewer than 6% of American adults had college degrees.[45] The combination country club and campus imagery is a provocative one and deserving of further investigation.

Alden Christie, an architecture student and Radburn resident, offered a more critical perspective in 1964. His comments may be taken as a sign of how given spaces functioned in ways that were not intended, *or* as a sign of their adaptability.

> Neighboring Radburn cul-de-sacs have no social connection. Interests are turned inward. The kitchen becomes the inelegant focal point for all outside activity, which consists of "across the pavement" contacts. . . . The children play more in the lanes than the parks . . . the automobile becomes, in fact, a member of the family . . . despite this, Radburn has always retained its validity as a place for young couples and small children. . . . The layout of the dwellings in the superblocks creates a network of intensely developed spaces which abruptly evaporate into a shapeless common, too vaguely defined to suggest an extension or expansion of private yards, too wide to command a directional tendency towards a focal point, too sparsely landscaped to invite a refuge from the tight complex of houses . . . the automobile has been made such a dominant feature of the Radburn scheme that life is more oriented towards the peripheral access road . . . than towards the common green."[46]

Although Radburn's designers hoped for an accommodation with the automobile, it was difficult for them to predict its overpowering role in modern society. The car is present there today, even ever-present, but it is put in a more modest place, recognized as necessity, but not a pervasive intruder. One can walk safely, one can be out of the view of the street, and if desired, one can walk down lanes or culs-de-sac. The Radburn plan offered a choice.

Garden city ideas went full circle, and the impact of Radburn was particularly strong in Europe, which was more receptive to planned community ideas. The recent evolution of new towns in Great Britain began with the passage of the 1946 New Towns Act, authorizing the government to site and establish new towns. The government reserved authority to review the plans, finances, and progress of each town. Once a new town was declared, land was expropriated from private landowners (with fair reimbursement) and handed over to an independent corporation that usually hired a planning staff to design the community. Although various existing conditions, regional economies, and unique sites contributed to the distinctive nature of British new towns, there were consistent characteristics. The new town nucleus was a pedestrian-oriented shopping, cultural, and service center. The residential areas were always (except in Cumbernauld) subdivided into neighborhoods of 5,000 to 10,000 people, usually with one or two elementary schools and small neighborhood commercial and community centers. In Howard's two formative experiments, the industrial areas had been located near to the center of the community, but this proved to be undesirable. In the postwar new towns industrial sites were relocated to the outskirts, close to motorways or railroads (a return to Howard's original diagram).

Open space layouts in England followed aspects of the work of Stein and Wright. The 1944 Dudley Report by the Central Housing Advisory Committee spoke of the striking advantages of the Radburn system, in terms of layouts and the superblock schemes. The ideas were only partially adaptable to a different culture and were adapted piecemeal. This is important to observe, for the critiques and kudos from abroad reflect distinctive cultural conditions. It was noted, for example, that the private garden was seen by most as a "basic English requirement," versus the semiprivate yards of the Radburn scheme. In their 1963 study of British new towns, Frederick Osborn and Arnold Whittick frequently made comparisons between Radburn and the block and open space layouts of the new towns. Like Radburn, houses fronted onto public walks, and cars entered auto courts from the rear. Each neighborhood was composed of a series of these tightly clustered housing groups. Perhaps a result of higher housing densities, the houses did not have immediate access to public parks as they did at Radburn. Instead, larger neighborhood groupings were surrounded by broad greens and, frequently, adjoining streamways, forests, or other landscape elements deemed worthy of preservation. The greens often led to the town center. One of the striking differences between these new towns and Letchworth and Welwyn Garden City was the addition of networks of open space. This invention by American planners—open space networks—directly influenced post-World War II British models, as well as new town plans in many other countries. Meanwhile, the greenbelt and its corollary, the town of limited size, were the most lasting contributions of the British to new town planning.

In the United States the use of the cul-de-sac, a hierarchical road system, and common open spaces, along with Perry's neighborhood unit plans of curved streets, became semiofficial doctrine. Radburn directly influenced the modest U.S. federal government experiments of town planning in the

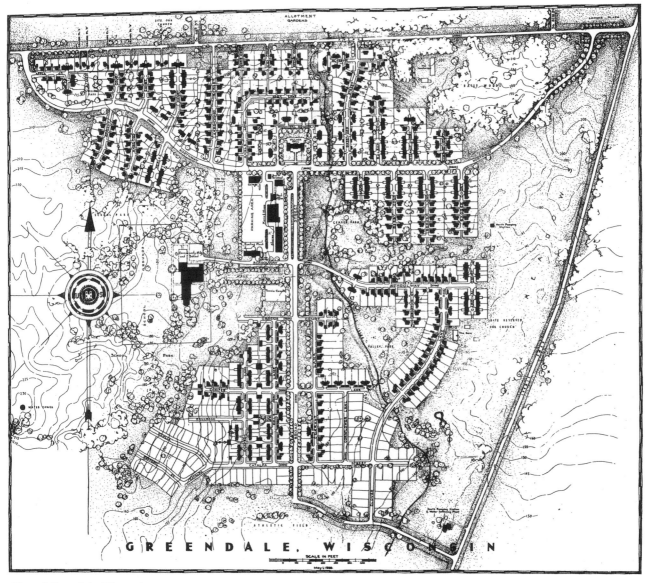

G R E E N D A L E, W I S C O N S I N

SCALE IN FEET
May 1, 1936

Plan of Greendale, Wisconsin.
Elbert Peets, 1938. From Paul D. Spreiregen,
ed., *On the Art of Designing Cities: Selected
Essays of Elbert Peets,* Cambridge: The MIT
Press, 1968.

1930s, the Greenbelt towns of the New Deal. In 1935, the Resettlement
Administration was established to create jobs through the planning, design,
and construction of new communities, while providing healthful low-rent
housing. Under Rexford Tugwell's leadership, Resettlement Administration
planners eagerly undertook the challenge to explore issues of good community design. Following the planning principles of the RPAA and, specifically,
the model designed at Radburn, they aspired to design an American Garden
City. The Greenbelt towns were satellite communities located in rural areas
and controlled in size by a greenbelt of public lands. They were built at
Greenbelt, Maryland; Greendale, Wisconsin; and Greenhills, Ohio. Most
housing was apartments and row houses, geared toward lower-middle-
income groups, and each community had services including schools, recreation centers, churches, and shopping. Typically, the physical organization
of Greenbelt town plans was determined by two independent public networks: walkways within green spaces connected all places of recreation,

education, and local service, and streets carried vehicles in and out of the community. These networks intersected at two places, the house and the shopping center. At home, the car would arrive and service the back door, and front windows overlooked the yard and the public green. The shopping and community centers were situated at the terminus of the public green and were equally served by streets and walkways. Elbert Peets's Greendale plan was indebted to Radburn, but in its more formal aspects also to Midwestern county seats and traditional village design.[47] The combination and multiplicity of sources anticipated the neotraditional designers of the 1980s. The Greenbelt towns represented one clear, simple conception of community life for the modern era, that a successful living environment could encourage a rich, public social life through well-connected private and public outdoor spaces, while simultaneously the automobile provided access to the wider world. The marriage of physical design and social ideals had more limited success. The Greenbelt towns had little diversity, they were home largely to couples with young children, blacks were excluded, and a working wife was reason for ejection. On the other hand, recent feminist writing, notably by Dolores Hayden in "What Would a Non-Sexist City be Like?" pointed to Radburn, recognizing in its plan the value of the potentials for social interaction and its communal values.[48] Ironically, the Greenbelt towns experiments influenced planning education and ideology throughout the world, but were destined to have little impact on the American public. The next major attempt at new town planning did not occur until the 1960s at Reston, Virginia, and Columbia, Maryland.

The lessons of Radburn are many, but it was Mumford who may have offered the best assessment: "What he [Stein] and Wright demonstrated are not forms to be copied, but a spirit to be assimilated and carried further, a method of integration to be perfected, a body of tradition to be modified and transmitted—and in time transmuted into new forms that will reflect the needs and desires and hopes of another age."[49] Portions of the plan, aspects of the idea, are found in virtually all planned (and unplanned) communities. Unfortunately, they are most often just pieces, segments of the idea: a cul-de-sac, an interior park, a superblock, or a walkway. Rarely do they have the thoughtful, carefully calibrated systemic integration of Radburn, evident in aspects ranging from the scale of rooms and their relationship to the yard and street, to the entire community plan.

FRANK LLOYD WRIGHT: BROADACRE CITY

Broadacre City was also a town for the motor age, but its architect, Frank Lloyd Wright, reached radically different conclusions in his visionary community design. Wright shared Mumford's analysis of the forces at work in modern society and also ascribed a predominant role to the new technologies. However, their differences lay in divergent visions of community and the role of technology. Wright's ideology was rooted in an individualistic ethic versus the social aspirations of the RPAA. His visions, so deeply embedded in American values, demand to be examined. Broadacre City at first glance looks like the postwar suburb, a low-density dispersion sprawled across the landscape, but a careful examination of the plan will show that there are important distinctions to be made between Wright's scheme and suburban reality.

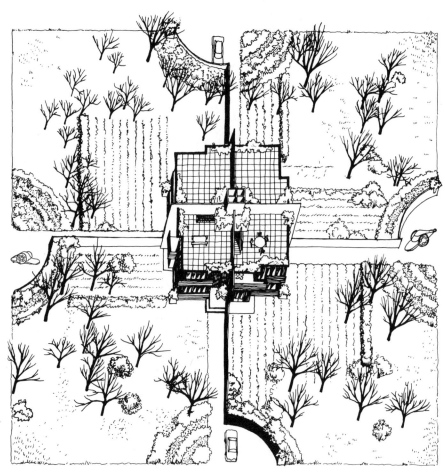

Broadacre City. House and yard prototype.
Cluster of four homes.
Kate Van Rooy.

Wright's Broadacre proposal was a response to the modern condition of the twentieth-century city, which he characterized as a menacing, cancerous growth. He sought a haven from urban centralization and its evils, from places he found "barbaric in the true meaning of the word."[50] In *The Disappearing City* of 1932 he first wrote about his Broadacre idea, but he would continue to ponder his proposal and elaborate on it throughout his life, including an illustrative version of the plan in *Architectural Record* in 1935 and another in *The Living City,* published just before his death in 1959. He visualized the scheme in drawings and in models constructed by his Taliesin apprentices, first displayed in 1935 at the newly completed urban complex of Rockefeller Center.[51] Wright produced drawings of the plan and continued to develop its many sections, often placing his built and unbuilt projects in the drawings. His was a contemporary response to a classical desire. "Here come the means to take all the real advantages of the centralization known as the city into the regional field we call the countryside and unite them with the features of the ground in that union we call modern architecture in that native creation we call the beauty of the country."[52]

In an echo of Mumford's analysis, Wright categorized the forces of change into three groups. First was individualized transportation, the automobile and the general mobilization of the human being. Second were advances in electrification and communication: refrigeration, heating, lighting, radio, telephone, and "soon television." Third was standardized machine-shop production: machine invention and scientific discovery.[53] These technological forces had transformed the verities of temporal and spatial relations, and optimistic modernists saw in these devices the potential to foster a new culture and way of life. Wright saw the possibility of an architecture whereby "the individual comes into his own" in cities where "no longer do human satisfactions depend upon density of population."[54] In Wright's decentralized vision city, suburb, and country would have an organic unity, reminiscent of what Mumford had described as planned regionalization. America's past and future would unite to create "the free city of democracy," and the technology of "Edison and Ford would resurrect Jefferson."[55]

The Broadacre City drawings are but an illustrative fragment of a continuous vision for the nation. Wright's intention was a national landscape plan, on the order of the Northwest Ordinance of 1785 and its survey system of township, section, and range. Wright placed Broadacre squarely into the Jeffersonian frame, requiring no change to the existing system of land surveys. The germs of Broadacre lay in Wright's noncompetitive entry to the 1913 City Club of Chicago competition for a housing development for a quarter-section of land. In this scheme, the urban grid is extended into a park and boulevard system with all houses no more than two blocks from a green space. Careful site planning and generous space gave the appearance of "well grouped buildings in a park."[56] At Broadacre the nineteenth-century railroad was gone, completely replaced by the automobile or airplanes. A 12 lane road linked the city to its surroundings. The city was then subdivided by a hierarchical gridwork of roads in a decentralized scheme with centralized elements. There were "small" or "little" components of houses, apartments, factories (with dwellings above), schools, cinema, clinics, and laboratories. Most homes were on one acre, but there were also apartments, "luxurious homes," and farms. There was a great emphasis on education, culture, and recreation. Larger factories were off the highway, but

Bird's eye view of the quarter section, Frank Lloyd Wright. City Residential Land Development Competition entry, Chicago, Illinois. © 1916 The City Club of Chicago. From Alfred Yeomans, City Residential Land Development, Chicago: University of Chicago Press, 1916, p. 97.

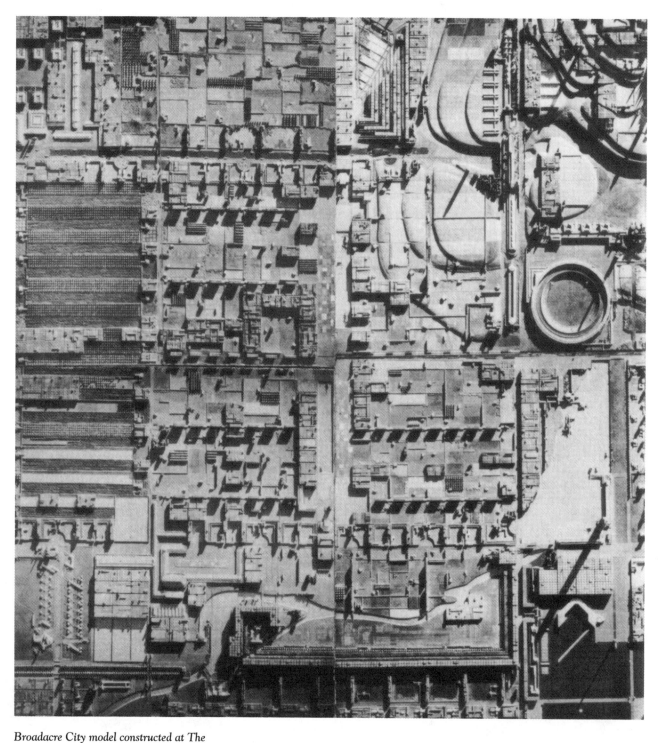

**Broadacre City model constructed at The
Hacienda, Chandler, AZ, 1934.**
From Frank Lloyd Wright, *The Living City.* New
York: Bramhall House, 1958, p. 66.
Copyright © 1958, The Frank Lloyd Wright
Foundation.

adjacent to vineyards and orchards. Perhaps most striking was Wright's awareness of, and provision for, land uses that became dominant later in the century. The gas station he described as a community center; there was an automobile inn off the highway, a market that anticipated regional shopping centers, a boulevard connector replete with zoo, aquarium, arboretum, and stadium. There were scientific and agricultural research stations, much like contemporary research parks. At the core lay schools with housing areas extending out a half mile, much like Radburn's neighborhoods. The county seat overlooked the lake, recreational facilities sat astride the creek, and a forested hillside was home to dwellings and schools. Small farms and the agricultural landscape framed and infiltrated the city.[57]

The name was telling: Broadacres, as Wright called it, was grand in scale, expansive—a city built around a module of one acre per household. He saw the name as referring to the broad freedoms the individual would experience. It also had the ring of a real estate development.[58] Of the plan, Wright would say that it was ". . . a free pattern. . . . of the ground and with the ground."[59] The model and plans have evoked many images. The city is composed much like a painting, with patterns that recall DeStijl compositions. It has the vibrancy of Mondrian's *Broadway Boogie-Woogie.* George Collins found it morphologically unique, with its origins in Wright's architectural and site-planning vocabulary, but surprisingly having no allusions or resemblance to either garden-city planning or neighborhood planning.[60] Perhaps Broadacres sources lie outside the city. Fishman notes the model's similarity to a fairground, in both its composition and the emphasis on recreational and educational facilities.[61] Portions have a campuslike character. Most significantly, one must look to the countryside, to the formal geometries of agricultural production, especially of the Midwest, with its multiple fields, squares, bands of crops, woodlots, hedgerows, isolated individual farmsteads, and rural roadways. The plan derives from the rural landscape as much as it does from urban grid patterns.[62] Grounded as it is in the Midwestern landscape and its pattern of house, field, woodlot, and road, beneath the Broadacre plan it is not hard to discern an idealized and modernized Wisconsin landscape. This is what Wright wished Chicago might become. "Looking down on the model it is almost impossible to distinguish among random nature, cultivated agriculture, or manmade buildings," wrote Walter Creese.[63] This is landscape made into cityscape, much as historian Albert Fein described Olmsted's urban visions.[64]

In Broadacre the home was "the most important unit in the city, really the center and the only centralization allowable."[65] One-acre plots for each family, large enough for intensive gardens, were Broadacre's basic building blocks. The interpenetrating spatial composition of Wright's open-plan architecture extended beyond the building walls. "The home would be an indoor garden, the garden an outdoor house," he wrote.[66] This low density yielded a "new scale of spacing" not confined to Wright's individualistic neo-Jeffersonian ideal of the modern yeoman.[67] There was a companion dimension: "the new standard of space measurement—the man seated in his automobile." Wright explained: "The fundamental unit of space-measurement has [so] radically changed that the man now bulks ten to one and in speed a thousand to one as he is seated in his motor car."[68] Broadacre assumed universal automobile ownership, and the houses themselves were classified as having from one to five cars. For Wright, mobility was natural and a fundamental human longing, and he often spoke of the mythic origins of civilization as a struggle between the cave dweller versus the more mobile tent dweller. He likened the freedoms of the driver to those of a captive bird whose cage had been opened, and he went as far as imagining personalized flight in small helicopters.[69]

Mobility, said Wright, is not entirely positive: "Perpetual to and fro excites and robs the urban individual of the meditation, imaginative reflection and projection once his as he lived and walked under clean sky among the growing greenery to which he was born companion."[70] Mobility needed to be guided and designed. "There is no more important function looking toward the city of the future than to get the best architects in the world interested in road building," he wrote.[71] These road builders would give order to the community and create a beautiful and efficient system where the machine was in its proper place. Part of the generation that witnessed the invention of the automobile, Wright imagined its most optimistic possibilities. Although the form was different, there was a kinship between his Broadacre model and that of Normal Bel Geddes's Futurama model presented at the General Motors Pavilion during the 1939 New York World's Fair.

The roads of Broadacre City united and separated areas and functions. Wright imagined the design of "spacious landscaped highways, grade crossings eliminated, 'by-passing' living areas . . . bright with wayside flowers, cool with shade trees," without telephone poles, wires, or billboards. These roads integrated all the diversified units of farms, factory, roadside markets, garden schools, and dwelling. The scale was new, and the city was now a region where each "citizen of the future will have all forms of production, distribution, self-improvement, enjoyment, within a radius of a hundred and fifty miles of his home now easily and speedily available by means of his car or his plane."[72] Wright anticipated the shopping strip and the regional shopping mall as new centers for commerce and expanded leisure possibilities. At his great Roadside Market, produce and products were to be sold in an atmosphere of entertainment. The Communal Center, near a major highway, would have "golf courses, racetrack, zoo, aquarium and planetarium . . . and a botanical garden," along with an art gallery and museum.[73]

The schools would be "garden schools" that "would be first, a park in the choicest part of the countryside, preferably by a stream or body of water [with] . . . enough ground for a flower and vegetable bed for each pupil alongside, with large play-spaces beyond that." All students would work the soil and learn to draw, because, he said, "eye minded is modern minded."[74] The Broadacre plan shows a stream running though the site and a dammed lake, reminiscent of the similar bodies of water found and created at Wright's Wisconsin Taliesin home. Alongside the water are found a pastoral park, music garden, baths, medical facilities, craft workshops, and the office of the county architect.

The park was not the primary green space. Wright's vision of an amalgam of city and country was not a scenic one, but one founded on a working landscape. This was not a garden city where landscape was primarily an amenity, or a suburb where people had the pleasures of living in the park. It was more a rural city with the character of living within a working countryside. Thus the farmer and the agricultural landscape became integral to the city and were no longer relegated to the hinterland. The proposal included intensive farming in greenhouses and farms of three to ten acres. Factories and offices were treated in a similar fashion, subdividing them into smaller units that were then reintegrated into the city. There were vineyards and orchards, shown as occupying almost 20% of the area of the plan. Having

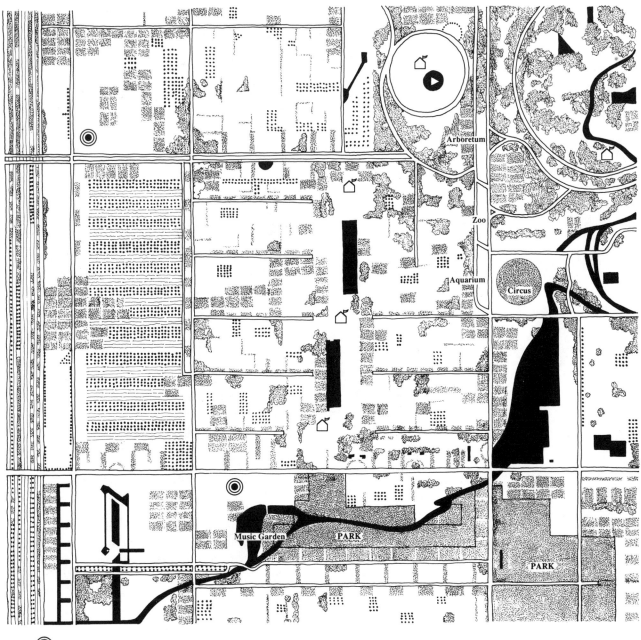

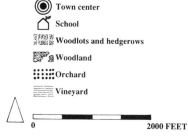

⊚ Town center

🏠 School

🌿🌿 Woodlots and hedgerows

🌳🌳 Woodland

▦▦ Orchard

☰☰ Vineyard

0   2000 FEET

Broadacre City highlighting agricultural land uses.
Kate Van Rooy.

the farmer in the city, Wright thought, "is a most welcome and perhaps the most attractive unit in all the structure of the city of the future."[75] High-rise buildings were isolated in parks, for Wright felt humanity had a "natural horizontality" and needed to stay close to "his birthright, the ground."[76] However, he did propose apartment living for those he described as "confirmed 'citified'."[77]

The boundary between landscape and cityscape is intentionally mooted at Broadacre in a spectrum that ranges from rural to urban. Wright's intentions were clear: "Broadacre City is no city at all in the sense that you are using the word. Broadacre City is everywhere or nowhere. It is the country itself come alive as a truly great city."[78] The agricultural landscape of fields, gardens, hedgerows, orchard, vineyard, and waterways, along with the technology of roads, the acre plots, and the institutional framework, gives the city its character. "Here architecture is landscape and landscape takes on the character of architecture by way of the simple process of cultivation."[79]

Wright postulated a hypothetical site for Broadacre. However, the preservation of existing landscape features is implied in the drawings and model, which exploit distinct sites of a forested hill and the shores of a lake and streams. "Woods, streams, mountains, ranges of hills, the great plains—all are shrines, beauty to be preserved. Architecture and acreage seen as landscape."[80] No cities would be alike, because they arise out of different situations that determine the shape and style of building. Reforestation, with woodlots as part of house and farm units, is found everywhere as a basic component of the plan. The term, urban forestry was not yet coined, but Wright proposed a program with government subsidies to plant "useful trees like white pine, walnut, birch, beech, fir" and fruit and nut trees. These would beautify the city and give it "character, privacy and comfort."[81]

Critics were contemptuous of calling Broadacre a city. George Collins called Broadacre "the Wrightian substitute for the city"; Meyer Shapiro called it a "shabby streamline utopia"; Wright biographer Brendan Gill found it a "homogenous non-city," which if built could be "a coast-to-coast, bumper-to-bumper Levittown."[82] Carl Feiss, although lauding Wright and his utopian desires, saw Broadacre City as "the subdivision plat for a middle-class suburb in Utopia." Recently, Robert Fishman, a more sympathetic suburban observer, saw in Wright's plan an optimism about design for a modern landscape that integrated "all the different functions of this new city into a viable whole" and a vision of "a stable landscape in which growth can be integrated and managed."[83]

Broadacre City is often described as if it were identical to the suburbs that developed after World War II. Some of the reasons are obvious. It was a decentralized, sprawling scheme. It was dependent on the automobile, acclaimed the car and the individual home. There was an orientation and celebration of leisure and recreation. However, in other ways it was a radical departure from the postwar suburb. Broadacre City was not a dormitory suburb. Its land uses were integrated, agriculture was integral to the community, and industry and commerce were equally present. The relationship of home and work was considered, as was the full array of human activity and services. In its inclusion of agriculture, its awareness of scale, and its attention to the virtues of the small, the plan was in many respects a true precursor to more recent sustainable city proposals.

Riverside and the nineteenth-century planned suburb set the basic planned parameters of suburban planning. They provided one model of integrated open space linking together house and garden, parkway and park. Riverside celebrates its origins at an annual Olmsted Day. Radburn aspired to a more democratic model of dwelling, and sought to accommodate the automobile while retaining the pastoral qualities of suburban life. Every July, Radburn celebrates a Family Day with elaborate celebrations. Broadacre City offered a more individualistic program, and represented a shift in the ideal, the rare model that confronted the rural aspect of the suburban equation.

NOTES

1. Leo Marx, *The Machine in the Garden: Technology and the Pastoral Ideal in America* (New York: Oxford University Press, 1964), p. 17.

2. John Archer, "City and Country in the American Romantic Suburb," *Journal of the Society of the Architectural Historians* **42,** No. 2 (1983):139–156.

3. Andrew Jackson Downing, *Rural Essays* (New York: Geo. A. Leavitt, 1869), pp. 236–243.

4. Susan Henderson, "Llewellyn Park, Suburban Idyll," *Journal of Garden History* **7,** No. 3 (1987):225.

5. Andrew Jackson Downing, *A Treatise on the Theory and Practice of Landscape Gardening* (New York: A. O. Moore, 1859), p. 568.

6. Robert Fishman, *Bourgeois Utopias: The Rise and Fall of Suburbia* (New York: Basic Books, 1987), p. 125.

7. Frederick Law Olmsted, "Memorandum Accompanying drawing for C.E. Norton, Cambridge, Mass." (February 8, 1868), in David Schuyler and Jane Turner Censer, eds., *The Papers of Frederick Law Olmsted,* Vol. 6, *The Years of Olmsted, Vaux and Company 1865–1874* (Baltimore: Johns Hopkins University Press, 1992), p. 257.

8. Charles Eliot, *Charles Eliot: Landscape Architect* (Boston: Houghton Mifflin, 1902), p. 214.

9. Frederick Law Olmsted, "To Calvert Vaux August 24, 1868" in David Schuyler and Jane Turner Censer, eds., *The Papers of Frederick Law Olmsted,* Vol. 6, *The Years of Olmsted, Vaux and Company, 1865-74* (Baltimore: Johns Hopkins University Press, 1992), p. 270.

10. Ibid., p. 280.

11. Fishman, *Bourgeois Utopias,* p. 127–129; and John Stilgoe, *Borderland: Origins of the American Suburb 1829–1939* (New Haven, CT: Yale University Press, 1988).

12. Ann Durkin Keating, *Building Chicago: Suburban Developers and the Creation of a Divided Metropolis* (Columbus: Ohio State University Press, 1988), p. 73.

13. Frederick Law Olmsted, "Preliminary Report Upon the Proposed Suburban Village at Riverside, near Chicago, by Olmsted, Vaux & Co." September 1, 1868, in David Schuyler and Jane Turner Censer, eds., *The Papers of Frederick Law Olmsted, Vol. 6, The Years of Olmsted, Vaux and Company 1865-1874* (Baltimore: Johns Hopkins University Press, 1992) p. 287.

14. Stilgoe, *Borderland,* p. 259.

15. Olmsted, "Preliminary Report Upon the Proposed Suburban Village at Riverside . . .", p. 287.

16. Ibid., p. 280.

17. Ibid., p. 288.

18. Ibid., p. 277.

19. Ibid., p. 285.

20. Albert Fein, *Frederick Law Olmsted and the American Environmental Tradition* (New York: George Braziller, 1972), p. 34.

21. Frederick Law Olmsted, "To Mary Perkins Olmsted," August 23, 1868, in David Schuyler and Jane Turner Censer, eds., *The Papers of Frederick Law Olmsted, Vol. 6, The Years of Olmsted, Vaux and Company 1865-1874,* (Baltimore: Johns Hopkins University Press, 1992) p. 266.

22. Olmsted, "Preliminary Report Upon the Proposed Suburban Village at Riverside," p. 279.

23. Henry Hubbard, "Land Subdivision Regulations," *Landscape Architecture,* (October 1925), 16, No. 1 p. 53.

24. Lewis Mumford, "The Fourth Migration" (1925), in Carl Sussman, ed., *Planning the Fourth Migration: The Neglected Vision of the Regional Plan Association of America* (Cambridge, MA: MIT Press, 1976), pp. 55–64.

25. Ebenezer Howard, *Garden Cities of To-Morrow,* F. J. Osborn, ed., (Cambridge, MA: MIT Press, 1965), p. 10.

26. Daniel Schaffer, *Garden Cities for America: The Radburn Experience* (Philadelphia: Temple University Press, 1982), p. 4.

27. Clarence Stein, *Towards New Towns for America* (1957; Cambridge: MIT Press, 1966), pp. 41–44.

28. Geddes Smith, quoted in Stein, *Towards New Towns for America,* p. 41.

29. Schaffer, *Garden Cities for America,* p. 157.

30. Stein, *Towards New Towns for America,* p. 66.

31. Ibid., p. 37.

32. Ibid., p. 41.

33. Schaffer, *Garden Cities for America,* p. 7.

34. Stein, *Towards New Towns for America,* p. 38.

35. Ibid., p. 53.

36. Eugenie Ladner Birch, "Radburn and the American Planning Movement: The Persistence of an Idea," *APA Journal* **46,** No. 4 (1980):435.

37. Schaffer, *Garden Cities for America,* p. 151.

38. Ibid., p. 175.

39. Marjorie Sewell Cautley, "Planting at Radburn," *Landscape Architecture* **2** No. 1 (October 1939):23–26.

40. Charles R. Wolfe, "Streets Regulating Neighborhood Form: A Selective History," in Anne Vernez Moudon, ed., *Public Streets for Public Use* (New York: Columbia University Press, 1991), pp. 110–122.

41. Stein, *Towards New Towns for America,* p. 57.

42. Ibid., p. 16.

43. "Community Patterns," *Architectural Forum* **44,** No. 4 (1936):247.

44. Schaffer, *Garden Cities for America,* p. 150.

45. Ibid., p. 174.

46. Alden Christie, "Radburn Reconsidered," *Connection* **7** (May 25, 1964):37–41.

47. Arnold Alanen and Joseph A. Eden, *Main Street Ready-Made: The New Deal Community of Greendale, Wisconsin* (Madison: The State Historical Society of Wisconsin, 1987), p. 37ff.

48. Cited in Lois Craig, "Suburbs," *Design Quarterly* **132** (1986):25.

49. Stein, *Towards New Towns for America,* p. 17.

50. Frank Lloyd Wright, *The Disappearing City* (New York: Walter Fraquhar Payson, 1932), p. 23.

51. Robert Fishman, *Urban Utopias in the Twentieth Century* (New York: Basic Books, 1977), p. 91.

52. Wright, *The Disappearing City,* p. 27.

53. Frank Lloyd Wright, "Broadacre City: A New Community Plan," *The Architectural Record* **77** (1935):244.

54. Wright, *The Disappearing City,* pp. 15, 24.

55. Frank Lloyd Wright, quoted in Patrick Meehan, ed., *The Master Architect: Conversations with Frank Lloyd Wright* (New York: John Wiley & Sons, 1984), p. 122; and Robert Fishman, *Urban Utopias in the Twentieth Century,* p. 123.

56. Alfred B. Yeomans, ed., *City Residential Development* (Chicago: University of Chicago Press, 1916), p. 99.

57. Wright, "Broadacre City" and *The Living City.* (New York: Bramhall House, 1958).

58. Fishman, *Urban Utopias in the Twentieth Century,* p. 121. Wright originally called it "the Usonian City."

59. Blair Brownell and Frank Lloyd Wright, *Architecture and Modern Life* (New York: Harper & Brothers, 1938), p. 318.

60. George R. Collins, "Broadacre City: Wright's Utopia Reconsidered," in Adolf K. Placzek, ed., *Four Great Makers of Modern Architecture* (New York: Da Capo Press, 1970), pp. 59, 68.

61. Fishman, *Urban Utopias in the Twentieth Century,* p. 66.

62. Denise Scott Brown, "Wright in the Rear View Mirror," *The New York Times* (September 12, 1993):56.

63. Walter L. Creese, *The Crowning of the American Landscape* (Princeton: Princeton University Press, 1985), p. 273.

64. Albert Fein, *Landscape into Cityscape,* (Ithaca, N.Y.: Cornell University Press) 1968.

65. Wright, *The Disappearing City,* p. 80.

66. Ibid., p. 45.

67. Ibid., p. 43.

68. Ibid., pp. 82, 20.

69. Ibid., p. 30.

70. Ibid., p. 3.

71. Ibid., p. 50.

72. Ibid., p. 44.

73. Ibid., p. 74.

74. Ibid., p. 79.

75. Ibid., p. 64.

76. Brownell and Wright, *Architecture and Modern Life,* p. 301.

77. Ibid., p. 70.

78. Ibid., p. 309.

79. Wright, "Broadacre City," p. 246.

80. Wright, *The Disappearing City,* p. 47.

81. Wright, "Broadacre City," p. 249.

82. George Collins, "Broadacre City," p. 55, and Brendan Gill, *Many Masks: A Life of Frank Lloyd Wright* (New York: G.P. Putnam's Sons, 1987), pp. 338, 508.

83. Robert Fishman, "The Rise and Fall of Suburbia," *Design Quarterly* **153** (1991):16.

4

INCREMENTS
The Subdivided Suburbs

In his 1953 satirical opera, *Trouble in Tahiti*, Leonard Bernstein described the early postwar suburb. The two sets were simple and cartoonlike, a backdrop of a city street in the rain and a child's sketch of a dream house. The estranged couple of the opera are recollecting the early hope and optimism of their marriage. Their problematic relationship is cut with interludes whose lyrics describe their life and its setting in "Sub-urb-i-a!—in Scarsdale, Wellesley Hills, Ozone Park, Highland Park, Brookline, Elkins Park, Bloomfield Hills, Beverly Hills, and Shaker Heights," where:

> Mornin' sun Kisses the driveway: kisses the lawn: Kisses the flagstones on the front lawn Of the little white house: Kisses the paper at the front door: kisses the roses around the front door of the little white house" . . .where there are, "Parks for the kids: neighborly butchers: Less than an hour by train," and they have a, "Lovely life: Happily married: sweet little son: Family picture second to none: It's a wonderful life! Up to date kitchen: washing machine: Colorful bathrooms, and *Life* Magazine, . . . Two door sedan and convertible coupe . . . Six days of work, fun every Sunday: Golf with the neighbors next door. Suburbia! Who could ask heaven for anything more?"[1]

For many of its first residents, the post-World War II American suburb of the detached single-family house achieved its promise—the best of city and country life in a home of their own. A new ranch-style house on its spacious lot provided the ideal environment for raising small children. Curving, curbless streets edged by open lawns created a spacious rural character while also providing an informal community open space for children's games and casual meetings. School yards and occasional parks added playgrounds and spaces for field sports. The memories of suburban dwellers of the 1950s and 1960s are filled with recollections of pickup ball games in the front yards, or games of hide-and-seek encompassing whole blocks. Located at the edge of the city, many new subdivisions were next to farms or undeveloped woodlands, often the most memorable open spaces of baby-boomers' childhoods.

How did it happen that houses and neighborhoods in New York State could be so similar to those in Ohio or southern California? Between 1945 and 1965, federal policy and national economy coincided to create a climate in which similar subdivisions enveloped the nation's urban fringes. At the end of World War II the country faced an uncertain economic future, severe housing shortages, and deteriorating urban centers. At the same time, victorious young G.I.s optimistically returned home to start families and

Ranch house and yard.
Kate Van Rooy.

careers. The housing industry, which had begun to develop into an impressive force prior to the 1929 stock market crash, blossomed once again with the support of the Federal Housing Administration (FHA) and the Veterans Administration (VA).[2] An unprecedented housing boom began, which continued unabated into the mid-1960s.[3] Land speculators, developers, and builders turned rural lands into subdivisions at an unprecedented rate, limited only by the availability of roads, power, water, and the distances people would commute. Few promised prospective buyers any community services; they sold only the house, yard, and street. (Many residents waited years for paved streets and city services.) Except for schools, the new suburbanites felt little need for the public services that local governments typically provide. Immediate family needs were met by the new house on its spacious lot, and the new car provided easy access to the city's shopping and cultural services. Only after the euphoria of a new life on the suburban frontier had subsided did residents pursue land use controls and municipal services such as new schools, parks, shopping, adequate roads, and organized recreation.

Subdivisions in each region had some unique qualities, perhaps in the site, the houses, or the resident population, yet there was a surprising resemblance between these new developments. There were two primary reasons: first, zoning laws and subdivision regulations throughout the nation were alike, based on guidelines distributed by national planning associations.[4] These laws designated mile after mile of land for single-family residential uses, allowing unplanned, incremental land subdivisions around the fringes of most cities. Second, the FHA rigorously enforced national standards for neighborhood planning and site and building design. Threatened with a refusal for mortgage insurance, subdividers and builders willingly followed the FHA's well-publicized guidelines.[5] Here they found simple, practical models of subdivision layout: gently curving streets with cul-de-sac ends, large lots, generous building setbacks, and centrally located parks, schools, and shopping centers. This landscape, which was home to two generations of Americans, provided the traditional home owner with a safe, secure family haven, a symbol of success, and a "good place to raise your kids."

SUBDIVIDING

From 1945 to the early 1960s new American developments were unkindly characterized as "cookie cutter" subdivisions, an incrementally developed fabric that was the result of the American subdividing process. Speculators purchased land in single ownership, often in agricultural usage, subdivided the property, and sold the resulting lots at significantly higher prices. Commonly, this occurred in advance of systematic land planning. The result was "a hopeless jumble of housing, industry, commerce and even agricultural uses,"[6] guided only by the availability of land for sale, road access, and the marketing savvy of the speculator. Subdivision developers commonly stripped sites of all vegetation prior to grading and constructing roads. They filled marshes and culverted streamways in an effort to maximize buildable land. By the time residents moved in, all traces of the natural landscape were obliterated and replaced with roads, driveways, houses, and lawns. What remained of the subdivisions' settings were their names and the names given to streets: "Park," "Forest," "Hills," "Meadows," and the like.[7]

Before World War II, subdividers were generally not builders; rather, they sold lots directly to private citizens for home sites, or to house builders who served both the speculative market and home owners. Some installed services and roads, but others sold only raw lots. Following the Depression and World War II, the pent-up demand for new housing was enormous. This created a market for a new breed of builders, and, with the assistance of FHA-insured mortgages, many subdividers and builders had an opportunity to both subdivide and build whole subdivisions, while the larger and more established speculators took on the development of entire communities.[8] Subdivision *developers* became commonplace. They created communities as grand as the Levittowns and subdivisions as modest as Portland's Vermont Hills by aggregating parcels of land, subdividing the land for sale to home owners or builders, installing services and roads, planting street trees, landscaping parks, dedicating school sites, and building shopping centers. Many offered a service to finance homes or to assist potential buyers in securing financing.

The FHA mortgage insurance program provided the financial impetus for mass suburban development, and its land planning service provided the design recipe. The final ingredient was the regulatory environment, wherein zoning laws and subdivision ordinances provided the ideal legal vehicle.

Zoning of already developed lands typically reinforced existing land use patterns, protecting the property values of upper-income residential areas by preventing nonconforming uses such as industry, high-density housing, and commerce. Zoning of as-yet-undeveloped lands designated great sectors of the urban fringe landscape for future uses, predominantly single-family housing. Commercial zoning would typically line roadways, blossoming at major intersections, to provide sites for shopping centers, whereas industry would be located on less attractive sites near major highways and railroads, even along rivers.

Governments in rural counties often had no zoning code nor any ordinances to control subdivisions prior to the earliest development activities. The mood of the populace in most areas was in support of new development. For the most part, developers were given a free hand. Only after an area was settled and the first few nonconforming developments were proposed would local residents push for the establishment of zoning to protect the quality of their neighborhoods and the value of their investments. In Oregon, the state did not authorize unincorporated areas to establish planning commissions until 1947. It then took up to five years for the counties surrounding Portland to establish their commissions and until 1961 for all to pass zoning codes.[9] Partially developed residential areas would be blanket-zoned for low-density, single-family housing, and commerce and industry would be allocated to predictable highway-related strips. Where ordinances and regulations existed, subdividers were required to meet minimum standards for lot sizes, building setbacks, street widths, intersection design, and the like. What was not controlled was the plan. Subdividers could meet the requirements of the codes and ordinances while still having flexibility in the layout of streets and lots.

Although most ordinances required the dedication of streets to the governing local jurisdiction, only a small minority included enforceable requirements for dedication of land for schools, parks, and community centers. Harold W. Lautner found, in a 1941 study of subdivision regulations,[10] that only 30% of the communities he studied, all with subdivision regulations, required the dedication of parklands in subdivisions. Fewer specified any clear quantitative requirement, and the number that mentioned the existence of a parks master plan was less than 25%. More commonly, suburban development occurred outside the city jurisdictions where few county governments had formalized planning. The FHA was the only body in these circumstances that had the clout to encourage subdividers to designate parks and open space.[11] Some developers agreed that parks would improve the quality of a neighborhood, thus increasing property values. Others chose to ignore the advice. As a result, the parks that existed formed an inconsistent patchwork pattern within the fabric of residential development, with tot lots and neighborhood parks being provided by some developers, but not by others. Schools were often the only public green spaces within vast residential landscapes.

Whole suburban regions often fell far below the national standards for per capita allowances of parks and open space. In 1958 the developed areas of Washington County, Oregon, west of Portland, had 2.4 acres of park and school grounds for every 1,000 persons.[12] At that time the National Recreation Association recommended 10 acres per 1,000 persons for parks and an additional 20 acres per 1,000 for larger regional parks. The region had only 8% of the recommended acreage of open space. Residents of Vermont Hills, Raleigh Hills, Cedar Hills, and the innumerable new subdivisions in the area had spacious yards, quiet streets, and, until the 1970s, access to golf courses, riding stables, farms, and wooded hillsides. Despite a minimal supply of parks facilities, they had the best of city and country life.

FEDERAL DESIGNS

By 1950 it was clear that America's preferred solution to urban problems was to attract young families to suburban areas and satellite settlements. The FHA worked hand in hand with federal urban renewal and highway-building programs to remove massive quantities of substandard housing ("slums") from central city areas and place new housing around the fringes.[13] The mortgage insurance program was viewed by developers, builders, and buyers as a mutually beneficial form of support. By choice, developers and builders could comply with FHA standards and qualify their homes for assistance. Home buyers were assured quality in both homes and neighborhoods, in addition to the opportunity to obtain low-interest loans. The program was a success. Between 1934 and 1970, the FHA was involved in mortgages for one-quarter of all new housing starts in the nation,[14] the vast majority of these new homes being constructed in the suburbs. Aided by the promise of low-interest FHA and VA loans, private builders were rapidly erecting single-family detached houses in new subdivisions. As fast as they could build, they had buyers in line.

When thousands of home buyers visited model homes, little did they realize that these nascent communities were guided by the FHA "model" for suburban communities. Through publications and conferences on land planning, information on neighborhood development and subdivision de-

The neighborhood appearance promoted by the U.S. Federal Housing Administration. From "Planning Profitable Neighborhoods, Technical Bulletin No. 7," U.S. Federal Housing Administration, 1938.

sign was disseminated by the FHA to the building industry, local governments, and the public.[15] The FHA Minimum Property Standards were often more detailed and more restrictive than local ordinances. Their guidelines promoted a streetscape style, either "continuous curvilinear," which was a modified gridiron, or "loops and culs-de-sac," a Radburn-type of heirarchical plan.[16] The net result throughout the 1950s and into the 1960s was that the FHA model for subdivision design was generally adhered to, with modifications for local conditions such as wider streets, reduction or elimination of parks and open space, or the deletion of sidewalks. A direct comparison of the design principles promulgated in FHA manuals with typical subdivisions of the early 1950s and 1960s indicates that the ideal suburban neighborhood that the FHA promoted had a significant impact on subdividers' designs.[17] Two widely distributed publications, *Planning Neighborhoods for Small Houses* (TB No. 5)[18] and *Planning Profitable Neighborhoods,* (TB No. 7)[19] contained written principles, diagrams, plans, and photographs of both good and bad community design. After 1938 developers' requests for prequalification of their subdivisions required review by the Land Planning Division. The developers were offered a carrot. Buyers had begun asking for assurances up-front that houses would be readily FHA approved,[20] and in response, FHA planners offered free advice on improving subdivision plans according to the FHA model. With adherence to this advice and FHA building codes, they would receive "conditional commitment." With at least one-quarter of their clientele interested in FHA-insured loans, developers would have been foolish to disregard FHA advice. Meanwhile, the FHA met their mandates to encourage quality homes and neighborhoods.

The design of orderly and distinguishable neighborhoods was the clear FHA message. FHA planners advised subdividers that neighborhood stability would result from locating adjacent to sympathetic neighborhoods, while assuring access to public transportation, schools, shopping, and recreational areas.[21] They differentiated between platted subdivisions and neighborhoods, places that retained some of the site's character and had more than houses. "Neighborhoods" included shopping, churches, schools, and parks. "The importance of distinctive neighborhood qualities lies not only in the initial appeal which is so vital a factor in marketing the development, nor in the increased security which derives from the safeguards created by careful planning, but also in the psychological reaction of the people who adopt the area for their home. Where a neighborhood can be identified and comprehended as such, the feeling of pride and responsibility which the owner has in his own parcel, tends to be extended to the neighborhood as a whole."[22] In the FHA philosophy, "subdivisions planned as neighborhoods are more profitable to developers, better security for investors, [and] more desirable to homeowners."[23]

Road layouts that were sensitive to site character and contour and placed homes along strictly residential streets were repeatedly emphasized.[24] Curving alignments would contribute neighborhood character, whereas gridiron plans were criticized as monotonous, costly, and dangerous. Through traffic was directed to arterial streets outside the development. For residential streets, the cul-de-sac was given special attention, because it reduced the paved area per lot, reduced traffic volumes, and could service lots on inaccessible parcels. Blocks were to be 600 to 1300 feet long by 200 to 300 feet wide, and lots were 50 to 60 feet wide by 100 to 120 feet deep. Sidewalks were promoted as important on heavily traveled streets; however, small residential streets could exist without curbs or sidewalks. On longer blocks, intermediate walkways were suggested to connect streets at the midpoint.

Developers were encouraged to provide central, accessible sites for schools, churches, and shopping areas, and examples were given indicating that these services should be located centrally and linked via neighborhood collector roads. However, there was also an underlying assumption that the ownership of automobiles by most suburban families removed the critical need for certain services. "In neighborhoods planned for higher priced

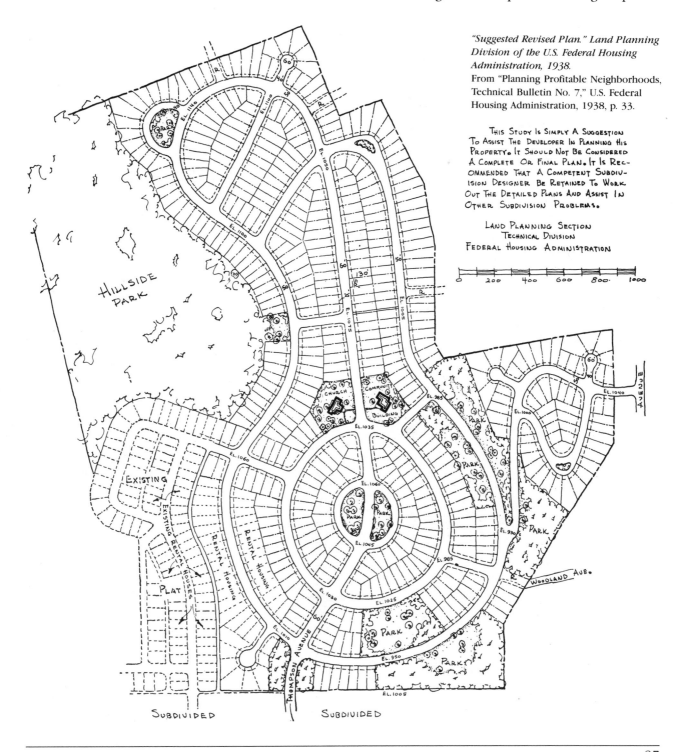

"Suggested Revised Plan." Land Planning Division of the U.S. Federal Housing Administration, 1938.
From "Planning Profitable Neighborhoods, Technical Bulletin No. 7," U.S. Federal Housing Administration, 1938, p. 33.

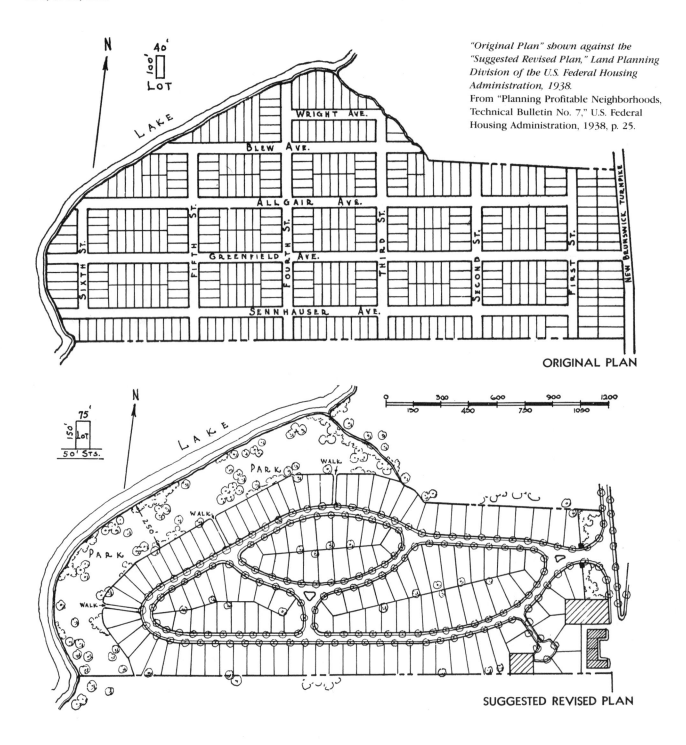

"Original Plan" shown against the "Suggested Revised Plan," Land Planning Division of the U.S. Federal Housing Administration, 1938.
From "Planning Profitable Neighborhoods, Technical Bulletin No. 7," U.S. Federal Housing Administration, 1938, p. 25.

ORIGINAL PLAN

SUGGESTED REVISED PLAN

homes, where shopping is done by car or telephone or dependence placed on delivery service, it is possible to omit local shopping facilities and to rely on distant commercial centers. In areas planned for low priced homes where shopping is done on foot and carried home, neighborhood centers should be provided in closer proximity to the home."[25] Along with most suburban planners and developers, the FHA assumed that highway-related regional shopping centers would adequately serve suburban dwellers—an attitude that eventually yielded diffused, disorderly locations of commercial and social services.

Parks were encouraged as "a definite community asset,"[26] and the preservation of natural features, with clear public access to them, was consistently stressed in FHA publications. Technical Bulletin No. 7 gave a more comprehensive view of the recommendations by providing numerous examples of neighborhoods redesigned by the Land Planning Division. Most of these examples showed both centralized park sites adjacent to schools and linear open spaces along streams or lakefronts. Streets often abutted public open spaces and parks to provide public access, and frequently easements were taken between lots for public pathways. The concept of public open space as a community network was consistently overlooked. FHA-designed parks were most often isolated parcels or leftover corners. Although the Radburn plan was mentioned in the guidelines, it was the traffic system, rather than the open space network, that was praised.[27] The FHA encouraged developers to take advantage of natural site features by furnishing both developed parks and linear natural areas; however, it skirted one critical lesson of Radburn: providing both safety and community vitality through a spine of interconnecting parkland. Also missing was a convincing argument that open space amenities were essential. A park was "a community asset," whereas the argument for streets with culs-de-sac and extra-long blocks was made in terms of "cost savings and safety." The greater conviction was in the economic argument. Although the more experienced developers understood that well-planned open space directly influenced neighborhood quality, which, in turn, affected their reputation, many neophyte builder-developers were more shortsighted.[28] When contemplated over the short term, parks consumed land that could be more profitably sold.

The FHA standards for natural open space, parks, school sites, and shopping areas were often more detailed and stringent than local subdivision ordinances and were viewed by many in the development community as extras rather than imperatives. Developers had to be concerned with marketing their "product" to maintain profitability and continue the process of land acquisition and development. The FHA "carrot," greater assurances of home sales, successfully changed the attitudes of many toward neighborhood amenities.[29] During this period, *House and Home,* a national magazine aimed at the home-building industry, both provided its readers with ideas and advice on sound, marketable site planning and house design ideas, and monitored the FHA and other national and regional regulatory agencies. Examples of their articles included "Five Prize Neighborhoods: This Year's NAHB Award Winners Show You How to Make a Better Setting for Your Houses"[30] and "Six Easy Lessons in Land Planning."[31] The latter article explained some of the current FHA site-planning concepts and promoted the land-planning service that the FHA provided. *House and Home* supported the basic FHA lessons, such as the benefits of longer, curving blocks that looked more attractive, yet were cost-effective, and the dedication of ravines, creekways, and naturally wooded areas for parks to increase immediately the market value of a neighborhood. The image of spacious, curving, tree-lined streets, orderly yards, forested backdrops, and picturesquely sited schools was known to be appealing to prospective buyers. Many developers followed the FHA standards, but others knew this quality could be achieved by the spacious design of streets and yards without dedicating extensive lands to public agencies. Many local governments, particularly county governments covering large unincorporated suburbs, supported this approach. "Suburban planners worried first about roads and sewers, second about zoning to protect new residential subdivisions, and only third about neighborhood amenities."[32]

Vermont Hills, Oregon: A house and yard.
Kate Van Rooy.

VERMONT HILLS, OREGON

Vermont Hills was a typical postwar subdivision, constructed between 1947 and 1951 in the euphoric post-World War II period. The site was atop rolling agricultural lands, a 10-minute drive west of downtown Portland and one and a half miles east of the prestigious Portland Golf Club. The developer, Commerce Investment, Inc., targeted young families and veterans with modestly priced "starter" houses prequalified for FHA assistance. The plan might have come straight out of FHA planning offices: streets were gently curving; blocks were 1,000 to 2,000 feet long; lots typically had 80 feet of frontage and were of 8,000 to 10,000 square feet. In the first phases of development, the land was subdivided into roughly 400 lots, with sites for an elementary school and adjacent park located on the north edge and small sites for an apartment building and shopping center on the south. Modest ranch-style houses were evenly spaced and generously set back from streets. Along one side of each street the developer planted red oaks, which residents interspersed with eclectic selections of northwestern plantings. The picturesque neighborhood was affordable and attractive to young middle-class Portlanders seeking escape from crowded wartime housing.

Narrow, curbless streets, gravel shoulders, widely spaced houses, and spacious undivided front lawns gave the streetscape an open, rural character, the pastoral antidote to the city that people sought. As they struggled to plant grass and a few trees and shrubs in the early years, residents recalled the rural flavor: "Everyone had big vegetable gardens; Dot had rabbits, pigeons, ducks and chickens; Strifes had a cow, Mr. Damerst had a goat and Charlie had horses."[33] Years later a landscape pattern emerged neighborhoodwide. Front yards were simply grass from street edge to front door,

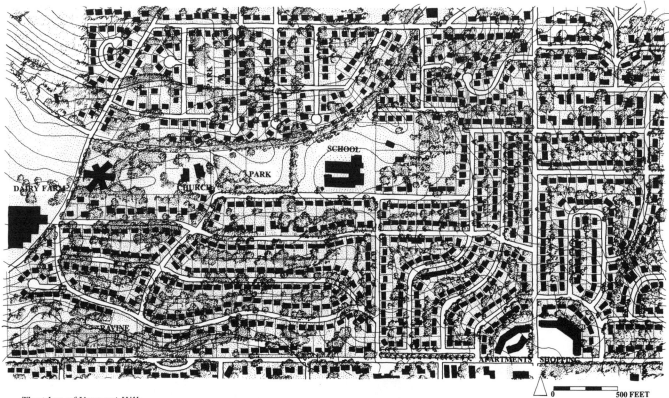

The plan of Vermont Hills.
Kate Van Rooy.

with foundation plantings or flower borders along walks and boundaries. Driveways led directly to garages on one end of the houses and provided spaces for games or car maintenance. Enclosed backyards had extensive lawn areas punctuated with swing sets, dog runs, vegetable gardens, and barnlike storage sheds. Patios were furnished with tables, chairs, potted plants, barbeques, and outside toys, and side yards were utility and storage spaces frequented by boats, campers, building materials, bicycles, and the like. Most backyards grew more elaborate as owners grew older or houses changed hands, with partially enclosed and furnished wood decks often replacing simple concrete patios. Residents now speak with pride about the mature landscape they have contributed to, boasting that they are having to take out trees and shrubs because some spaces are so overgrown.[34]

In recollecting their own and their children's outdoor activities, the residents recall spending much of their personal and family time in the yard or on the street. "It was a great place to raise kids."[35] Cats slept in the street and kids played kick-the-can and hide-and-seek in the continuous space from front door to front door. Today people use this public space extensively. Cars are frequently parked on gravel shoulders as well as in driveways, inasmuch as many of the one-car garages have been converted into rooms. Front yards are used for children's play, car washing, and yard maintenance, and people commonly have cross-the-hedge conversations. Residents are quite fond of the curbless streets and feel very comfortable walking dogs, jogging, and playing on the streets. Backyard accoutrements still show that more private family activities are centered here: gardening, toddler play, sunbathing, and eating.

Southwest Nebraska Street, Vermont Hills.
C. Girling.

Several other significant open spaces were as memorable as yards and streets. Children made frequent forays to a creek bottom in the southwest corner of the community for crayfish and private "kid" play. A portion of this area remains in public ownership, although formal public access was never established. Pendelton Park, developed several years after the first residents moved in, was a safe destination for older children who "spent their lives there"[36] playing pickup ball games. North of the park and adjacent to the school, there was a forested ravine that was the community woodland, site of many forts and informal trails. A privately owned dairy bordering Vermont Hills, was an important educational and social center during the children's formative years. Alpenrose Dairy opened its land and barn to exploration by neighborhood children, providing exposure to a working farm. The dairy was renowned in the region for holding week-long Fourth of July celebrations including displays, pageants, and fireworks. For Vermont Hills, the dairy was a community center cum 4-H Club.

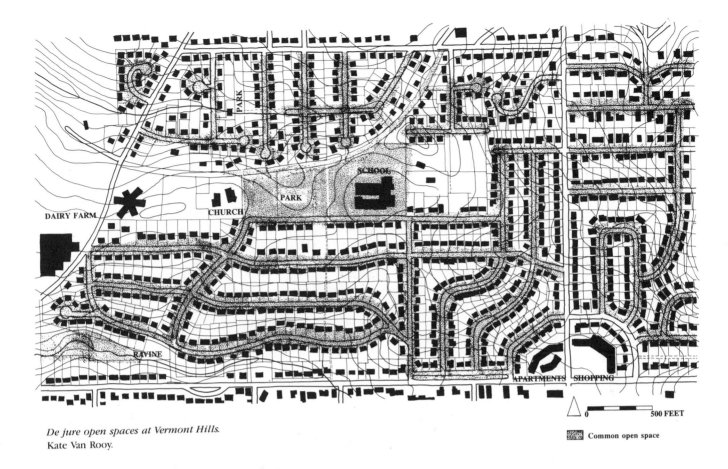

De jure open spaces at Vermont Hills.
Kate Van Rooy.

▦ Common open space

0   500 FEET

De facto open spaces at Vermont Hills.
C. Girling.

LEVITTOWN

Federally promoted patterns of development were not exclusive to the West. Across the continent, on Long Island, New York, a similar but much larger community was constructed at the same time as Vermont Hills. In 1949, *Architectural Forum* reported on America's largest housing project on Long Island, where "two years ago it was potato farm"; off Hempstead Turnpike, there stood "a whole city of bungalows . . . a curious dreamlike quality of endlessness and timelessness. You could literally go miles in any direction without reaching the end of these impassive rows of little houses. There are 6,000 of them and they are as identical as so many Ford cars parked on some giant parking lot." The report noted "an eerie similarity" and "something military" about the place.[37] The military association was not only in its seeming regimentation, but in the new inhabitants, for most were veterans, workers in the defense industries located on Long Island, or among the legions of daily commuters into New York City. Virtually all qualified for low-interest VA and FHA loans. In less than five years—between May 7, 1947, when plans for Levittown (or Island Trees, as it was first named) were announced, and November 20, 1951—17,447 homes were built.[38] Costs were kept low by large land purchases and mass purchasing of building materials, including the developers' production of their own lumber on the West Coast. The Levitt organization streamlined house building into 26 assembly-line operations, with crews moving from lot to lot. At its peak, 150 houses were completed per day. Levittown, Long Island, and the two subsequent Levittowns in Pennsylvania and New Jersey became home to thousands. They also became the archetype and a stereotype, a synonym for the mass-produced postwar suburb.[39]

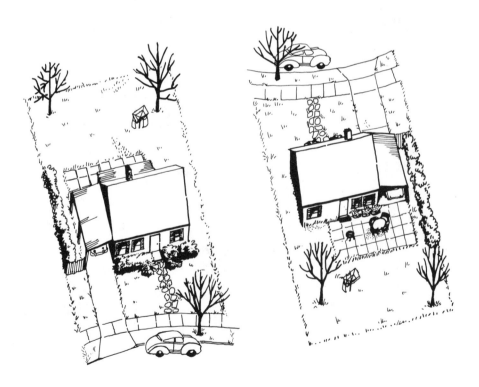

Levittown: A house and yard.
Kate Van Rooy.

What did people buy? They bought a small house on a modest lot in a new community, within commuting range of New York City. The site had been farmland, but the area was rapidly suburbanizing. They also purchased a stake in an instant community. Much like the "instant cities" of the American West, where the process of community building was compressed into a brief period of time, the suburban communities of the merchant builders offered an instant community, a place where the settlement process was accelerated.[40] At Levittown the pioneers arrived en mass, much like participants in a gold rush, finding a ready-made community to fulfill their desires for a home of their own and more.

The typical postwar builder was the large-scale "merchant builder," who by 1949 accounted for 80% of new homes. The most successful of these builders were Levitt & Sons, the father Abraham and his sons, William, the businessman and promoter, and Alfred, the designer. Their first houses were Cape Cod-style homes with kitchen, living/dining room, two bedrooms, and bath for a cost of $6,990. The home was 750 square feet on a 60-by 100-foot lot. (The average new home in 1992 was 1950 square feet, 250% larger.) There was no basement, but an expansion attic, which for another $350 would be finished, adding 178 square feet more. There was no garage. The house came with the latest "extras" built in: range, refrigerator, kitchen cabinets, bookshelves, metal venetian blinds, and washer. Deluxe models, 401 square feet larger, were available for another $1,300.[41] Early homes could be rented, but by 1949 they were for purchase only, with the Ranch model the new offering. The Ranch had a third bedroom, a fireplace, and a carport. Built-in televisions were standard, a new window to the outside world. Sixteen-foot picture windows provided grand views of the neighborhood and, equally, put the family on view.[42] Reflecting on moving to Levittown in the early 1950's, forty years later Fred Lofsvold was struck by how people referred to houses in the manner of automobiles. Each was given a model name and a year, and people awaited the appearance of next year's models.[43]

At their subsequent developments the Levitts would perfect their formula. In 1951 they colonized Bucks County, Pennsylvania, with the construction of Levittown II. The houses were on wider 70-foot lots with carports,[44] and by 1953 the fastest selling house in the United States was the new "Rancher," an improved version of the "Levittowner."[45] More luxurious models were included in their "Country Clubber" line. The Levitts knew their clientele well. In 1955 they offered a three-bedroom Jubilee Model in honor of the twenty-fifth anniversary of the company for $10,990, complete with attached garage, and still with an expansion attic. That year the firm started 4,900 homes at Levittown II, making it the nation's largest builder.

The Levitts did not leave the landscape character to chance. Levittown was promoted as "A Garden Community."[46] Their vision coincided with that of the purchasers. The raw tracts of the suburban frontier needed to be domesticated. In 1952, *House and Home* reported that at Levittown II, "every house will have its own 'park' when all the trees are grown," and that "trees and shrubs will make this the most completely landscaped city in the country; evergreens screening houses, around each lot, plus thousands of street trees. In addition to the slow-growing evergreens already planted, each back yard will get three fruit trees."[47]

Lease agreements obligated tenants to maintain the landscape. As Barbara Kelly noted in her Levittown study, "Lease agreements . . . later covenanted into the deeds . . . reinforced Levittown as a document for what

"Every house will have its own park."
House and Home, 11 (6) December 1952,
p. 83.

most Americans believed a home and community should be. The young, nuclear families, in their similar (but distinct), privatized (but conforming) houses, living in their do-it-yourself domesticity, were the ideal model for the young, American family of modest means in the postwar period."[48] Even after the Levittown Property Owners Association took over from the Levitts, it retained most of their mandates.[49] No fences were allowed, and hedges were restricted to a height of three feet; permission was needed to paint exteriors, grass was to be cut weekly from April to November, and no more than two pets were permitted.[50] The restrictions became petty. Wash was not to be hung out on weekends. Outdoor wash was a private affair, and for recent city dwellers—65% of Levittown's early residents had moved from apartments—hanging wash was an urban icon, and a lower-class one at that.[51] Levitt suggested using portable lines.[52] Of course, dryers would soon bring this activity indoors. Backyard fences were later added as lots were enclosed (for privacy, to supervise children, and to keep dogs in) and as backyard pools proliferated.

Yards were spatially differentiated between front yard and back. The front was public and social space, neat, open to the street, and similar to everyone else's front yard. The back was the family space, utilitarian in its service to barbeques, children's play, and vegetable gardens. Front and back also prescribed male and female domains: Echoing the ancient practice of men working in the fields, the lawn was male territory, and social norms made its care obligatory.[53] Men were responsible for the basic structure of building and property, while women handled decorating: furniture and drapery inside and flowers outside.[54] Male domesticity was reinforced in do-it-yourself activity, expansions and remodeling of the house and yard. In this low-density world the "front lawn would begin to pinch-hit as the suburban equivalent of the corner bar."[55] W.D. Wetherell's marvelous short story, "The Man Who Loved Levittown," describes the early pioneering days

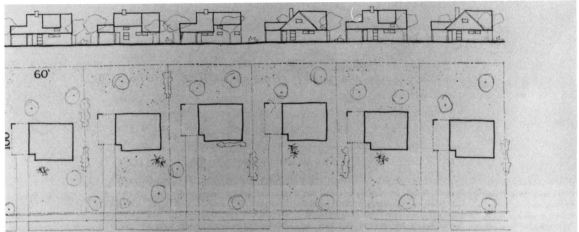

IN LEVITTOWN NO. 1 the same basic story-and-a-half house, with four elevation changes, was repeated more than 14,000 times. To give an impression of variety and keep his houses from looking like so many peas in a pod, Levitt curved his streets and staggered his setbacks.

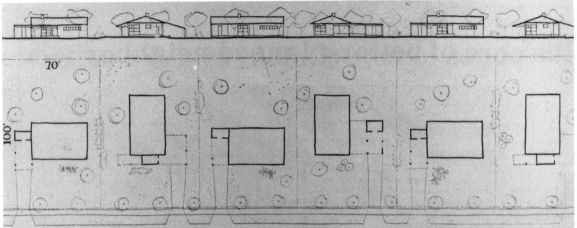

IN LEVITTOWN NO. 2 Levitt stuck to the same basic house within each section of his community. He started with his one-story models (shown here) and made them look different by turning them long and narrow end to the street, and varying carports, setbacks and color.

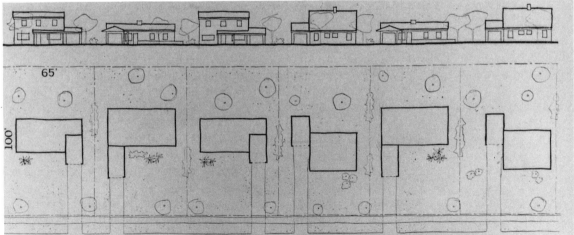

IN LEVITTOWN NO. 3 three different models—different in size, type, price, and looks—are mixed on the same street. This is a major departure for Levitt, who in his previous Levittowns (below) built the same basic house over and over again in the same section.

Levittown streetscapes,
House and Home, 14 (2), August 1958, p. 78.

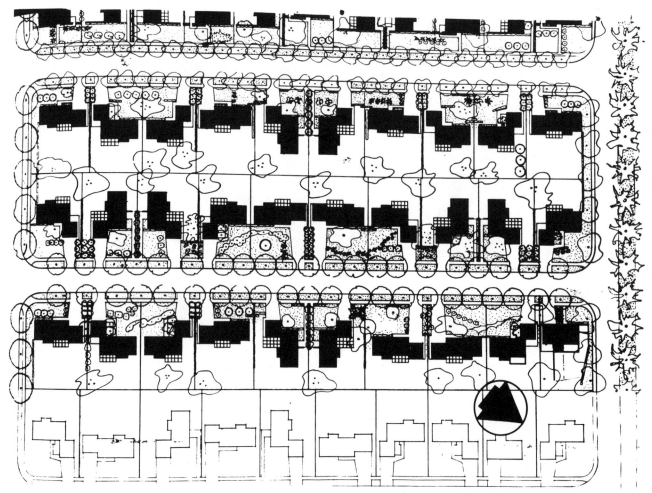

Mar Vista, Los Angeles, 1949.
Architect: Gregory Ain; builder: Advance Development Co. "Variations on the basic house type were fitted to the site and to each other like an intricate puzzle to avoid the usual subdivision monotony,"
Architectural Forum, 90 (4), April 1949, p. 107.

when there were no hedges and "everyone's home was your home; we all walked back and forth like it was one big yard."[56]

Cars were originally parked on the street or next to the house, later under carports and then in garages. In the early stages Alfred Levitt had to fight his father and brother, who argued for garages. He insisted, "Until people are decently housed, I believe we have no moral right to house autos."[57] The architecture easily accommodated their addition. David Popenoe in his study of the Pennsylvania Levittown noted that many carports had been converted to living spaces, leaving the streets lined with parked cars at night and on weekends, some even parked in front yards.[58] The street, at generous suburban dimensions and with low traffic volumes, was suited for the storage of automobiles, but was ideally auto-free. Cars on the street were viewed as an aspect of urban life most of the residents wanted to avoid.[59]

Bare fields rapidly gave way to houses that replicated the look of a Monopoly board, but plantings soon transformed them into individualized green settings. As Levittowns progressed from I to II to III, the parklike setting was increasingly supplemented by designated parks and open spaces. The initial Levittown grew incrementally, mostly as a result of ad hoc measures, but later communities offered a more complete plan as part of the purchase price. At Levittown II, 250 acres of "forest preserves" were part of the community plan, partially acting as buffers between neighborhoods.

"Village Greens" comprising a local shopping center, swimming pool, playground, and sometimes a school were built. On Long Island, the local Village Greens fared poorly economically as large new shopping centers drew their customers, so in Pennsylvania the Levitts relocated shopping to their own regional shopping center that served Levittown and beyond. Levittowns had no "downtown," but many centers: a shopping center, city hall, school fields, parking lots. For most Levittowners, their home was the center of the community.[60] *House and Home* reported that in Pennsylvania, "in contrast to Levittown I, there will be no small parks, where there is nothing to do but sit. The Levitts discovered on Long Island that people prefer to sit in their own yards, will go off to a park to swim, play games or for special facilities."[61] In Pennsylvania the Levittown Public Recreation Association controlled five Olympic-size pools and pavilions, picnic areas, and playgrounds. At one time half the residents were members, but that number declined to one-quarter by 1973 as children grew older (10- to 15-year-olds were the primary pool users). By that year, 10% of the homes had their own pools.[62]

Levittown in its early phase, 1949,
Architectural Forum, 90 (4), April 1949,
p. 85.

Alfred Levitt remarked, "Father has always been a neighborhood man. In all our developments, he always got a swimming pool and meeting house in right away and landscaped to beat hell."[63] "We learned that housebuyers want to be identified with a neighborhood, not a subdivision."[64] So the Levitts constructed neighborhoods. The new community of Landia represented their ideal. Although it was never built, many of its ideas were incorporated into the Pennsylvania and New Jersey communities. Landia was to have 1,750 houses in seven neighborhoods of 90 to 350 houses with "every community facility": tennis courts, town hall, schools, railroad station, preschool nursery, pools, baseball fields, and ice skating ponds on frozen recharge basins. A modified greenbelt pattern was to be incorporated between neighborhoods, each with a clear main street with loops around it.[65] At Levittown II, as it was first known, neighborhoods were built around eight "master blocks" for 400 to 600 families. At the center of each was a swimming pool and recreation area.[66] There were 40 named neighborhoods averaging 430 homes, ranging in size from 51 to 990 homes.[67] In an attempt to reinforce neighborhood identity, all the street names in a neighborhood began with the same letter. Thus, in Stonybrook there were Spiral, Spring, Shelter, Sunset, Shadetree, Summer, Stream, Strawberry, Sugarmaple, and Shepherd.[68] In New Jersey the entire town was divided into neighborhoods of 1,200 to 1,500 homes; each had its own park, and the neighborhoods were separated by greenbelts. The symbols of community were clear: the single family home, education, leisure, and amenity.

In 1950, William Dobriner described a walk down a Levittown street. He was still impressed by the "newness of it all: freshly painted houses with western pine exteriors; the ruts that guided the '47 Chevys and Fords up to the carports; grass, growing braver each week; skinny saplings, three to a house, standing like embarrassed sentinels along the curving sidewalks." Ten years later the newness had been worn away: "Many of the brave saplings died; few were replaced. Some streets are almost treeless; others, apparently because the nursery stock was healthy, are verdantly suburban. Foundation plantings now obscure the windows and curl up under the eaves."[69]

The Levitts built Levittown, but it was then rebuilt. Barbara Kelly offers a thesis regarding Levittown that places the home owner on equal footing with the Levitts as the designers of the community. Houses were designed first by the developers and then redesigned by the owners. They were the coproducers of the domestic environment.[70] Her architectural observations are most astute. The stylistic progression at Levittown led from the basic Cape Cod fundamental house unit, in the first stage, to the ranch house. To these Kelly adds a third "style," the owner-redesigned unit, putting the owners as shapers of their domestic environment on a par with the architect-builder of the community.[71] Within a decade the home owners redesigned the interiors, exteriors, and yards of their homes. The expansion attics were completed, carports and garages built, rooms added, walks and patios constructed, trees planted. Building suppliers and nurseries kept do-it-yourselfers busy. Houses were furnished and fixed, decorated and individualized. Homes assumed the personalities of their owners through individual building projects and family enterprises.[72] Within eight years, 66% of the expansion-attic homes had three or more bedrooms, expanded from the original two.[73]

Attentive to critiques of monotony, in the Pennsylvania development the Levitts turned one-half of the houses sideways, offered four carport

Levittown house and yard, after residents' additions and remodeling.
Kate Van Rooy.

variations, and seven colors of siding and trim.[74] Only one house in 28 was identical. As Gans noted, "none of the adults who thought Levittown dull ascribed the dullness to architectural homogeneity."[75] The stereotype of ticky-tacky identical homes, and people, was belied by even a cursory examination in the field. The setting proved to be a ripe forum for an assertion of American individuality. Twenty three years after completion an observer commented, *"None* of the houses looks like any other. . . . Almost every single one of them has been added on to, extended, built out, remodeled to the max. The roofs have developed so many dormers it seems like they've grown dormers on dormers. . . . And those once pathetic saplings have grown and flourished into fifty thousand shade trees spreading and merging, casting cozy coverings of shadows and privacy over rococo renovation."[76]

Levittown residents were able to purchase the "Dream House" basics, a stripped-down house and lot. These postwar pioneers were suburban home-steaders, converting and taking possession of their newly settled territory. They invested in the modest frames of tract houses provided by Levitt and Sons and converted the place into a prosperous middle-class community. The residents' rebuilding made it into the "better" neighborhood most desired—they built the community they aspired to, a place, in appearance, that had the trappings of the suburban ideal of the nineteenth-century suburb.[77] It was a middle landscape for middle-of-the-roaders.

In the 1950s critiques of suburbia became commonplace, and Levittown the butt of jokes. Ron Rosenbaum, a Long Island native, wrote, "Of all the burbs in burbdom, none was more scorned and reviled, none more notoriously, quintessentially burbish, none the target of more ridicule and revulsion than that first, postwar mass produced middle-class commune called Levittown."[78] The prejudice against the suburb, especially by taste-makers and designers, was pervasive. Some of the criticism was well grounded and thoughtful, but much of it was elitist and intellectual snobbery in regard to suburbia and, especially, mass-market housing. The emphasis on superficial appearance forestalled serious commentary and critique.

Herbert Gans's sociological classic, *The Levittowners,* studied the final Levittown in New Jersey, where he lived for two years beginning in June 1958. (The community later reverted to its original name of Willingboro.) Gans was particularly interested in the relationship between the form of the community and its social patterns. He discovered that "functional neighboring," the people with whom one actually talked, typically extended only three to four houses down the street in either direction, and that the key social unit was the subblock of houses adjacent to and facing each other. Here friendships were formed, neighboring and mutual help occurred. This was true especially for women and children, whose territory and options were restricted.[79] Gans reported, "Although they are laid out according to the precepts of the traditional neighborhood scheme, the individual neighborhoods do not affect people's lives . . . they are too large for social relations . . . too similar to each other to encourage identification, and without distinctive social or political functions which might spawn neighborhood groups."[80] The school, found at the neighborhood core, had not become a local focal point, but its meeting rooms were used every night by community-wide, not neighborhood, groups. These were communities for traditional nuclear families. In the early phases Levittown succeeded with young upwardly mobile families with small children. In 1950 one-third of the residents were under age five; by 1960 a third were still under ten. What became the neighborhood center was the pool, particularly for teenagers.

Adolescents were not satisfied with Levittown life. Numerous suburban studies indicate that it is adolescents who find the suburban environment most difficult. Many discover that there is "nothing to do," and that without transportation, they cannot get to stores and recreational facilities. Even if the desired activity is just "hanging out," one must get to the proper location, and transportation is a major problem, especially for those below driving age.[81] Single parents, working mothers, the elderly, and minorities were barely accommodated. Moreover, Levittown was exclusively white. In 1957 the first African-American family to buy a house in Levittown, Pennsylvania, found its home stoned.

Herbert Gans's conclusion about Levittown, "Whatever its imperfections, Levittown is a good place to live," was verified by many other sociological studies. It is interesting to note that in 1966 Robert Venturi, in *Complexity and Contradiction in Architecture,* wrote, "Main Street is almost right," an appreciative recognition of the American commercial and civic vernacular. Venturi and Denise Scott Brown soon went on to study Levittown with their Yale students. Such an investigation was rare. By and large, the design community ignored and often reviled the suburbs, despite the fact that it was there that much of their work was occurring. Perhaps a more sympathetic and less prejudiced reading of the suburban scene would have encouraged different design responses.

The residents and the Levitts knew better, and, partly in defense, mythologized their own community and its growth out of the potato fields. The community myth spoke of "the rural roots of the community, the benevolent builder, the pioneer spirit among the residents, the joy of single family dwellings, the collective activity among the homeowners as they worked to impart an individuality thorough remodeling and landscaping, and the struggle for upward mobility through material goods."[82] Critics focused on the static image, the foreshortened telescopic view, and few appreciated the community's true dynamics. As Kelly notes, "The reality of the suburban experience is as much the product of the redesigned environment as it is of the FHA-designed, builder delivered subdivisions that formed its roots. Indeed, the reshaping of the environment by the residents was a key factor in shaping the suburban experience."[83] In W. D. Wetherell's short story "The Man Who Loved Levittown," Tommy DiMaria reflects on his pioneering days: "Cabin cruiser, porches, garages . . . you name it, we built it. That's why this little boxes stuff was pure phooey. Sure they were little boxes when we first started. But what did we do? The minute we got our mitts on them we started remodeling them, adding stuff, changing them around." He adds later, with pride, "We were cowboys out there. We were pioneers."[84]

The massive subdividing phenomenon that swept post-1945 America created an indelible new national landscape. Fueled by the ideal that each American family should be able to own a private home on an individual lot in a safe, spacious, and homogeneous neighborhood, postwar suburbs throughout the nation were constructed as if from a mold. Rural lands were developed in a patchwork pattern. Following major roads, commercial strips provided one predictable order. Each residential neighborhood, platted by an individual subdivider, was a unique enclave, similar in design yet rarely planned to connect with or complement others. "Somewhere along the way the suburban dream turned into the subdivision nightmare, the dreary look-alike developments, the slums of the future, the 'slurbs'," wrote architecture

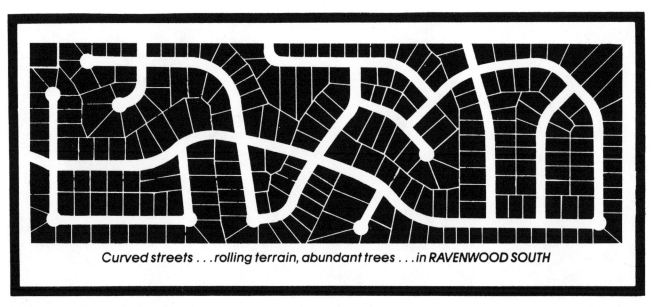

Curved streets . . . rolling terrain, abundant trees . . . in RAVENWOOD SOUTH

Realtor's advertisement, Springfield, MO,
1990.

critic Ada Louise Huxtable in 1964.[85] It was the repetitious design that drew such criticism; however, this effect was short-lived. Home owners immediately began to change their houses and yards, and within 10 years, most of these communities had lost their early cookie-cutter quality and became a collection of individualized homes. The builder provided the package, parts, and some directions, but it was the residents who completed the picture.

In the 1950s suburbs, private developers created communities out of aggregated private lands. Public agencies were in their formative stages, scrambling to meet basic needs such as road construction and sewerage. Developers and consumers were primarily interested in maximizing the size and influence of the private domain. In Vermont Hills and surrounding suburban developments, the most memorable, most used open spaces were informal aggregations: front yard, street and driveway; backyard, woodlot, creek, and adjacent farm. Designated open spaces such as parks were well utilized for specific activities, but the enduring outdoor activities were the games and chance meetings in the front yard and street, explorations along undeveloped creek bottoms and woodlands, and rural experiences associated with the neighboring farm or ranch. The street and continuously connected front yards took on the role of community open space in their provision of spacious verdure, visibility of neighbors, even a safe place for children's games. De facto open space played a much more significant role in both community and individual life than did the planned park. Parks were isolated elements in the community, whereas the street and associated front yards were the open spaces that knit the community together. In these suburbs, the "backbone" of the neighborhood became the street and its associated front yards, thus reversing the vision of Stein and Wright (see Chapter 3). The crescent and cul-de-sac of the American suburb was the neighborhood meeting ground.

With financial backing from the FHA and the VA, the private housing industry transformed urban fringe areas into what is now considered the quintessential suburb. Subdividers and developers, influenced by FHA interpretations of Radburn and the Greenbelt towns, embraced the casual style

*Continuously connected front yards of the
subdivided suburbs.*
C. Girling.

of curving streets, spacious lots, and the ranch house. No one took responsibility for community-scaled planning. A precarious balance developed as streams were still running, orchards still producing, and woods still wild. For a moment, the suburban best-of-both-worlds promise was realized. But it was soon lost, as subdivisions, shopping malls, and freeways slowly engulfed the remaining rural and wild places that suburbanites had sought. In a classic version of the "tragedy of the commons," the suburban dream became a victim of its own success.

A few began to question the pattern and the process, especially the unplanned, willy-nilly outward expansion. In 1961, critic Jane Jacobs expressed anger toward the rapid suburbanization of fringe areas when she wrote:

> And so each day, several thousand more acres of our countryside are eaten by bulldozers, covered with pavement, dotted with suburbanites who have killed the thing they thought they came to find. Our irreplaceable heritage of Grade I agricultural land (a rare treasure of nature on this earth) is sacrificed for highways or supermarket parking lots as ruthlessly and unthinkingly as the trees and woodlands are uprooted, the streams and rivers polluted and the air itself filled with gasoline exhausts (products of nature's manufacturing) required in the great national effort to cozy up with a fictionalized nature and flee the "unnaturalness" of the city. The semisuburbanized and suburbanized messes we create in this way become despised

by their own inhabitants tomorrow. These thin dispersions lack any reasonable degree of innate vitality, staying power, or inherent usefulness as settlements.[86]

Her harsh critique, and others that soon followed, jolted the planning profession and building industry leaders into investigating alternatives to the subdivision. Articles and publications about cluster subdivisions and planned unit developments that consumed less land and preserved natural open spaces began to appear. William H. Whyte[87] promoted "linkages" of open space in planned subdivisions. He advised planners to first save or recapture natural landscape corridors, then to plan coherent new subdivisions. Similarly, the American Society of Planning Officials wrote about "nets" of open space.[88] The scale of planned communities also grew. While cluster subdivisions and PUDs provided new models for small-scale developers, the large-scale merchant builders continued to flourish and began to explore models borrowed from abroad. By 1963, two New Towns were under way and the building industry entered a new era that emphasized rational planning procedures and very large, preplanned communities with extensive open space systems.

NOTES

1. Leonard Bernstein, *Trouble in Tahiti* (New York: G. Schirmer, Inc., 1953), p. 6–8, 10, 61–67.
2. The 1934 National Housing Act established a mortgage insurance program, administered by the newly created Federal Housing Administration, which offered low-interest loans giving middle- and lower-middle-income people opportunities to purchase housing supplied by private industry. The Veteran's Administration offered G.I.s similar loans after World War II.
3. Marc A. Weiss, *The Rise of the Community Builders: The American Real Estate Industry and Urban Land Planning* (New York: Columbia University Press, 1987), Chap. 6.
4. Donald A. Krueckeberg, ed., *Introduction to Planning History in the United States* (New Brunswick, NJ: Center for Urban Policy Research, 1983), p. 8.
5. Peter G. Rowe, *Making a Middle Landscape* (Cambridge, MA.: The MIT Press, 1991), p. 204; Robert Fishman, *Bourgeois Utopias: The Rise and Fall of Suburbia* (New York: Basic Books, 1987), p. 175; and Weiss, *The Rise of the Community Builders*, p. 148–149.
6. Fishman, *Bourgeois Utopias*, p. 190.
7. Kenneth Jackson, *Crabgrass Frontier: The Suburbanization of the United States* (New York: Oxford University Press, 1985), p. 273.
8. Weiss, *The Rise of the Community Builders*, p. 160–162.
9. Carl Abbott, *Portland Planning, Politics and Growth in a Twentieth-Century City* (Lincoln: University of Nebraska Press, 1983), p. 234–240.
10. Harold W. Lautner, *Subdivision Regulations: An Analysis of Land Subdivision Control Practices* (Chicago: Public Administration Service, 1941), p. 177.
11. Weiss, *The Rise of the Community Builders*, p. 142.
12. *Proposed Zoning Ordinance for Beaverton [Oregon]* (Beaverton, OR: Beaverton City Planning Commission, 1976).
13. Fishman, *Bourgeois Utopias*, Chap. 6.
14. Eugenie Ladner Birch, "Radburn and The American Planning Movement, The Persistence of an Idea," in Krueckeberg, ed. *Introduction to Planning History in the United States*, p. 133.
15. Weiss, *The Rise of the Community Builders*, p. 158.
16. For greater depth of discussion of the roots of FHA street patterns, see Rowe, *Making a Middle Landscape*, p. 205, and Anne Vernez Moudon in the chapter entitled "The Evolution of Common Twentieth-Century Residential Forms: An American Case Study," in J. W. R. Whitehand and Peter J. Larkham, eds., *Urban Landscapes: International Perspectives* (New York: Routledge, 1992).

17. Ibid.
18. U.S. Federal Housing Administration (FHA), *Planning Neighborhoods for Small Houses, Technical Bulletin No. 5* (Washington, DC: Federal Housing Administration, 1934).
19. U.S. Federal Housing Administration, *Planning Profitable Neighborhoods, Technical Bulletin No. 7* (Washington, DC: Federal Housing Administration, 1938).
20. Weiss, *The Rise of the Community Builders*, p. 147.
21. Federal Housing Administration, *Technical Bulletin No. 7*.
22. Federal Housing Administration, *Technical Bulletin No. 5*, p. 28.
23. Federal Housing Administration, *Technical Bulletin No. 7*, p. 4.
24. Ibid.
25. Federal Housing Administration, *Technical Bulletin No. 5*, p. 26.
26. Federal Housing Administration, *Technical Bulletin No. 7*, p. 13.
27. Federal Housing Administration, *Technical Bulletin No. 5*, p. 24.
28. Weiss, *The Rise of the Community Builders*, p. 142.
29. Ibid., p. 152.
30. "Five Prize Neighborhoods," *House and Home* **11,** No. 3 (March 1957): pp. 116–121.
31. "Here Are six easy lessons in Land Planning," *House and Home* **12,** No. 2(August 1957):160–164.
32. Abbott, *Portland Planning*, p. 245.
33. A meeting was held between the authors and 14 residents of Vermont Hills in February 1992. The majority of attendants were original residents of the community. May Krinke and Karine Myrin organized the meeting.
34. Ibid.
35. Ibid.
36. Ibid.
37. "The Builder's House 1949," *Architectural Forum* **90,** No. 4(April 1949):85.
38. Harold L. Wattel, "Levittown: A Suburban Community," in William Dobriner, ed., *The Suburban Community* (New York: G.P. Putnam's Sons, 1958), p. 288.
39. William Dobriner, *Class in Suburbia* (Englewood Cliffs, NJ: Prentice-Hall, 1963), p. 85.
40. Kenneth I. Helphand, *Colorado: Visions of an American Landscape* (Niwot, CO: Roberts Rinehart, 1991), p. 321.
41. "A Complete House for $6,990," *Architectural Forum* **86,** No. 5(May 1947): 70–73.
42. Barbara M. Kelly, *Expanding the American Dream: Building and Rebuilding Levittown* (Albany: State University of New York Press, 1993), p. 84.
43. Fred Lofsvold. Interview, Summer, 1993.
44. "$9,990 Levitt Houses Boast 70′ Lots, Levittown, PA," *Architectural Forum* **95** (October 1951):217–219.
45. "The Fastest-Selling Houses in the USA," *House and Home* **4,** No. 2(August 1953):126–130.
46. Kelly, *Expanding the American Dream*, p. 35.
47. "Biggest New City in the US," *House and Home* **2,** No. 6(December 1952):83, 86.
48. Kelly, *Expanding the American Dream*, p. 87.
49. Ibid., p. 63.
50. David Popenoe, *The Suburban Environment: Sweden and the United States* (Chicago: University of Chicago Press, 1977), p. 116.
51. Wattel, "Levittown," p. 288.
52. Kelly, *Expanding the American Dream*, p. 68.
53. Herbert Gans, *The Levittowners* (New York: Pantheon, 1967), p. 268.
54. Kelly, *Expanding the American Dream*, p. 78.
55. Ibid., p. 71.
56. W. D. Wetherell, *The Man Who Loved Levittown* (Pittsburgh: University of Pittsburgh Press, 1985), p. 14.
57. "The Builder's House 1949," p. 88.
58. Popenoe, *The Suburban Environment*, p. 116.
59. Kelly, *Expanding the American Dream*, p. 145.
60. Gans, *The Levittowners*, p. 282.
61. "Biggest New City in the US," p. 82.
62. Popenoe, *The Suburban Environment*, p. 136.
63. "The Builder's House 1949," p. 91.
64. "Levitt's Landia," *Architectural Forum* **94,** No. 2(February 1951):140–148.
65. Ibid.
66. "Biggest New City in the US," p. 80–91.

67. Popenoe, *The Suburban Environment*, p. 113.
68. "Biggest New City in the US," p. 82.
69. Dobriner, *Class in Suburbia*, pp. 100, 105.
70. Kelly, *Expanding the American Dream*, p. 3.
71. Ibid., pp. 56–57.
72. Gans, *The Levittowners*, p. 277.
73. "How Levittown Disproves the Cynical Prophets," *House and Home* **12,** No. 5(November 1957):54.
74. "Biggest New City in the US," p. 86.
75. Gans, *The Levittowners*, p. 282.
76. Ron Rosenbaum, "The House That Levitt Built," *Esquire* **100,** No. 6(1983):388.
77. Kelly, *Expanding the American Dream*, pp. 17, 114.
78. Rosenbaum, "The House That Levitt Built," p. 378.
79. Gans, *The Levittowners*, pp. 156, 279.
80. Ibid., p. 279.
81. Ibid., p. 206.
82. Kelly, *Expanding the American Dream*, p. 149.
83. Ibid., p. 160.
84. Wetherell, *The Man Who Loved Levittown*, p. 6.
85. Ada Louise Huxtable, "'Clusters' Instead of 'Slurbs'," *The New York Times Magazine* (February 9, 1964):37–44.
86. Jane Jacobs, *Death and Life of Great American Cities* (New York: Random House, 1961), p. 445.
87. William H. Whyte, *Cluster Development* (New York: American Conservation Association, 1964).
88. Frederick H. Bair, *The Open Space Net* (Chicago: ASPO Planning Advisory Service, 1968).

5
LINKAGES
Community Planning

F or those who could be there, life in the suburbs was great. The American Dream was made real as hundreds of thousands of families succeeded in buying homes in attractive, safe neighborhoods.[1] The significant and recognized costs were the extensive environmental costs of incremental suburban development. The unplanned North American megalopolis was headed for disaster—pathos, gridlock, and poisoning were the predicted outcome. In confirmation, Rachel Carson's 1962 best-seller, *Silent Spring*,[2] forecast worldwide environmental disaster if current patterns of development, agriculture, and energy production were continued. In the early 1960s, Jacobs, Carson, Whyte, and innumerable others popped the balloons of postwar optimism.

By the early 1960s national-level planners collaborated with the building industry to research and publicize alternatives to the subdivided suburbs. Conference papers and journal articles closely tracked the British new towns, as well as projects in Scandinavia, Holland, and Canada. The American Society of Planning Officials (ASPO), the Federal Housing and Home Finance Agency, and the Federal Housing Administration (FHA) worked with industry representatives such as the National Association of Home Builders (NAHB) and the Urban Land Institute (ULI) to research both the physical form of new development and the language for state and local ordinances. Through education and publicity they encouraged communities to undertake comprehensive planning for land use, transportation, infrastructure, recreation, and open space. These agencies provided guidelines to the comprehensive planning process, as well as model legislation for cluster subdivisions and, later, for planned unit developments (PUDs), creatively planned residential areas that exhibited economies of layout while retaining areas of open landscape.[3] One of the most consistent messages was that preserving open space was both environmentally and economically beneficial. Many communities adopted the legislation, thereby giving developers the opportunity of flexible planning and higher densities in exchange for providing public open space. With costs of all aspects of community development rising, developers welcomed the economy of clustering buildings—by the early 1970s cluster subdivisions and PUDs added new housing and community forms to the mix of suburban options.

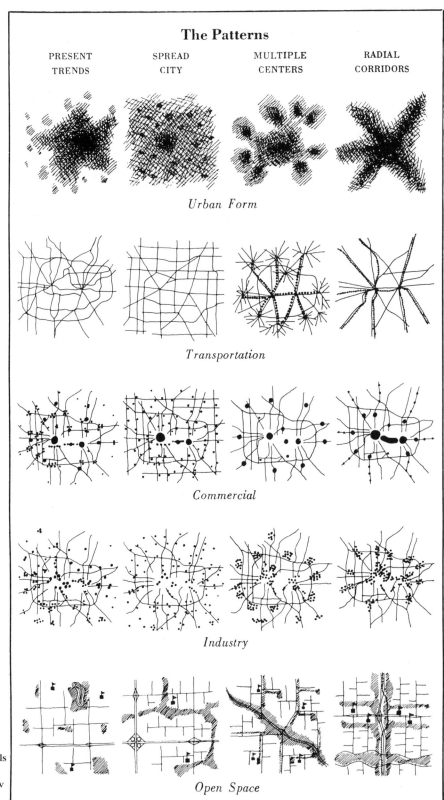

The Patterns

PRESENT TRENDS   SPREAD CITY   MULTIPLE CENTERS   RADIAL CORRIDORS

Urban Form

Transportation

Commercial

Industry

Open Space

"An inter-agency land use-transportation planning program for the Twin Cities metropolitan area (Minneapolis-St. Paul), 1964."
From American Society of Planning Officials Newsletter, November, 1964, Chicago: American Society of Planning Officials, now known as the American Planning Association.

CLUSTER SUBDIVISIONS

Cluster subdivisions (or cluster developments) provided legal loopholes that allowed developers to create areas of clustered higher-density development in exchange for preserving open space, all within a single development.[4] Two features were critical. Houses would be clustered into small groups or modules, which reduced the total lengths of roads and the extent of corresponding infrastructure. Individual lots were significantly smaller; however, each cluster of houses was separated by space that could be common land for the enjoyment of the residents. Conventional large-lot subdivisions often were built under subdivision regulations that prescribed minimum lot sizes, most commonly to assure adequate spacing for on-site septic systems.[5] Maximum allowable densities were based on a division of total acreage by minimum lot size, and many developers took a similar straightforward approach to subdivision layout. Parcels were typically divided into as many equal-sized lots as would fit, with little regard to topography or other landscape characteristics. Cluster subdivisions allowed the flexibility to group houses, respond to difficult site conditions, and reserve portions of the property for common open space. By maintaining the same overall density formula for the site, sewage systems could still be provided safely. Both developers and the community would benefit from more economical layouts and the qualities gained when features such as streams and woodlands remained for everyone's enjoyment.

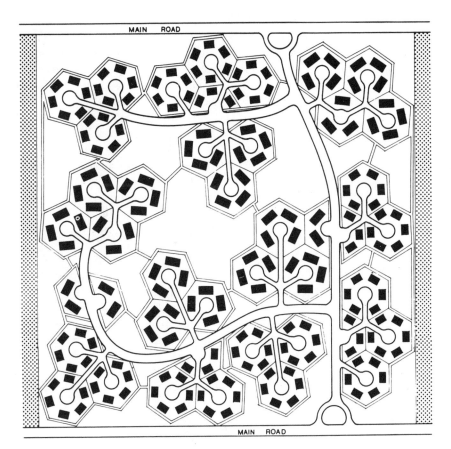

Cluster housing layout.
From Gideon Golany, *New Town Planning: Principles and Practice,* New York: John Wiley and Sons, 1976, p. 229.

In addition to reducing the costs of large-lot development, Jon Rosenthal, of the ASPO, was intent on convincing the development community that it was possible to retain the rural character of low-density developments. He mentioned Radburn as a model of cluster housing where "park land is always close at hand."[6] However, he was careful to point out the difference between the landscaped parks at Radburn and the natural features that he suggested preserving. He cited several examples in which streamways, woodlands, and hillocks were left intact, providing a natural backdrop to the new housing. Land not sold for lots would be in common ownership, whether by a residents' association or by the local government, assuring its future as a natural area. Rosenthal also mentioned the additional opportunities for "sociability"[7] that common open spaces might provide.

A problem with preserving open space in small cluster developments was the limited extent of their natural open spaces. These were fragments of much larger natural systems, which really needed preservation to be anything other than local amenity. William H. Whyte argued in favor of clustering dwellings for reasons similar to those of the ASPO: conservation of land for open space, reductions in roads and infrastructure, and a stronger sense of community. But he also identified a community-scaled need for open space "linkages" that could extend beyond individual developments, in effect connecting whole communities, both human and natural. "The open space of a cluster subdivision may be functional in itself, but it becomes far more so if it is tied in with other open spaces—with community parks, with schools, and with the open spaces of other cluster developments."[8] The great opportunity of clustering, said Whyte, was for communities to plan linked open space systems ahead of development, then encourage developers to align their open spaces within the community framework. The landscape would determine the location of open space linkages by the very existence of riparian corridors. The community would accept nature's framework, then fill in elements such as parks, schools, and community centers. Whyte's book was full of examples of cluster subdivisions, which were beginning to address the larger-scaled linkages he was promoting. He praised the new towns of Reston, Virginia, and El Dorado Hills, California, for their extensive systems of linked open spaces and cited the progressive open space planning going on in the counties of Santa Clara, Santa Barbara, and Monterey in California.

Whyte's ideas were not new. He raised once again arguments made by the Regional Planning Association of New York in the 1920s and even earlier by Frederick Law Olmsted. Whyte's arguments, however, were directed toward 1960s development conditions, and he provided both developers and community planners with workable proposals reinforced by innumerable examples. He forcefully argued that open spaces, from intimate yards to public parks and nature preserves, had to be linked with each other to best serve urbanized populations. He argued that a spacious landscape quality would best be achieved not by setting aside large tracts for parks, but by utilizing both natural and human-made corridors to connect a series of smaller spaces. Reston and Columbia provided widely publicized examples. The new towns exemplified the benefits of such open space systems and proved that with advance planning they were achievable, at least in private developments. In 1966, the ULI study, "Open Space Communities in the Market Place," confirmed that well-designed open space communities such as Radburn, Reston, and Miami Lakes in Florida were attractive to prospective home buyers and that in the majority of these communities, open space

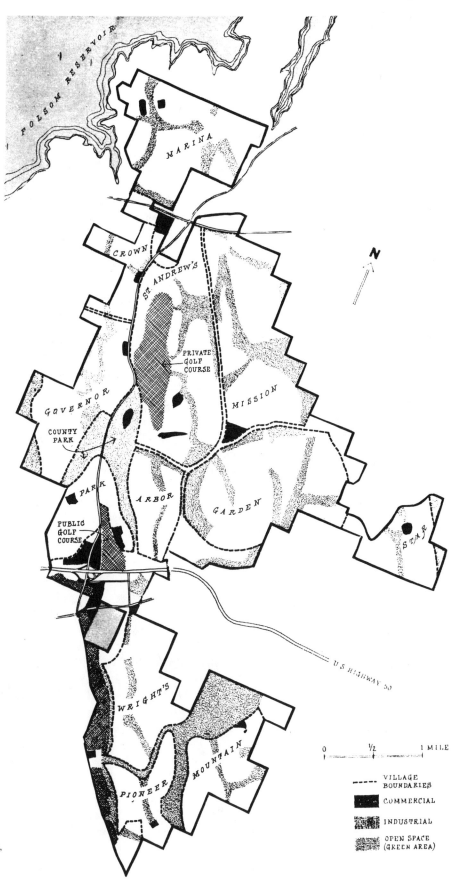

Plan of El Dorado Hills, California.
House and Home, Vol. 23, No. 3, March,
1963, p. 106–115.

contributed to the development's marketability. The new development style called "open space communities" swept the nation by the late 1960s, compelled by evidence that buyers wanted more natural and recreational open space near their homes.[9]

PLANNED UNIT DEVELOPMENTS

Touted as an ideal alternative to the subdivision for America's small builders,[10] the planned unit development (PUD), a small-scale planned community characterized by attached single-family or multifamily housing and small open space reserves, appeared concurrently with cluster developments. Articles in planning, design, and law journals throughout the 1960s promoted this new form of planning law, because it addressed small-scale projects, encouraged innovation, and provided local jurisdictions with a device for increasing density while procuring needed open space.[11] The smaller scale of PUDs allowed the planning through build-out cycle to be drastically shortened, thus bringing them within the financial capabilities of small and midsized developers. By the early 1970s PUD legislation had been adopted nationwide by local jurisdictions.[12]

The primary objective of the PUD ordinance in the early years was to introduce flexibility into the approvals and development process. It gave planning officials the power to negotiate with developers while allowing the developers to explore new building and site designs. The ASPO recommended that ordinances include design goals and guidelines that had to be met by the developer.[13] Community officials would then review plans and completed projects to assure compliance, thus maintaining closer contact with housing development "in the field." Many jurisdictions also included a phase of public review within the approvals process, giving local residents an opportunity to voice their support or concerns.[14] Developers were allowed tremendous design flexibility and suddenly had the same proactive

A PUD with ganged parking.
C. Girling.

relationship with planning officials that community builders had. They were asked to meet certain density requirements, limit negative impacts on neighbors—especially those of parking and traffic—reveal potential impacts on urban services, reduce environmental impacts, and provide certain amounts of public or semipublic open space. Neighborhood stores, churches, and day-care facilities were often allowed on the site. Housing mixes were encouraged. For example, in the Eugene, Oregon, ordinance, density was calculated in points per gross acre, with points assigned to numbers of bedrooms. No mention was made of building types or numbers of units per acre, giving the developer great flexibility in determining the composition and design of apartments and houses. There was leeway in street and parking layouts, and innumerable experiments were tried. With densities high, parking was a challenge. In the stereotypical PUD, cars were clustered in lots set between blocks of buildings, tucked under the dwelling in a garage, or aligned as head-in parking along the roads. The latter examples were often favored because they brought people's cars closer to their dwellings; however, the resulting streetscape had the character of a long parking lot.[15] Many developers maintained these vehicular areas as common property (owned by a representative home owners association) so that they did not have to meet stringent engineering regulations.

The ASPO[16] placed landscape preservation as a high priority for all PUD legislation. It recommended specific language in ordinances to protect natural amenities and encouraged communities to include clear definitions of "open space," with specific quantity and quality standards to address issues of usefulness. Upon acceptance of such ordinances, the ASPO said, local planners would finally have a significant level of control over open space in suburban America. Promoters assured that the resulting developments would fit the local conditions by preserving natural areas and being responsive to site conditions. The higher densities of most PUDs would be compensated for by providing each dwelling with a small private yard and extensive common green spaces for games and larger gatherings.

Despite the best of intentions, a national pattern emerged that had several negative characteristics: entry drives often looked like parking lots or, in upscale developments, uninterrupted lines of garage doors; walls, berms, and planting along public streets enclosed the development but excluded outsiders; complex, awkward configurations of drives and housing were difficult to navigate, even with the map found at the entry to the community; weakly defined yards backed onto undifferentiated green space; and common open spaces were never developed, but remained as green wastelands. Landscaped and maintained by the home owners association with a primary objective of tidiness, the grounds often had an impersonal, institutional quality.[17]

The proportions and delineation of private outdoor spaces and common open areas constituted a key dilemma. If private yards were heavily enclosed, the adjacent common space was often perceived as "leftover." If entirely unenclosed, both would be exposed and rendered unusable. The result in many PUDs was common areas left as ill-defined "viewing" space, intended to give the impression of spaciousness, yet so exposed that people were uncomfortable using them. The character of these common spaces often determined the overall character of the development. Naturally treed areas could give the whole development a "woodsy" feeling. The addition of paths and a hands-off approach to maintenance yielded an intriguing and useful landscape. Open sites posed more difficult problems, as planting was

Weakly defined yards and undeveloped open space in a PUD.
C. Girling.

often crucial for screening and the partial enclosure of private areas. A natural landscape character was less apparent, and developers typically felt that they needed to create character to sell the units. Taken to extreme, this led to the construction of incongruous projects such as the mission-style "South of the Border" garden apartments near the prairie city of Winnipeg, Canada.

Two Eugene, Oregon, communities provide examples of the "best" PUD attributes in their handling of open space. Edgewood Townhouses was one of Eugene's earliest PUDs, tentatively approved in 1968 while the PUD ordinance was still under consideration by the city council. The site was located in a tight valley in Eugene's wooded South Hills. Landscape architect Lloyd Bond, together with architects Morris and Redden, decided to make the narrow but active stream the focus of the project while maintaining the site's wooded quality. They determined that houses would face onto public paths and automobiles would be stored in private garages surrounding rear car courts. In doing this, they avoided one of the great pitfalls of PUDs, the confusion of back and front, car and pedestrian, private and public space, and the resulting lack of clarity about how outdoor spaces might be used. Using Eugene's common street-and-alley model, the designers squeezed the whole composition into a very small space, with private courtyards situated between the garages and dwellings. The stream drained a much larger basin than the project site, so it was important that a riparian easement be maintained to stabilize the stream banks and protect the adjacent homes. Pathways, originally intended to be public but now designated as private, were aligned along both banks. At the center of the development, the Edgewood

A home at Edgewood Townhouses, Eugene, Oregon.
Kate Van Rooy.

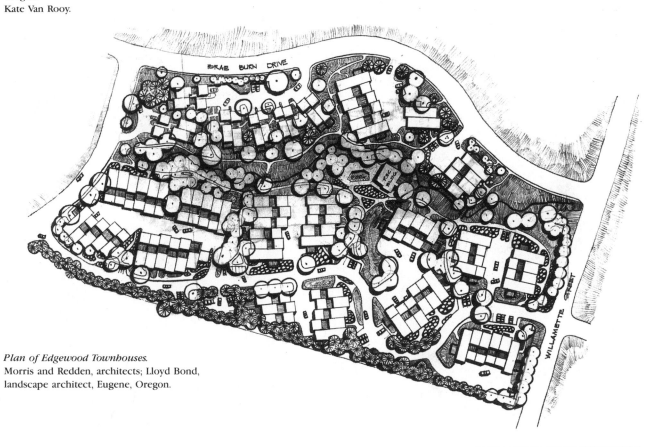

Plan of Edgewood Townhouses.
Morris and Redden, architects; Lloyd Bond, landscape architect, Eugene, Oregon.

pool and meeting hall were sited adjacent to the stream. West of the site where the stream originated, a public nature trail was retained. East of the site the stream was culverted and absorbed into the city's underground stormwater system. Now, 25 years later, courtyards are personalized and common areas mature, yet neat. In 1982 jurors awarded the project an American Society of Landscape Architects design award, stating that they were "very impressed with [the] siting and the landscape architect's role. Density was superbly dealt with, [and it had] an extremely well done planting plan."[18]

In the tight circumstance of many PUDs, size, scale, and distance of outdoor space is crucial to successful design. Private space must be adequately screened from public view, yet common space must remain both physically and visually accessible. For safety's sake a person's eyes must be on the streets;[19] so must his or her gaze fall on common green spaces. The courtyards of Edgewood Townhouses provided an excellent example of how outdoor space in a PUD can be successfully delineated from very private yards to public areas. However, the residents' desire to privatize the streamway path is an indication of a significant weakness in one area. Dwellings were sited as close as 10 feet to the public pathway, without adequate screening between the path and the front door. Such a condition can appear threatening, in that people unknown to a resident can be only a few feet from the front door. In such a situation, an additional layer of screening would have reduced feelings of exposure and vulnerability to intruders.[20]

Edgewood Townhouses.
C. Girling.

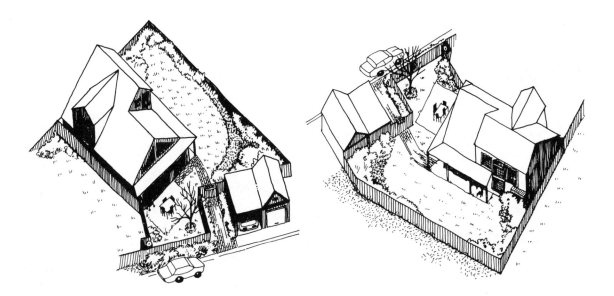

A home at Champignon, Eugene, Oregon.
Kate Van Rooy.

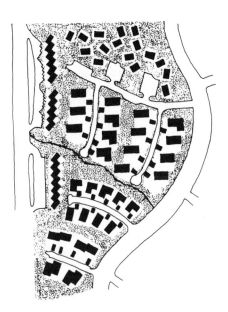

Common open space

0   500 FEET

Plan of Champignon. Threshold Architects;
Peter Thompson, landscape architect.
Redrawn by Kate Van Rooy from Threshold
Architects drawings.

Champignon, a small development located in a growing "up-scale" area of Eugene, provides an example of how the PUD law could encourage innovative design. Spyglass Development Co. recognized an unaddressed niche in Eugene's housing market—singles, couples without children, and formerly marrieds—and created a PUD with three different housing types to meet their needs. Threshold Architects led the design team, assisted by landscape architect Peter Thompson. Threshold applied Christopher Alexander's Pattern Language to the project, incorporating many "patterns" into the project.[21] The site was at the foot of a steep butte and had sloping and level, as well as wooded and open areas. The wooded portion of the site was a majestic grove of Oregon white oaks whose root systems were very sensitive to disturbance or changes to the water table. Responding to the site's conditions, the architects proposed four "identifiable neighborhoods"[22]: cottages for singles and formerly marrieds in the oak woods, two neighborhoods of zero lot-line single-family houses on the open, level ground (though few families have ever lived in the project), and row houses for small families and couples along a street.

Sixteen 1,000-square-foot cottages were nestled within the oak grove. Employing light post-and-beam structures that hardly touched the ground, each cottage was intended to be a "tree place"[23] within a "garden growing wild."[24] All land in the cottages area was held in common, and the private spaces for the cottages were a screened deck and a front porch. Although obviously a semiprivate realm, the oak forest was left open to public access. In the streets of the single-family area the architects sought a "path shape"[25] and scale for the street, with the intent of creating a "positive" outdoor space. Small garages and private terraces enclosed narrow, richly paved streets, giving them the quality of well-cared-for alleys. Gateways were placed on the street edge, between the terraces and the garages. The scale and juxtaposition of elements created a street in which cars, cyclists, and pedestrians were made equals, amicably sharing the street.

Some critical connections, however, were left incomplete. Pathways originally intended to connect the four neighborhoods were not constructed. Although everyone else can circulate on the internal roads, residents of the row houses have to cut through planting beds to reach other

119

The common street at Champignon.
C. Girling.

areas. Common green spaces fell prey to a frequent dilemma of PUDs. Yards were fenced to give them enough privacy for dining or sunbathing, leaving the "quiet backs"[26] with no apparent purpose. An all-too-frequent example is that a streamway was preserved where it crossed midway through the site, only to be culverted under adjacent developments. Although the streets are a locally acclaimed success, the green open spaces are disconnected strips of lawn and a discontinuous former stream, made all the more evident by the lack of any other connected green space in the surrounding neighborhood.

New discoveries often promise us much greater solutions than they deliver. PUDs were anticipated to be a solution to suburban sprawl and landscape disfigurement. The sprawl of large-lot subdivisions would be ameliorated by increased densities, reduced land consumption, and the creation of community open space. Everyone thought that by giving developers (and their designers) more control and having planning departments review PUD proposals, the standards of community design would improve. These aspirations were not fulfilled. The population of San Jose, California, doubled during its "PUD period" from 1965 to 1985. This community provides a vivid example of the cumulative effects of PUDs. In a study prepared for the San Jose Department of City Planning, Daniel Solomon and Associates, stated that although there were innumerable cases of well-designed projects,

> What recent housing tends not to address . . . are the relationships of dwellings to one another within a project and the quality of community that new housing creates in aggregation. . . . At its most negative this community takes the form of isolated enclaves, separated from adjacent properties by perimeter parking drives and walled off from public streets and adjacent properties. . . . The public world is reduced to walls and garages, and the isolated nature of the housing enclaves tends to deprive them of context, history and community.[27]

The PUD suffered from the same problems as the subdivision. Multiple, introverted, isolated projects were constructed. Development continued to outstep planning, especially in regard to communitywide networks of open space and nonvehicular circulation. As more and more communities like San Jose evolved, it became evident that the linkages of which Whyte spoke were missing.

AMERICA'S NEW TOWNS: RESTON AND COLUMBIA

Ideas about new town design moved quickly from Europe to America and back again. Ebenezer Howard's Garden Cities formed the germ of Western new town theory, but there were other significant influences. Residential open space networks, derived from Olmsted's greenway designs, were used by John Nolen at Mariemount and Kingsport[28] and by Clarence Stein and Henry Wright at Radburn. These models directly influenced post-World War II British new towns, as well as new towns in Europe, Australia, and other lands abroad.[29] Meanwhile, the greenbelt and its corollary, the town of limited size, were the most lasting contributions of the British to new town plans.[30] Finland's Tapiola borrowed concepts from both the British garden cities and Radburn and was destined to influence America's later new towns. Tapiola was one of the first new towns to have a clearly stated environmental ethic. In addition to creating a well-balanced population and economic self-sufficiency, its planners were concerned with preserving vast amounts of the site's woodlands to create a community in nature. Through writings by American planners Paul Speiregen[31] and Wolf Von Eckert,[32] the unique natural qualities of Tapiola were brought to the American planning community.

It was two enlightened private developers who bucked the tide of development and began America's two renowned European-style new towns. Reston, Virginia, and Columbia, Maryland, were both planned to be economically self-sufficient communities with their own quasi-governments

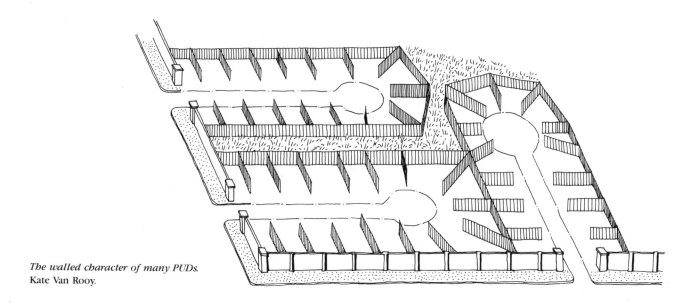

The walled character of many PUDs.
Kate Van Rooy.

Wooded open space at Tapiola, Finland.
C. Girling.

and a range of jobs for their populations. Both were located within commuting distance of Washington, D.C. The developers, Robert E. Simon and James Rouse, were compelled by the idea of creating complete new towns and went far beyond their colleagues in the development industry. Influenced by the well-publicized new towns in Great Britain and Scandinavia, they employed teams of planners, architects, and sociologists to scientifically plan every aspect of these communities. They redefined "village," "neighborhood," and "community" and identified shopping and service as the significant foci of community life. Perhaps most important, they envisioned new ways of living that would highlight recreation within vast networks of open space. In the process, they proved that it was possible in America to create new communities without direct government support.

Reston was conceived by developer Robert E. Simon in 1962, and Columbia by James Rouse in 1963. Both developers were well aware of contemporary new towns in Europe. Each aspired to create an American interpretation of the European new town—a product of private industry rather than government programs. Borrowing from the accepted European defini-

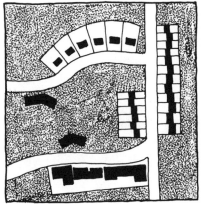 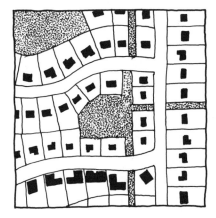

EUROPEAN NEW TOWN **AMERICAN NEW TOWN**

American vs. European new towns: In America, land was sold to private landholders unless given protected status, as with public streets and open spaces. In European new towns, land was a public resource. Small parcels within the public fabric were sold to private interests. Kate Van Rooy.

tions of "new town," Simon and Rouse emphasized balanced, preplanned, and contained communities composed of a full range of economic, social, educational, recreational, and housing opportunities.[33] Unlike the British, both were confident that private, *for-profit* companies could produce such communities. These developers hired large teams of environmental and behavioral planners to develop early concepts and lay out their plans. Reston was originally planned for 75,000 people, and by 1992 had reached 54,000. Columbia, originally designed for 110,000, reached 73,000 by 1992.

Reston, Virginia. C. Girling.

Robert Simon's vision for Reston was a townscape so compelling and complete that a diverse population could live and work there for their entire lives.[34] For him this meant that the town would provide a diverse range of housing types and settings, entertainment and recreation, professional services, jobs, shopping, and churches. Simon felt that the times demanded a community focused on outdoor recreation. Although he appreciated the rolling woodlands and meadows of his site, he directed his planners to design all open spaces with purpose—each type of open space identified was to have a specific role related to the community's plan. The resulting plan comprised both active and passive recreational spaces, including golf courses, parks, tot lots, swimming and tennis centers, wooded and meadow areas with trails and picnic sites, and a 71-acre nature center.

Simon hired more than 35 consulting firms, including land planners, architects, engineers, economists, lawyers, and various social planners. Reston's development predated Ian McHarg's groundbreaking work, *Design with Nature*,[35] by seven years, but reflected a similar sentiment in its use of a comprehensive planning approach and its sensitivity to landscape features. While physical designers analyzed the site and identified major open space corridors and developable areas, social planners worked to define the elements of neighborhood, community, and town. Lawyers worked with Howard County to develop a planned community ordinance that would protect the surrounding rural areas while providing the company maximum freedom in configuration, density, and mixes of land uses.[36]

The plan for Reston was composed of seven villages, an industrial corridor along the Dulles freeway, and a town center (which was not opened until October 1990). Each village was sited around a distinctive landscape feature, such as the artificial Lake Anne. These centers were connected by a high-density housing "sinew,"[37] a continuous band of multifamily housing that paralleled an open space corridor. Each village housed 12,000 people in apartments, row houses, and single-family houses. Village centers (four by 1992), were mixed-use areas with apartments, shops, and offices, all focusing on a public plaza. Most village residents would be within walking range of the center, and planners envisioned lively activity day and night.

PUD-like enclaves formed the smallest grouping of dwellings at Reston, a corporate form of neighborhood. For added diversity, these were designed by different architects and built for different markets. Each had a unique look, composition, and name and separate entryways off the looped collector streets. Composed primarily of town houses and garden apartments, they were the predominant form of housing at Reston.[38] Most were characterized by tightly grouped buildings that fronted on narrow entry drives and parking and backed onto small private yards adjacent to common open space. In some cases the open space was a golf course or public park. In others, it was a lake or a natural corridor with walking or biking trails.

The circulation system resembled the Radburn model, with a hierarchy of roads to reduce traffic on residential streets and separated pedestrian paths passing through the public open space network. Vehicular connections were made with amply landscaped loop roads that led from the village center around each village and back again. Narrow local roads or cluster parking lots served the housing enclaves. The Reston Parkway provided a major north-south connection through the town, tying all to the town center as well as to several local highways that traverse the town from east to west.

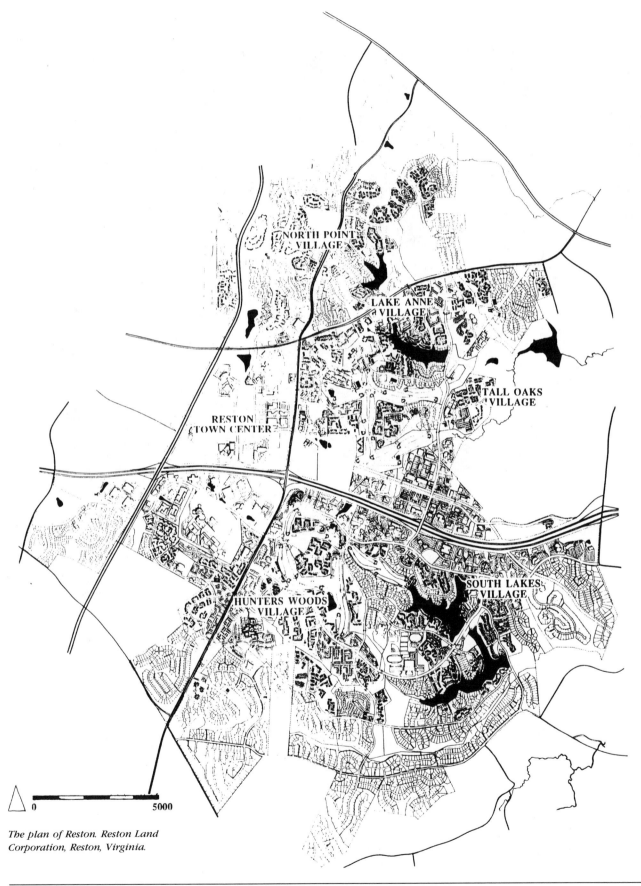

*The plan of Reston. Reston Land
Corporation, Reston, Virginia.*

Waterside park at Reston.
C. Girling.

Reston's open spaces were selected prior to siting buildings, to take best advantage of natural features. Three streams were reserved for natural corridors, and four lakes were created in low-lying areas. A total of 23% of the land area was dedicated to common open space.[39] Public, semipublic, and private open spaces linked together to form a townscape predominated by woodlands and water. Today the Reston Association has a renewed commitment to the conservation of natural areas and has embarked on an aggressive management plan focused on respecting natural processes. The plan emphasizes a hands-off approach to "natural areas"[40] and discourages the use of chemical products on all common lands. Exceptions are made for highly maintained sites such as playing fields. Various promotional brochures educate home owners about how to encourage lands to succeed from open ground through meadowland stages, to the climax of northern hardwood forests that originally covered the site. The Reston Association also sponsors a year-round environmental education program at the community's nature center.

In sharp contrast to the natural areas were the village plazas and the town center. These provided a taste of urbanity, with restaurants, shops, and movie theaters spilling onto public plazas. Lake Anne Village Center[41] terminated one end of the lake with a public dock below the plaza. Surrounding the plaza was a semicircle of shops with second-story apartments overlooking the plaza. Office buildings and an apartment tower completed the enclo-

Open space plan of Reston.
Kate Van Rooy.

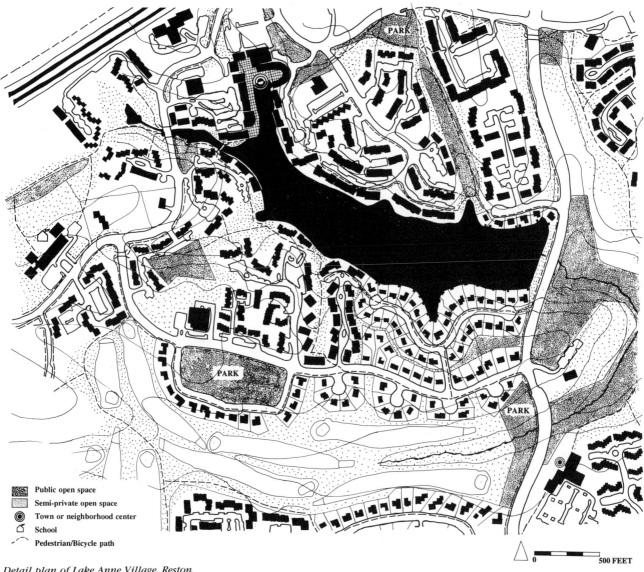

Public open space
Semi-private open space
Town or neighborhood center
School
Pedestrian/Bicycle path

0   500 FEET

Detail plan of Lake Anne Village, Reston.
Kate Van Rooy.

sure of the plaza, while providing a modest population to patronize the shops. Reston waited 25 years for its town center—a grid-based design with a hotel, office buildings, shops, restaurants, and an eleven screen cinema housed in neoclassical buildings. The focus of Reston's new town center is the half-mile long Market Street, a pedestrian street that terminates at Market Square.[42]

Robert Simon had a strong interest in the outdoors and was committed to the idea that country living should indeed provide access to both planned recreation and undeveloped landscapes. His primary contribution to the continuum of new community development in the United States might be seen as the physical plan that brought together principles that planners had been pursuing since the Radburn days: a complete town with all the physical, social, and employment opportunities of small-town Ameri-

Lake Anne Village Center, Reston.
Kenneth Helphand.

ca, composed in a plan that integrated a full complement of housing types and densities and all the services needed for daily life. The final achievement in Reston was the recent construction of a "downtown." With it came the recognition that for urban dwellers, open space is a continuum: from the most public spaces in the streets of downtown to the most private in one's backyard. Equally important is the continuum from the geometry and style of highly urbanized settings to the organic order of natural landscapes.

In his speech "How to Build a Whole City from Scratch," James Rouse said that his goal for Columbia was "a series of small communities separated by topography, highways, public institutions, greenbelts, and united by a center that provided cultural, educational, and recreational facilities for many."[43] Like Simon, Rouse hired a large interdisciplinary team to plan Columbia, using a highly innovative working process. After the preliminary site analysis was complete, the community plan was designed in a series of 2½-day group sessions. The team, composed of planners, developers, and advisors from government, family life, recreation, sociology, economics, education, health, psychology, housing, transportation, and communication represented their areas of expertise. A number of innovative plan arrangements and social services arose out of the approach: new groupings for public school grades were tested in Columbia; a preventative health care program was instituted; a cooperative ministry of churches was instituted to coordinate social services and supply some low-rent housing; many of the cultural and recreational activities were dispersed into the neighborhoods or villages, rather than trying to centralize them.

Called a "system of overlapping communities,"[44] Columbia's physical plan evolved from the early conception of its social institutions. It differed from Reston in the purposeful inclusion of the neighborhood as a social grouping and a place where residents would meet on a regular basis. Seven villages of 15,000 persons were divided into three to four neighborhoods of

The lakefront, Columbia, Maryland.
Kenneth Helphand.

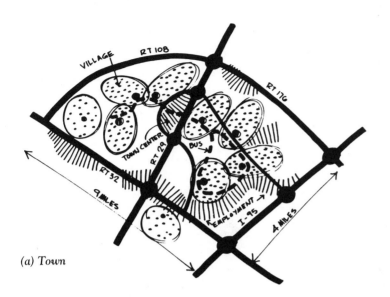

(a) Town

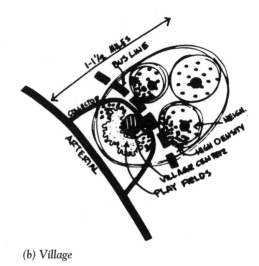

(b) Village

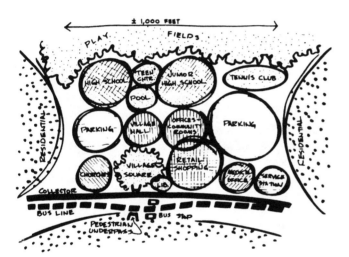

(c) Village Center

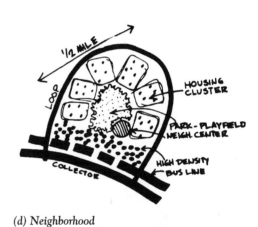

(d) Neighborhood

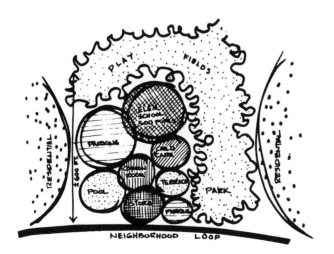

(e) Neighborhood Center

(f) Housing Cluster

Concept diagrams for Columbia.
From Morton Hoppenfeld, "A Sketch of the Planning–Building Process for Columbia, Maryland." Reprinted by permission of the *Journal of the American Institute of Planners*, Vol. 33, No. 6, November 1967, pp. 398–409.

between 600 and 800 apartments, town houses, and detached homes. Each neighborhood center had a community building and swimming pool near the elementary school, affording better opportunities for expanding the curriculum of the school and providing after-school care. A smaller social division was also planned. Within each neighborhood, housing clusters were grouped around a common yard, providing the opportunity for casual acquaintance or pickup games. The daily activities of young parents and their children formed the nucleus of the neighborhood: elementary school, day care, park, summer swimming, and the convenience store. Like Radburn, the neighborhood was sized so that young children walked or biked a maximum of one-half mile to school. Villages centers served older children, as well as the weekly needs of most residents. They included a supermarket, banks, medical offices, specialty stores, secondary schools, and townwide recreational and religious facilities.

Rouse, recognizing that in the 1960s the traditional main street was found in the suburban shopping mall, made Columbia's town center an enclosed mall. The mall layout is conventional, a large, low building surrounded by parking. Separated by its extensive apron of parking, it has no pedestrian connections to surrounding town center facilities: a central park, a waterfront park, a music pavilion, a community college, hotels, office buildings, and major medical facilities. At Columbia's core, the automobile dominates. The focus is parking, not park.

In the early 1960s people assumed that their leisure time would continue to increase, as predictions were made of the six- or seven-hour workday and the four-day workweek. Columbia, having been planned in this climate, has a surprisingly exhaustive list of recreational opportunities. The summer 1992 *Newcomers Guide to Columbia and Howard County* listed the following recreational resources for Columbia: 2,500 acres of open space with more than 50 miles of trails, 3 man-made lakes, 7 developed parks and 128 tot lots, 21 neighborhood pools and an indoor swim center, an ice rink, 2 tennis clubs, 2 fitness clubs, a golf course, a horse center, one nursery school (run by the community association), 20 before/after-school programs, a youth resource center, and a center for the arts.[45]

Columbia's rolling and partially forested site was laced with intermittent streams, creeks, and two channels of the Patuxent River draining toward the southeast corner of the site. These waterways formed the primary network of public open space. Within their corridors were pedestrian and bicycle trails and, in some locations, equestrian trails. All major parks and many village centers with schools, parks, and swimming pools were sited along these streamway corridors, reinforcing the open space system. The subsidiary open spaces or "common yards" located within each housing cluster often linked in some fashion with the streamway corridors, so that most residents had pedestrian or bicycle connections from their homes to neighborhood schools and shops and the communitywide open space network (see pages 41 and 44). Cluster-to-cluster connections were also made with pedestrian easements, thus a secondary network was created that links residential areas to each other. A drainage system has dispersed sources and a confluence, and so does Columbia's open space network. Unfortunately, the open space confluence does not coincide with the town's center, making it difficult in many cases for residents to walk or bike there. Similar problems can be found at the village scale, where some neighborhood centers have only vehicular connections to village centers, or some housing clusters are poorly connected to both neighborhood and village centers.

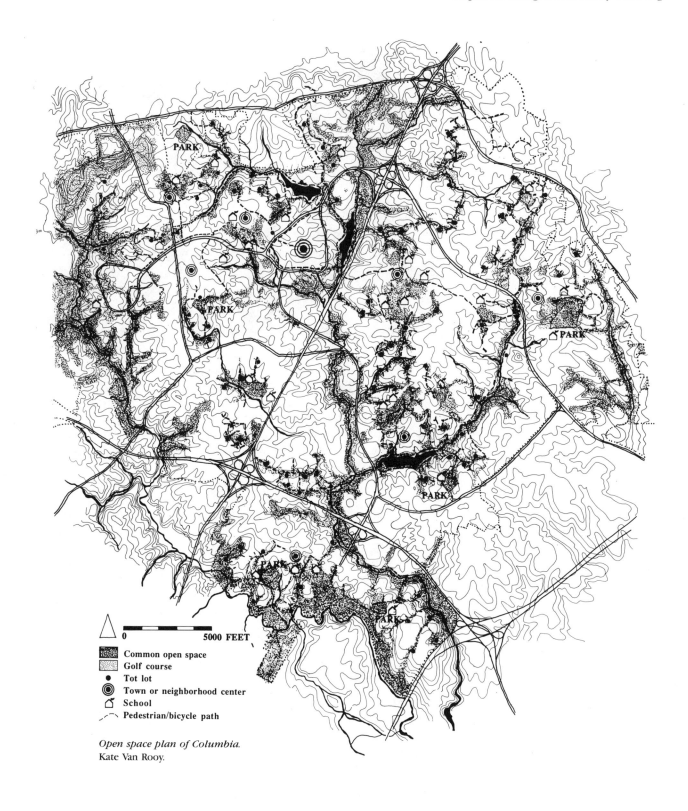

△ 0 _____ 5000 FEET

▦ Common open space
▦ Golf course
● Tot lot
◎ Town or neighborhood center
⌂ School
⌇ Pedestrian/bicycle path

Open space plan of Columbia.
Kate Van Rooy.

Secondary pedestrian circulation network at Columbia.
Kenneth Helphand.

Although its physical plan had distinct disadvantages, particularly the reinforcement of automobile dependency, and its appearance was blandly conventional, Columbia's contribution to the new communities movement —in fact, to several national institutions—was its sophisticated social planning. Studies of Columbia consistently remark that its social institutions and many ad hoc community organizations were operating as soon as the first residents moved in, in 1967. Some authors contend that its social planning led the way for several national trends[46]: its unique health maintenance organization led the nation in preventative health care; its system of many small schools and a new clustering of grade levels (1–5, 6–8, 9–12) has now become a standard nationwide; its interfaith religious centers were some of the earliest in the nation; and its mall-as-center recognized that America's shopping streets were moving indoors and the nature of community spaces was being redefined. Columbia, like Reston, was not a radical experiment, but a modest manipulation of urban conventions at all scales. In both cases, modesty was critical to market appeal, on which the developers were dependent.

LEGACIES OF PLANNED COMMUNITIES

The new towns of the 1960s contributed several important concepts to the continuum of new community development in America. Most important, they revived thought and discussion about community form, population, and politics, again raising the question of how design contributes to the creation of good communities. They emphasized "scientific" planning, or what would now be called interdisciplinary planning. They revived the central role of a network of open spaces and public lands in the structure and life of communities and crystallized the role of the village or town center as a cultural, community service, and shopping center. However, the development of new towns required vast resources. They were too big and clumsy for most of the development industry and took too long to reach maturity for a culture compelled by instant gratification.

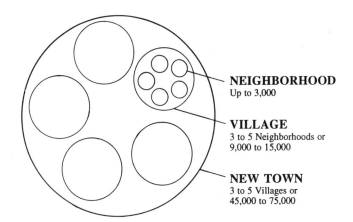

NEIGHBORHOOD
Up to 3,000

VILLAGE
3 to 5 Neighborhoods or
9,000 to 15,000

NEW TOWN
3 to 5 Villages or
45,000 to 75,000

Common population breakdown for neighborhood, village, and new town in the United States.
Compiled from several sources by C. Girling.

In their 1976 comparison of new planned communities and conventional subdivisions, Raymond Burby and Shirley Weiss found that planned communities indeed had better land planning, superior recreational facilities, safer and easier pedestrian routes, reduced automobile travel, improved living environments for low- and moderate-income people, and a more diverse population in terms of race and age.[47] However, conventional subdivisions were generally as successful as planned communities in evaluations of housing and neighborhood livability, participation in community life, provision of services, participation in governance, and perceptions that the neighborhood was a good place to raise children. Planned and conventional communities were also rated relatively equal in appearance and nearness to the outdoors and the natural environment. New planned communities were particularly weak in meeting residents' expectations for the provision of medical and social services. Thus, although their physical aspects may be superior, the social aspects of new communities were found wanting. Similarly, Richard Brooks concluded in his study that we should no longer assume that if we develop a superior town plan, strong community values will result.[48] Rather, a much broader set of social and governmental institutions, far beyond the reach of any physical planner or developer, influences the degree to which a locale achieves community—the problem is much bigger than the place itself.

The experimentation with how to subdivide a community into villages and neighborhoods was important in adopting Clarence Perry's earlier theories and applying them in the marketplace. Between Reston and Columbia alone numerous compositions for neighborhood and village centers were tried, many of which met with resistance from potential tenants, particularly retailers, grocers, and school districts. These groups were evolving very different theories of distribution for their services, such as highway-oriented superstores and corporate convenience stores and wanted nothing to do with preconstructed spaces, for they had patterned designs of their own. Such major commercial centers were slow to arrive. Community developers could not subsidize such enormous undertakings as commercial centers. Often they needed specialty developers to take on these projects, which would occur only after a population base existed.

From a physical planning point of view, cluster subdivisions, PUDs, and new towns had successes. Between 1960 and 1975 the seed planted at Radburn flowered. The potential of planned open space networks was realized in several different forms in the new communities. Common open space once again became a recognized and valued attribute in residential environments. In PUDs and cluster subdivisions, it was limited in scale and also in use; however, in the new towns, planners experimented with a broad range of landscape types and uses for open space. Although Americans never accepted the British idea that new towns should be publicly owned and controlled—that private houses and yards would be patches within the public fabric—many recognized the value of reserving a network of landscape resources in common ownership. At Reston in particular, the full range of open space opportunities, from yard to park to natural preserve, was made available to its residents, and accompanying this landscape were recreational and educational programs. In recent years the Reston Association has emphasized environmental education programs, intended to give the residents a deeper appreciation of the Reston landscape while improving everyone's landscape maintenance habits. What people gained with the open space networks of the new towns was, first and foremost, access to natural lands—a townscape set within nature—vast choices of recreational activities, and separated pedestrian and bike paths leading to significant community nodes.

In the increasingly competitive housing markets of the 1970s and 1980s, developers turned to the advertising industry to assist with marketing. Advertisers helped their clients to select the most marketable lessons learned from new towns to apply to thousands of master-planned communities developed across the nation over the next 15 years. The aspiration to create complete, diverse, economically and politically independent communities was boiled down to lifestyle themes tied to recreation and family type. The result in the 1980s was a plethora of planned communities ranging in size from PUDs of a few acres to 10,000-acre master-planned communities, each geared to a narrow market niche. Although initially seeming to match the quality of physical environment provided by the new towns, they proved to be even more socially limiting and contributed to an unprecedented level of mobility among suburbanites.

NOTES

1. Scott Donaldson, *The Suburban Myth* (New York: Columbia University Press, 1969).
2. Rachel Carson, *Silent Spring* (Greenwich, CT: Fawcett Publications, 1962).
3. Examples of such studies include Urban Land Institute, *New Approaches to Residential Land Development, A Study of Concepts and Innovations, Technical Bulletin No. 40* (Washington, DC: Urban Land Institute, January 1961); Jan Krasnowiecki and Richard F. Babcock, *Legal Aspects of Planned Unit Residential Development, Technical Bulletin No. 52* (Washington, DC: Urban Land Institute, May 1965); Carl Norcross, *Open Space Communities in the Market Place, Technical Bulletin No. 57* (Washington, DC: Urban Land Institute, December 1966); Frank S. So, David R. Mosena, and Frank S. Bangs, *Planned Unit Development Ordinances, Report No. 291* (Chicago: American Society of Planning Officials, Planning Advisory Service, May 1973).
4. Jon Rosenthal, "Cluster Subdivisions," *Information Report No. 135* (Chicago: ASPO Planning Advisory Service, 1960). This report clarified terminology and promoted cluster subdivisions, defining them as alternatives to standard subdivisions, which allow variances on the street layout and lot sizing to reduce development costs while preserving open space, pp. 2–4.
5. Ibid, p. 13.
6. Ibid, p. 4.
7. Ibid, p. 28.
8. William H. Whyte, *Cluster Developments* (New York: American Conservation Association, 1964), p. 78.

9. Norcross, *Open Space Communities in the Marketplace,* pp. 4–6.

10. So, Mosena, and Bangs, *Planned Unit Development Ordinances,* p. 1.

11. Robert W. Burchell and James W. Hughes, *Planned Unit Development New Communities, American Style* (New Brunswick, N.J.: Center for Urban Policy Research, Rutgers University, 1972), p. 1.

12. Ibid, p. 178.

13. So, Mosena, and Bangs, *Planned Unit Development Ordinances,* p. 25.

14. Ibid, p. 14.

15. Solomon and Associates, *Toward Community: Residential Design Guidelines of the City of San Jose* (unpublished, 1986).

16. So, Mosena, and Bangs, *Planned Unit Development Ordinances,* p. 30.

17. Daniel Solomon, "Life on the Edge: Toward a New Suburbia," *Architectural Record* **176,** No. 13 (November 1988):63–67.

18. "ASLA Merit Awards," *Landscape Architecture* **72,** No. 5 (September/October 1982):99.

19. Jane Jacobs, *Death and Life of Great American Cities* (New York: Vintage Books, 1961); and Anne Vernez Moudon, *Public Streets for Public Use* (New York: Columbia University Press, 1987).

20. Clare Cooper Marcus and Wendy Sarkissian, *Housing as If People Mattered* (Berkeley: University of California Press, 1986), p. 78.

21. Christopher Alexander, Sara Ishikawa, Murray Silverstein, *A Pattern Language* (New York: Oxford University Press, 1977). A design model that follows the typical design process from site selection to the details of interior design, giving very specific guidelines for the design of each element. The guidelines, shown in parentheses in this book, are called "patterns."

22. Ibid, Pattern #14.

23. Ibid, Pattern #171.

24. Ibid, Pattern #172.

25. Ibid, Pattern #121.

26. Ibid, Pattern #59.

27. Daniel Solomon and Associates, *Toward Community,* p. 2.

28. See Chapter 7 for coverage of Nolen's work.

29. Frederic J. Osborn and Arnold Whittick, *The New Towns: The Answer to Megalopolis* (New York: McGraw-Hill, 1963), p. 257; and Shirley F. Weiss, "New Towns—Transatlantic Exchange," *Town and Country Planning* **38** (September, 1970):374–381.

30. Osborn and Whittick, *The New Towns,* p. 150–163.

31. Heikki von Hertzen and Paul D. Speiregen, *Building a New Town: Finland's New Garden City Tapiola* (Cambridge, MA: The MIT Press, 1971).

32. Wolf Von Eckardt, "The Community: Could This Be Our Town?" *The New Republic* **151,** No. 19 (November, 1964):17–24.

33. Carlos Campbell, *New Towns: Another Way to Live,* (Reston, Virginia: Reston Publishing Company, 1976), p. 18; and James Rouse, "How to Build a Whole City from Scratch" (Address to the National Association of Mutual Savings Banks, May 17, 1966).

34. Campbell, *New Towns Another Way to Live,* p. 32; and Robert Simon, "Planning a New Town—Reston, Virginia," *Proceedings, American Society of Planning Officials Conference, Boston, April 5–9, 1964* (Chicago: American Society of Planning Officials, 1964).

35. McHarg, Ian, *Design With Nature* (New York: John Wiley and Sons, 1992).

36. Edward Carpenter, "Brave New Town," *Industrial Design* **11,** No. 3 (March 1964):62–67.

37. Term used by William Conklin, architect, in "Reston: An Answer to Suburban Sprawl: Urban Living in the Country," *Architectural Record* **136,** (July 1964):119–134.

38. Robert Simon, "Planning a New Town—Reston, Virginia."

39. In Reston, and in most American planned communities, open space is held in common ownership by a home owners association. Fees assessed against each residence pay for their operation. Although rarely controlled, these lands and facilities are intended for use by residents only, not the general public. *Semipublic* refers to facilities that have restricted access, such as tennis and swimming clubs. Residents generally have to pay additional fees to use these facilities.

40. Reston Association, *Open Space Guidelines,* an unpublished document updated in the spring of 1993.

41. Designed by architects Whittlesey and Conklin. See "Reston: an Answer to Suburban Sprawl," *Architectural Record* 136 (July 1964) 119–134, and "Lake Anne Village Center: A Planned Community Nucleus," *Progressive Architecture* 47, No. 5 (May 1966):194–201.

42. Robert L. Miller, "Dropped in on Suburbia," *Landscape Architecture* 82, No. 3, (March 1992), 54–57.

43. James Rouse, "How to Build a Whole City from Scratch."

44. Morton Hoppenfeld, "A Sketch of the Planning-Building Process for Columbia, Maryland," *American Institute of Planners Journal* 33, No. 6 (November 1967):398–409.

45. All of these facilities are under the management of the Columbia Association, which oversees all public grounds, runs the cultural and recreational programs, and maintains design control over the community.

46. Richard Oliver Brooks, *New Towns and Communal Values: A Case Study of Columbia, Maryland* (New York: Praeger Publishers, 1974), pp. 8–16; Richard Oliver Brooks "Interpretation: Social Planning in Columbia," *American Institute of Planners Journal* 37, No. 11 (November 1971), p. 373–379; and Gurney Breckenfeld, *Columbia and the New Cities* (New York: Ives Washburn, Inc., 1971), p. 291–301.

47. Raymond Burby and Shirley F. Weiss, *New Communities U.S.A.* (Lexington MA: Lexington Books, 1976), p. 381.

48. Brooks, *New Towns and Communal Values,* pp. 197–199.

6
THEMES
Technoburbs and Ecoburbs

"Entice 'em with Advertising" exhorted the *Professional Builder* in March 1974. "We must sell lifestyle and emotion to be successful," the authors went on to say, encouraging developers to "sell people *before* they saw the property" [author's emphasis]. In an era of theme parks, communities also adopted themes, whereby projects were given personalities conceived by marketing strategists. As the recession set in that year, developers recognized that to survive they had to become more competitive. In stepped the advertising industry, working hand in hand with planners and realtors. This is not to say that sound principles of community planning were not adhered to, only that those features understood as particularly marketable by the real estate industry, such as distinctive, safe, emotionally appealing characteristics, would be especially important. Planned communities, ranging from a hundred acres to thousands of acres, were becoming commonplace throughout the nation, and most had professionally designed open space systems that connected extensive numbers of recreation facilities. Their popularity coincided with a recession and with developers' needs to realign their priorities and listen to marketing strategists.

Developers used a cohesive theme to create a distinctive and memorable "package" of buildings, landscaping, graphics, signage, and advertising, which together established the community's image.[1] Such attention to everything from lettering on signs to the look of the landscape was in itself a selling point, an indication that the developers had thought of everything. At Woodbridge in Irvine, California, the SWA Group designed just such a package for the Irvine Company. The overall landscape image was one of a picturesque suburb in the Olmstedian style. A pastoral scene of naturalistic lakes edged by grassy slopes and trees was showcased from carefully planned viewing spots along the shoreline. Despite the plain, ranch-style houses that lurked beyond, gently curving boulevards bordered by estate-quality duplexes gave an impression of a venerable community, a Riverside, Illinois, or the nearby Palos Verdes. The graphics and signage used natural wood and simple, bold symbols, giving the project a contemporary lift. The Irvine Company continues to pursue this themed approach to its projects, and its most recent extravaganza illustrates the point well. Newport Coast, a luxury community located immediately south of Newport Beach, harkens back to an idea that has been used in California real estate for a century. "Homes, estates and villas will color the hillsides in the spirit and tone found at the *Mediterranean Sea*," states the oversized glossy brochure.[2] The sales office for this project is a "gallery," its walls lined with large oil paintings by local artist Ron McKee. Commissioned by the Irvine Company, the paintings depict families happily playing at the beach, on the golf course, or walking

Woodbridge, Irvine, California.
©Tom Lamb/The SWA Group, Laguna Beach,
California.

the canyon trails. Housing prices begin with $300,000 "homes" and progress to $1 million, one-acre "estate" lots in the exclusive seaside Pelican Point neighborhood. Classically styled accoutrements such as gate houses, walls, lighting, and signage provide an aristocratic quality while the semi-arid coastal landscape stands in for the Mediterranean shore.

There were patterns to these themes, or so discovered Clare Cooper Marcus and several colleagues as they studied model homes in the Bay Area from 1981 to 1986.[3] Although their intent was to uncover incongruities between the written advertising and the implied messages of model homes, they discovered several recurring promotional themes. Not surprisingly, most predominant was the marketing of nature through names, slogans, imagery, and landscaping. Since the suburban genesis, proximity to nature in pastoral, sylvan, or rural surroundings has been a compelling desire. Builders and developers, shrewdly appealing to this romanticized ideal, have consistently used natural themes for naming their projects and the streets within them. For example, residents of Woodbridge will live on Firwood, Beachwood, Ashwood, or Wildwood Streets. By the mid-1970s it was commonplace to name a development after a nearby landscape feature, such as "Meadows," "Hills," "Woods," and "Creeks," and the favorite namesakes for streets were local trees: "Birch Bay," "Cottonwood Drive," or "Cherry Lane."

Real estate marketers sold an idea of living close to nature, but often the natural landscapes did not exist.[4] The "nature" that most commonly existed

Painting of Los Trancos Canyon, Newport Coast, Irvine, California.
By Ron McKee.
Source: The Irvine Company.

was professionally designed landscaping installed around the model home, often supporting the style of the house, such as formal gardens around "Tudor" homes or desert gardens around mission-style ranchettes. The other "nature" they presented was the coveted view through the picture window—nature pictorialized. Any scene would do, whether a valley landscape, an ocean or lake, or a city skyline. Nature was loosely interpreted. At Woodbridge, landscape architects created a new nature, one that needed aggressive maintenance. In other places, there was a distant view. In both cases, nature was scenery, "out there," a setting for home and neighborhood.

The out-of-doors did not mean scenery alone. Developers promoted leisure activities beyond the home and lot.[5] Yard work, gardening, and other activities related to the home, acclaimed as virtues of suburbia earlier in the century,[6] were not mentioned either in the literature or by salespersons. Perhaps, like housework and chores, yard work was losing its associations with family life. All too frequently landscape tasks were hired out, while families filled their time with organized sports, lessons, or bike excursions. Direct contact with nature was also overlooked. Instead, promotional materials provided extensive lists of nearby activity centers such as swimming pools, tennis courts, golf courses, and fitness clubs. These facilities were accessible only by car, and when researchers searched for walking or bike paths, they rarely found them.

As community development became a corporate enterprise in the 1970s, less emphasis was placed on social innovation or civic life. "Market-based community planning is limited by nature because it focuses nearly exclusively on those regional needs and trends that may affect the value of the master-planned community's products. Therefore, the amount and quality of open space, employment and commercial facilities, and balanced housing are considered only insofar as they improve the development's market potential."[7] Even at Irvine, considered by many to be a new town, the developers admit to having "exported" the more difficult social amenities such as cemeteries, prisons, hospitals, and congregate care facilities. Retail services common to strip commercial areas, such as automobile service shops, second-hand stores, roadside eateries, and bars, were also exported. By 1980 the industry had developed sophisticated models for identifying market sectors and meeting their expectations.[8] With evocative names, songs, imagery, and extravagantly decorated and landscaped model homes, developers sold a lifestyle engendered by the setting they created.

MASTER-PLANNED COMMUNITIES

The largest and most sophisticated of the themed developments were master-planned communities (MPCs). MPCs had their roots in the large planned communities of the 1920s and the new towns of the 1960s. The term was coined by planners in the mid-1970s to describe planned communities that were significantly larger than planned unit developments (PUDs), yet less comprehensive than new towns, and were planned in the whole before construction.[9] Whereas new towns were planned as small cities, with a full range of services for their residents, solid employment bases capable of supporting their populations,[10] and the intention of evolving self-government, MPCs were generally more limited in scope. Many were built within commuting distance of major metropolitan areas and had little or no office, warehousing, or industrial lands. Most addressed several very specific market niches, defined by income level, personal or family status, likes and dislikes with regard to activities, and general qualities of neighborhood and house,[11] whereas new towns were geared toward a broad spectrum of the population in an effort to create balanced demographics. MPCs varied dramatically in size. Communities as small as 400 acres and as large as 65,000 acres have been termed MPCs by both scholars and developers.[12] The final caveat concerning MPCs, which distinguishes them from other new communities, was that they were privately developed, often by very large corporations intent on making a profit. This required that they address upper-income populations and limit commercial enterprises within the community to those they knew their populations would support financially.[13]

MPC developers amassed and preplanned extensive tracts of land in exurban areas. They were welcomed by local governments, which saw multifaceted developments as contributors to the local economy. With the cooperation and modest financial support of governments, the developers installed the community infrastructure, the landscaping of public corridors and parks, and built commercial and business centers. Construction of MPCs was phased over 10 to 20 years, with the supply of houses matching market demand, and many of the largest communities are still in the process of development. As the population increased, so did the need to supply services. Service centers, often called "village centers," containing shops, bank, salons, cleaners, and now video stores, were commonly included. In the largest communities, major shopping and business centers, a "town center," would be needed. Woodbridge's "center" was a corridor between two boulevards, with clothing stores, restaurants, retail services, schools, parks, medical offices, and seniors' housing, all terminated by a strip mall.

Common open space was and remains a mandatory component of MPCs. Developers provide it both because buyers expect it as part of the package and because many local governments require 30% to 40% of the gross site area to be reserved as open space. The construction of golf courses is a popular strategy for meeting these requirements. In Moudon's study of sixteen Puget Sound MPCs,[14] five included at least one 18-hole golf course. In these five communities, whose open space ranged from 20% to 63% of the total site area, golf courses accounted for as much as 65% of the open space. In recent years, as the Department of Environmental Quality more actively enforced the Clean Water Act and as governments at all levels enforced the preservation of sensitive natural areas, developers have been quick to utilize such lands to meet open space requirements. In 1960s communities grass-and-trees parks were the most common form of open space. In MPCs, large passive greens were replaced by golf courses and natural areas, leaving a void at the traditional center, the recreational community park.

The terms *village* and *neighborhood* were commonplace in the MPC vocabulary, but applied with scant attention to social theory.[15] Village and neighborhood compositions were more likely to be based on the limits of local regulations, site characteristics, and the corporate marketing agenda. Villages typically remained the largest subunits of the community, and neighborhoods were their subdivisions. At Woodbridge, a *village* within Irvine, the site's quadrants were subdivided into 10 to 16 neighborhoods, each with roughly 600 people, the equivalent of Columbia's housing clus-

Aerial drawing of one quadrant of Woodbridge.
©The SWA Group, Laguna Beach, California.

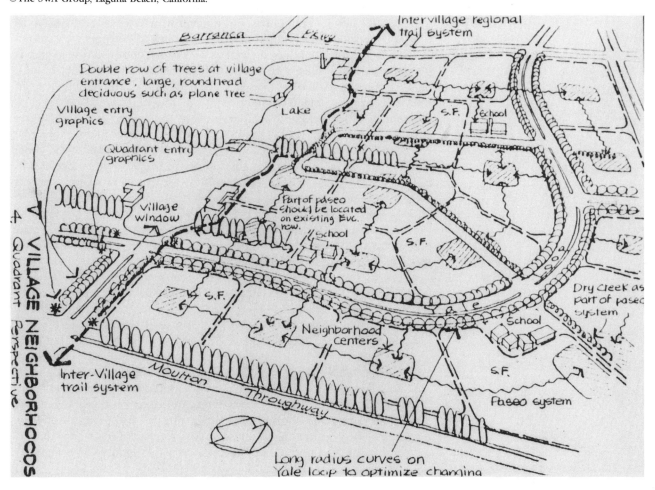

ters (see Chapter 5). The 42 "neighborhoods" had minimal provisions: a neighborhood park and pool; only one neighborhood in seven had an elementary school. Neighborhood size was determined by a geometric subdivision of the plan to offer people smaller associations than those provided by the entire village of 26,000 people. The neighborhoods intentionally coincided with builder parcels; thus each would have a unique identity as a result of different building and landscape designs.

The MPC was the profit-driven *product* of a corporate developer.[16] Typically located in suburban or exurban areas, these communities were often targeted toward specific segments of the population such as seniors, or a market group defined by a favorite activity such as golf or boating. They were designed as "total" environments—packaged living—landscapes "which were openly merchandised, landscapes in which the distinctions between public and private [were] blurred, and landscapes in which management [dominated] design."[17] Homes were not just shelter. Their purchase had proven to be a rewarding investment strategy. Houses bought in the early postwar years had increased steadily in value in most cities, and for the middle class the twofold gain of having good shelter while earning retirement income was extremely compelling. Protecting the monetary value of homes had been a concern of the housing industry since early in the century when codes and deed restrictions became commonplace. In the 1970s developers expanded their role on behalf of the home owner. They offered a secure shelter-cum-investment package whereby image, status, and security were purchased with a dwelling.[18]

How did developers control the long-term maintenance of neighborhood quality and housing value? Built into all sales agreements were design guidelines to direct builders, as well as covenants, codes, and restrictions (CC&Rs) to control the future actions of home owners. The CC&Rs, in turn, required the formation of home owners associations, which enforced design guidelines and maintained common lands. Their work assured that the environment would develop in conformity with the image designed by the corporation. Because MPCs often had up to 20-year build-out periods, the corporation was not only protecting property values on behalf of the home owners, but was also protecting the future marketability of its project. In fact, in many master-planned communities, control of the home owners association remained with the developer for many years, with the resident board members gradually replacing developer's appointees on a per capita basis. At The Woodlands, Texas, residents finally took over all but one board position of The Woodlands Community Association in 1992, 18 years after the first people had moved in.

Security came in several forms. Investment security was one attraction of MPCs, but the more significant form of security sold to home buyers was the perception of safety: freedom from the fear of known and unknown dangers, particularly urban violence and drug trafficking—a safe place to raise one's children. MPCs were bounded, and separate from adjacent communities, promoting the image of the country estate, with walls, gates, and key cards providing exclusivity, privacy, and physical safety. The degree of enclosure and security has become a symbol of the relative cost and status of a development. As these trends intensified in recent years, physical boundaries were strengthened, thus eliminating the possibility of connections between adjacent communities. In the early days of Irvine, arterial and collector roads with bermed and landscaped verges next to high masonry

Irvine collector street.
©Tom Lamb/The SWA Group, Laguna Beach,
California.

walls formed persuasive boundaries. In the 1980s walled or "gated" neighborhoods became commonplace, with higher-value developments receiving
greater attention to security. Single-family detached housing at Irvine's
Tustin Ranch was typically found within gated developments, whereas the
town house developments were walled without gates, and the apartment
communities had neither walls nor gates. Pelican Point has 24-hour guard
service based in elaborate gate houses. Complete security means complete
enclosure. With one, or at most two, entrances for both cars and pedestrians, the advertised amenities of acres of open space and bike trails are
walled out—still other destinations accessible only by car. At Tustin Ranch
open space is found primarily in the guise of the members-only golf course,
also walled and gated, and bike routes are lanes along collector streets
where people drive at 50 miles per hour. Even neighborhood pools are
gated, and for members only. Journalist David Guterson, writing about
Green Valley, Nevada, summed up the ultimate effect: "In the wake of our
contemporary trembling and discontent, [Green Valley's] pilgrims have
sought out a corporate castle where in exchange for false security they pay
in personal freedoms; where the corporation that does the job of walling
others out also walls the residents in."[19]

THE TECHNOBURB: IRVINE, CALIFORNIA

By 1980 the post-World War II suburbs had been superseded by a new urban form, which Robert Fishman called "technoburbs."[20] Technology has always been the suburban handmaiden, but as in many aspects of modern culture, technology's impact has lately been accelerated. Technoburbs were made possible by the proliferation of freeways (and the concurrent explosion of the automobile population) and the development of sophisticated communications networks that make it possible for business and industry to prosper in dispersed locations. These suburbs are no longer dependent on the central city for their existence—they are now semiautonomous. They are located within metropolitan regions, but well beyond central cities. As socioeconomic entities, they offer a full range of housing options accompanied by shopping malls, schools, parks, hospitals, businesses, and high-tech industrial parks.

Development patterns in technoburbs appear to be a jumble of housing, industry, commerce, and even agriculture.[21] Shopping malls are the focus of a nascent community life.[22] It is the automobile and limited access highways that determine the basic framework. Freeway interchanges are the most valued locations for shopping centers, hotels, office buildings, and warehouse-type retailers. Along freeway corridors are business "campuses," warehousing, and industrial "parks." Former country roads and highways, upgraded to arterial standards, lace the interstices, linking walled communities.

The Irvine Ranch, covering much of Orange County in California, was an intentional technoburb conceived long before most urban geographers recognized the pattern. From its inception, the ranch was planned as a dispersed, low-density exurban region. The earliest plans showed a network of "villages" interspersed with industrial, research, and business parks, shopping centers, and a university campus. No town center was planned, and none exists to this day.[23] Rather, networks of arterial roads, freeways, open space corridors, telephone and computer cables weave together the widely separated parts of this planned technoburb.[24]

The Irvine Ranch, managed by the privately owned Irvine Company, remained primarily agricultural through the 1950s. Los Angeles had reached its northwestern borders, and the company was receiving numerous offers from developers. Rather than sell, they decided to develop the land themselves in a planned, orderly manner, giving planning and design responsibility to the James Irvine Foundation, a nonprofit trust formed in 1937. In 1959 the company donated 1,000 acres to the University of California for its Irvine campus, while being well aware of plans for two major freeways connecting San Diego and Los Angeles, both of which would pass through the central valley portion of the site. The Irvine Ranch stretches from the foot of the Santa Ana mountains in the north through the flat central plain of 53,000 acres to the coastal San Joaquin Hills. Site of the earliest development, the central plain was originally grazing land before its conversion to more intensive uses, citrus orchards and row crops, in this century. The San Joaquin Hills and the Santa Ana foothills are in the semiarid coastal region, with grasses and chaparral on open sites and sycamore and live oak communities in seepages and drainages within the steep canyons. Newport Bay, an ecologically important but disturbed marine estuary, cuts between the coastal hills almost to the central plain.

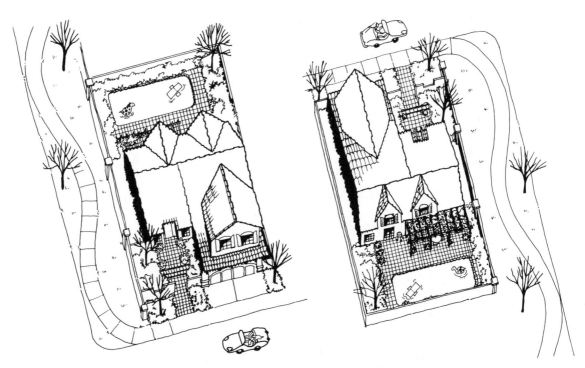

*Mediterranean styled house and yard,
Irvine, California.*
Kate Van Rooy.

William Periera developed the first land use concept in 1960, a new community composed of a loose fabric of villages. University Village, adjacent to the campus, and Woodbridge, on the north side of the Santa Ana Freeway, were the first of several villages initiated in the early 1970s in Irvine's central plain. Throughout the 1970s growth occurred around Woodbridge, in nearby hills and around existing communities: Santa Ana (the county seat), Tustin, and two resort communities, Newport Beach and Laguna Beach. By 1991 housing, business parks, and industrial areas had blanketed most of the flat, easily developable lands, and plans were under way to develop several hilltop communities. The population of Orange County had exceeded two million.[25]

The "outer city,"[26] as corporation planners called it, included multiple nuclei of business, industry, shopping, and services spread across the ranch. Two major industrial sites were sited adjacent to military bases located roughly where the San Diego Freeway crosses the western site boundary and where the Santa Ana and San Diego Freeways intersect at the eastern boundary. Between these industrial areas, extending from the base of the Santa Ana foothills to Newport Beach, were the residential villages, ranging in size from 600 to 2,000 acres. Each was to be unique, with themes or focal points derived from the setting to differentiate one village from the other: the views afforded by hilltop living, the pastoral quality of golf course settings, or the marine attractions of water-oriented settings. Each would be serviced by a school, shopping, and parks. Buffered boundaries of landscaped roadways, drainage corridors, canyons, golf courses, or water bodies separated the villages.

An early environmental analysis and land use study conducted by the SWA Group identified one of the most unique and successful planning ideas to be incorporated at Irvine. Accepting the policy of dispersed villages already adopted by the company, the SWA Group sought strategies for knit-

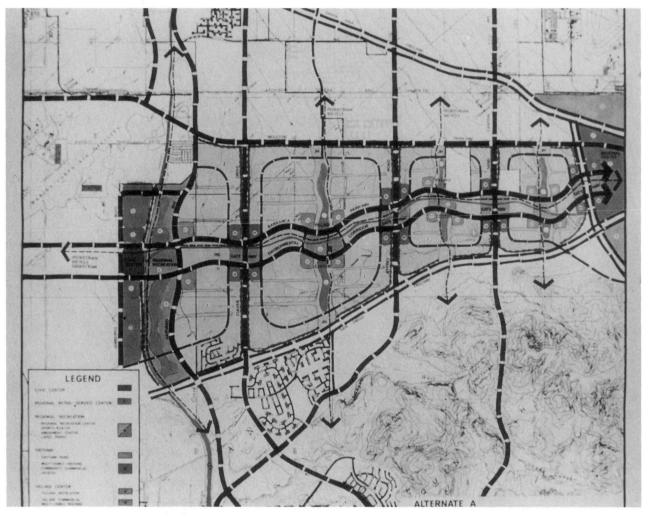

Proposed village linkage system for Irvine.
©The SWA Group, Laguna Beach, California.

ting the villages together, while simultaneously employing the connections for recreational purposes. SWA proposed using the two major drainageways that extended around Irvine's central plain as major open space and activity corridors. Pathways for bikes and walking would follow these drainages, providing green connections from one village to the next. The primary corridor ran east to west, aligning the channeled San Diego Creek, and was to be the location of "activity corridors." Village-scale services such as shopping, schools, offices, and medical facilities were placed within these linear spaces. Artificial lakes became minor north-south corridors that formed the recreational heart of each village. Woodbridge, the first village based on SWA's study, fully incorporated the activity corridor concept. Communities to the east and west also utilized activity corridors, but the north-south lakes and the corridor SWA proposed at the base of the Santa Ana foothills were never pursued.

Located on dead, flat land, formerly planted in row crops, Woodbridge was characterized by two simple landscape features, a windbreak of large

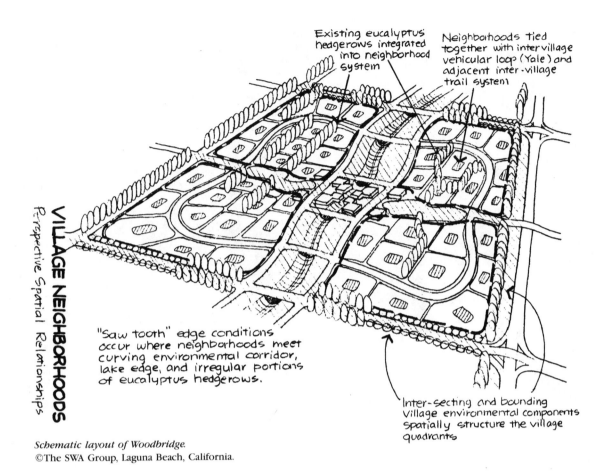

Existing eucalyptus hedgerows integrated into neighborhood system

Neighborhoods tied together with inter village vehicular loop (Yale) and adjacent inter-village trail system

VILLAGE NEIGHBORHOODS
Perspective Spatial Relationships

"Saw tooth" edge conditions occur where neighborhoods meet curving environmental corridor, lake edge, and irregular portions of eucalyptus hedgerows.

Inter-secting and bounding Village environmental components spatially structure the village quadrants

Schematic layout of Woodbridge.
©The SWA Group, Laguna Beach, California.

eucalyptus trees running through the site roughly east to west, paralleled by the San Diego Creek several hundred feet to the south. The community's landscape feature was to be the north-south axis of lakes, which crossed the activity corridor at the midpoint of the site. Here, SWA sited the village shopping center and the proposed community park. A grand boulevard was designed to loop around the site, linking each quadrant to the activity corridor. With its duplex and triplex manors overlooking sweeping lawns, Yale Loop was the signature of the community, distinctly reminiscent of Olmsted's Riverside (see Chapter 3). Innumerable small neighborhoods lay behind Yale Loop. Based on a simple grided organization, these small enclaves of roughly 250 dwellings created a complex fabric of varying housing types and densities. Each the product of a different builder, contemporary West Coast-styled town houses could be found next to split-level ranchers.

The landscape of Woodbridge remains the unifying fabric for a diversity of buildings. It includes a range of interconnected public, semiprivate, and private open spaces ranging from the central community park and lakes and the public pathway system to limited-membership pools, tennis courts, beaches, and, finally, private clubs and individual yards. Providing consistency throughout the community and changing little with the seasons, the entire context is one of lush lawns edged by curving borders of trimmed evergreen shrubbery. Much of the public open space around the lakes and along San Diego Creek is passive greenspace—lawns with trees, and paths running through it. Private yards are small and fenced. A unique feature of the earliest phases was the requirement that lakeside fences had to be transparent above a certain height. This assured views from yards to the

Yale Loop at Woodbridge.
©Tom Lamb/The SWA Group, Laguna Beach,
California.

lakes, but also widened the perceived open space around the lakes when viewed from the opposite bank. Two sandy beaches on the shores of North and South Lakes, borrowed pieces of the familiar California coast, have over the years become settings for *the* social sphere during the summer months. Groups representing all walks of community life congregate daily at the beaches, a scene recalling the social role played by Radburn's pools (see Chapter 3). Food, toys, and beach furniture accompany them for the day's outing. At the center of each neighborhood are the park, a small lawn with minor play facilities, and the neighborhood pool, gated and for the exclusive use of neighborhood residents. These pools are also busy on summer days; being closer to home they provide an opportunity for a quick swim.[27] Like Radburn, Woodbridge has a separated pedestrian circulation system. "Paseos" form a fine grid of narrow paths throughout the site, linking one neighborhood park to others and the elementary schools to the neighborhoods they serve. They also tie into the major pathways along the lakes and the activity corridor. Using these paths, people can walk or bike from home to schools, shops, doctors' offices, parks, or even to the adjacent village.

Woodbridge's designers placed great emphasis on the creation of Woodbridge's boundary and set a strong precedent for later Irvine villages.[28] They believed that Woodbridge's identity as a discrete community would be enhanced if it had a strong boundary. The community was encircled by arterial roads on three sides and the Santa Ana Freeway along the south. The boundary they designed, called a "green wall," needed to visually mark the village's edges while also reducing the noise from high-speed arterial roads and a freeway. The solution was a high, heavily planted earth berm with a meandering path along the outside. Except for vehicular entry points on

Recreation at Woodbridge.
C. Girling.

A boundary of Woodbridge.
©The SWA Group, Laguna Beach, California.

three sides, Woodbridge was not only bounded and marked, but physically enclosed. The critical break in the enclosure was the activity corridor that penetrated the green wall at the east and west, linking Woodbridge to its adjacent neighbors. The Irvine Company has since determined that people seek even greater "security," and in most cases have eliminated intravillage connections, thereby walling residents in as well as walling strangers out.

AN IRVINE TOUR: JUNE 1991

The day I went out to explore Irvine Ranch, I had one additional objective—I needed an oil change on the car. I looked at the land use map I had received from The Company and saw along my route innumerable thin red strips, commercial zones in my experience. My first stop was Woodbridge, the early pace-setting planned community originally conceived by SWA for The Irvine Company. It was as I had imagined, almost. Based on one article in Moudon's Master-Planned Communities, *I immediately understood the basic plan as I drove into the development. The elegant loop roads took me through the neighborhoods, and the two main east-west roads led to all institutions, service centers, and the shops at the village center. I was most impressed by the pedestrian circulation system. I could wander through the neighborhoods, following narrow pathways from one to the next, passing school yards and neighborhood pools. My first surprise was that the pools were semiprivate, fenced, and signed "for neighborhood residents only." Troops of bicyclists frequently passed me on the larger paths. Later I found out that these were often people from adjoining villages who frequented Woodbridge for its pleasant and extensive bike paths. I easily found the distinctive wood bridge, namesake of the community, and one of the "beaches" conceived to be activity foci. From outside the locked gate I watched hundreds of members picnicking, sunning, swimming, and playing. Back on the pathway, I headed for the village center, a more public eating and shopping hub that bridged the two lakes. From a high vantage point on a beautiful café terrace, I could survey the length of the north lake. It was picture perfect, a serene lake surrounded by an apron of manicured greenery and the occasional waterside condominium development. Walking back to the car, through a different set of neighborhoods, it suddenly occurred to me: my whole experience of Woodbridge was of a carefully designed and professionally maintained landscape. Not a blade of grass was out of place, not an ill-suited plant found in a garden; in fact, I wasn't sure I had seen a real garden—the kind that average people plant and tend.*

I was sure that the commercial strip I had seen along Culver Drive, just west of Woodbridge, would yield the Pit-Stop I was after, but despite finding one well-designed and inconspicuous gas station that provided no service, I was disappointed—this was a strip-mall of specialty shops and one supermarket. I moved on to the Irvine Visitor Center at Tustin. After gathering all the promotional literature they had and talking to the friendly senior citizen working at the center, I headed off to see Tustin Ranch, a new golf course community, and several other new developments around Tustin. What I found was disquieting. Whereas Woodbridge was a clustering of somewhat distinct neighborhoods, interconnected by "paseos," and a public open space system around the lakes, Tustin was a series of small walled, and often gated, neighborhoods, more like PUDs. Within each was the neighborhood green, a lawn around a fenced pool— "private, for members only." It was difficult to find evidence of the open space network that I had seen on Irvine master plans, except for the golf course. It also was private, and I felt like a trespasser when I stopped along the entry drive to take photographs. I was becoming irritated by the unending well-maintained landscapes—I found no blade of grass untended, no variety nor impetuous discontinuity. Did everyone conform? Were there no landscape rebels?

Unable to go on, if only because I was barred by the gates of these neighborhoods, I decided to pursue my other task in earnest. Surely around the Tustin Auto Center and the adjacent mall, the only commercial area for miles around, I would find my Pit-Stop. Alas, the auto center was a car-mall with the newest models displayed in glass houses around a neat loop road, and the shopping mall included only tasteful shops and a couple of carefully designed fast-food restaurants. I followed the 15-mile commercial-industrial edge of Irvine back to the Pacific Highway at Newport Beach to no avail. After scouring Newport Beach for the inevitable, yet nonexistent, highway strip of all western coastal towns, I headed back to Laguna Beach, a resort town out of the control of the Irvine Company, where the attendant at a familiar looking Shell station agreed to change my oil the next morning. After having driven more than 50 miles around the Irvine Ranch, I came away convinced that anything messy, dirty, or tasteless was not allowed, that every shingle and shutter, every shrub and succulent was professionally designed, installed, and maintained. The Irvine Company's corporate image predominated, and thus it has remained for more than 15 years.[29]

Communities can be overplanned and overdesigned, the quality a bit too picture perfect, the place too often treated like a product. Extreme landscapes emphasize inherent contradictions, such as that in the Nevada Desert, where the American Nevada Corporation's Green Valley is a "mirage," one that consumes enormous quantities of scarce water and energy to support a pleasant, upscale existence for more than 32,000 middle-class Nevadans.[30] Irvine today presents an extreme example of where a repeated pattern of master-planned communities can take us: walled paradise next to walled paradise, all with the sterility of golf course greens, connected by equally monotonous roads: no litter allowed, either natural or human, no spontaneity, no nature—an engineered life.

THE ECOBURBS: VILLAGE HOMES, CALIFORNIA, AND THE WOODLANDS, TEXAS

No period of time is monolithic in character. All have many currents running through them. Although the technoburb is currently dominant, there are recessive alternative trends, such as the communities we call "ecoburbs." These attempt, through environment-sensitive planning and design to reduce the impacts of development on natural resources. The ultimate objective of such communities is to encourage residents to pursue an environmentally sensitive, "sustainable" lifestyle. From individual action to local, regional, and national initiatives, sustainable development proponents believe that we could drastically reduce the environmental impacts of urbanization through policy, planning, and design decisions that influence the way we all live.[31] Planning and design principles that have generally been accepted as essential to sustainable development include the planning of land uses and transportation systems to encourage walking, bicycling, and mass transportation; location of land uses on the most tolerant sites; on-site recycling and reuse of water and organic materials; on-site water purification by natural means (scale may vary); protection and regeneration of natural topsoils; elimination of many or all chemical pesticides, insecticides, and fertilizers; and on-site alternative energy production used in concert with energy conservation (i.e., the use of passive solar heating and natural cooling).[32]

Most master-planned communities developed since 1970 have used some form of environmental planning, whereby lands are studied through a rational process to determine both sensitivities and tolerances for differing types of development. Popularized by Ian McHarg's book *Design with Nature,*[33] by the early 1970s the environmental planning process was incorporated into regional planning and landscape architecture education throughout the country. What, then, allows only some of these master-planned communities to be defined as "ecoburbs"? These are suburban developments which not only adhered to the ecological planning process, but have adopted sustainable development principles. Residents of such communities accept a more ecologically sensitive lifestyle—they live by principles originally conceived by project planners. Like many energy systems, some of the resident actions are passive, whereas others require active participation. Those living within a forest learn to respect forest ecology by retaining forest litter on the ground and learning to live with raccoons, deer, and other creatures. Those living in solar houses operate blinds and windows daily to allow the house to respond to weather conditions. Others commit themselves to participation in community agriculture.

These authors found only one successful, thriving ecoburb, Village Homes, a small but significant PUD in Davis, California, built in 1975.[34] Others, including The Woodlands, Texas, exhibited strong ecological principles during planning, but have veered away from the ideology in recent years. Throughout the late 1970s and early 1980s, many efforts were made to establish such developments. In *Sustainable Communities,* Sim Van der Ryn and Peter Calthorpe[35] identified several urban and exurban projects that exhibited sustainable principles; however, few succeeded in addressing the balance between resource consumption and production that they advocated. In the early flowering of the environmental movement, numerous demonstration projects were instituted throughout the nation. Projects such as The Integral Urban House in San Francisco demonstrated self-sufficient systems and practices to help make families less dependent on outside resources. Marin Solar Village, designed by Van der Ryn, Calthorpe, and their students at the University of California, Berkeley, was intended to be a sustainable community that exhibited permanence and balance between people and jobs, local production and consumption, and natural and human communities. Permanence was defined as the ability of the community to be self-sustaining, physically and culturally, the result of balancing resource input with output and cooperating on community enterprises. For example, waste water from homes and industry was to be reused for agriculture, then cleaned on-site before spilling into the adjacent bay. Although efforts were made to secure funding for the project, it was never built. Cerro Gordo near Cottage Grove, Oregon, has suffered a similar fate. Its proponents are still promising that it will be the first sustainable community in the nation; however, almost 20 years after its initiation only a handful of houses have been constructed on the 1,160-acre site.[36]

Village Homes

The realized project of Village Homes, constructed five years before Marin Solar Village was planned, exhibited many of Van der Ryn and Calthorpe's sustainable development principles. A fraction of the size of the later project, it included 217 homes on 70 acres. Designer-builder Mike Corbett had aspirations to build a community that not only conserved and cleaned water, but also used both passive and active solar energy, produced more food than its residents could consume, and included the residents in managing their community's resources. In addition to having sound environmental ideals, Corbett found a site well suited to his small environment-sensitive PUD. On flat terrain, in an amenable climate and in close proximity to downtown Davis and the University of California at Davis, it afforded its residents opportunities to use bicycles extensively—and many do.

Village Homes, as a concept, addressed a profound issue related to sustainable development—a belief in the principle of the commons—whereby the commons was understood to be the world's natural resources, finite in supply, and therefore, by necessity, carefully managed by all.[37] At Village Homes, commons was not only an ideology, but a physical attribute. A unique and very successful innovation regarding land ownership was devised. In addition to the two popular forms associated with PUDs, private property and association-owned common lands, Village Homes has a

Passive solar house and yard, Village Homes.
Kate Van Rooy.

155

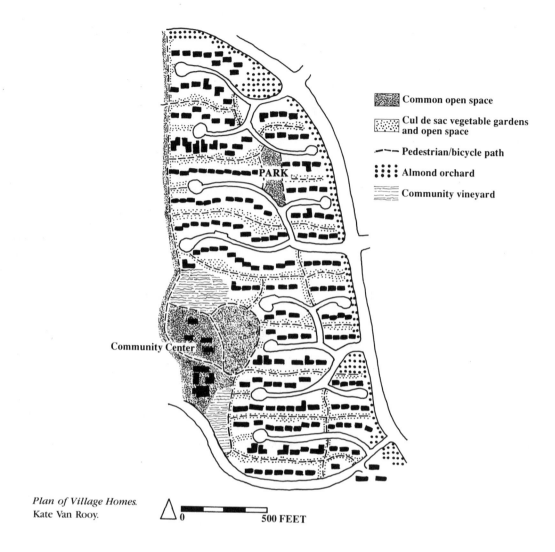

Common open space

Cul de sac vegetable gardens and open space

Pedestrian/bicycle path

Almond orchard

Community vineyard

PARK

Community Center

Plan of Village Homes.
Kate Van Rooy.

0   500 FEET

Section through the commons at Village Homes.
Kate Van Rooy.

third category, which is common land owned by smaller groups of eight families. The houses are sited on 4,000-square-foot lots with an area to the rear (if front is the carport side) which is jointly owned by the smaller groups. Like Radburn, both front and rear yards became living spaces (see Chapter 3). The front yard, located between the street-side carport and the house, was a small fenced courtyard—the most private yard. The backyard was a narrow space between the house and the commons, often left without fences. Design and landscaping of these common areas were left to the owner groups, resulting in each having a significantly different character.

Common area, Village Homes.
C. Girling.

Common area with drainageway, Village Homes.
C. Girling.

Some are intensive vegetable gardens, some have evolved into elaborate perennial gardens, and still others have large play areas. The car was kept in its place on narrow, richly planted residential culs-de-sac, while gardens, paths, and streams predominated. A surface drainage system sufficient to accommodate local rainfall meandered through common spaces, seasonally swelling in low-lying areas.

Corbett and his partner, Judy Corbett, and several close associates created a place in which all residents collaborated on community management. Their community focused on agriculture as a belief, an activity, a resource, and a product. Roughly 20% of their 70-acre site was devoted directly to row crops, vineyards, and orchards. (A proportion similar to Broadacre City.) In addition, many of their street trees were fruit trees, and many households collaborated on personal vegetable plots close to their homes. Residents of Village Homes proclaim it to be a very successful model. Most focus their energies and attention on working with their immediate neighbors in planting, maintaining, enjoying, and harvesting their mini-commons, and their home owners association pays full-time gardeners to care for the acres of common agriculture and green space. Theirs is literally life in a garden, in a way reminiscent of the cottage gardens of England, Israeli kibbutzim, and Radburn.

The Woodlands

The Woodlands, a master-planned community north of Houston, Texas, was called "the first city plan produced by ecological planning."[38] Ian McHarg, author of its "Ecological Plan,"[39] successfully proposed to owner George Mitchell that adherence to his ecological planning methodology would allow the development of a unique, environment-sensitive community without compromising the corporation's profits. The cornerstone of McHarg's concept was the implementation of a natural or surface drainage system, necessitating the extensive preservation of riparian areas and all but eliminating the use of engineered drainage systems. Although the term *ecological* was associated with the project, its orientation was clearly toward the preservation and conservation of nature. Its goal was not to be sustainable by altering or impacting resident life styles. The Woodlands might have become a near-ecoburb, but for the corporation's recent turn away from McHarg's principles.

George Mitchell began plans for a new community in his native Houston-Galveston area in 1964 with the purchase of the Grogan-Cochran Lumber Company along the new I-45 corridor, 27 miles north of Houston. Mitchell ultimately acquired 25,000 acres. Interested in qualifying for funding under the 1968 New Communities Act,[40] Mitchell began to research new towns, especially Rouse's Columbia, Maryland. After rejection of his first submission to the Department of Housing and Urban Development (HUD),[41] Mitchell realized that he would need a highly qualified consultant group to obtain federal funding for the project.[42] In 1971 he succeeded on his second try with a team including architect and planner William Pereira of Los Angeles, environmental planners Wallace McHarg Roberts and Todd (WMRT) of Philadelphia, engineering consultants Richard P. Browne Associates of Columbia, Maryland, and marketing consultants Gladstone Associates of Washington, D.C.[43] Mitchell had sought out McHarg's firm with the conviction that preservation of the forest on his site was critical, and it was

The Woodlands, Texas.
C. Girling.

McHarg's environmental planning methodology which led the team to create a unique new community.

While the other consultants began their preliminary proposals, WMRT conducted an extensive ecological analysis of the site. The process included an inventory of the site's natural systems with the assistance of local environmental experts, followed by the use of computer models to speculate on the impacts of the proposed land uses.[44] In the inventory summary, WMRT identified the surface hydrology as the most sensitive natural system on the site: "In the Woodlands then, water became the integrating process which explained the nature of the site. Through the flow of water over the ground, the movement of water in the ground, and the effects of water on soil and vegetation, one can understand the interactions of nature and how to complement them."[45] McHarg's idea was to mimic the natural hydrologic cycle found on the site with a modified natural drainage system.

The carrying capacity of the site's numerous landscape units were evaluated to determine areas most suitable for development. Areas within the 100-year floodplain were protected along with soils of high permeability, because they would play a crucial role in recharge. Areas with density and diversity of vegetation and/or high habitat value were also preserved. Each proposed land use was classified according to the amount of site clearance it required and the impact it would have on natural systems. Impact was then compared with the tolerances established for each landscape unit, based on combined soil and vegetation factors. The mapping process revealed developable areas, which were then assigned the most suitable type of development and an allowable percentage of clearing.[46]

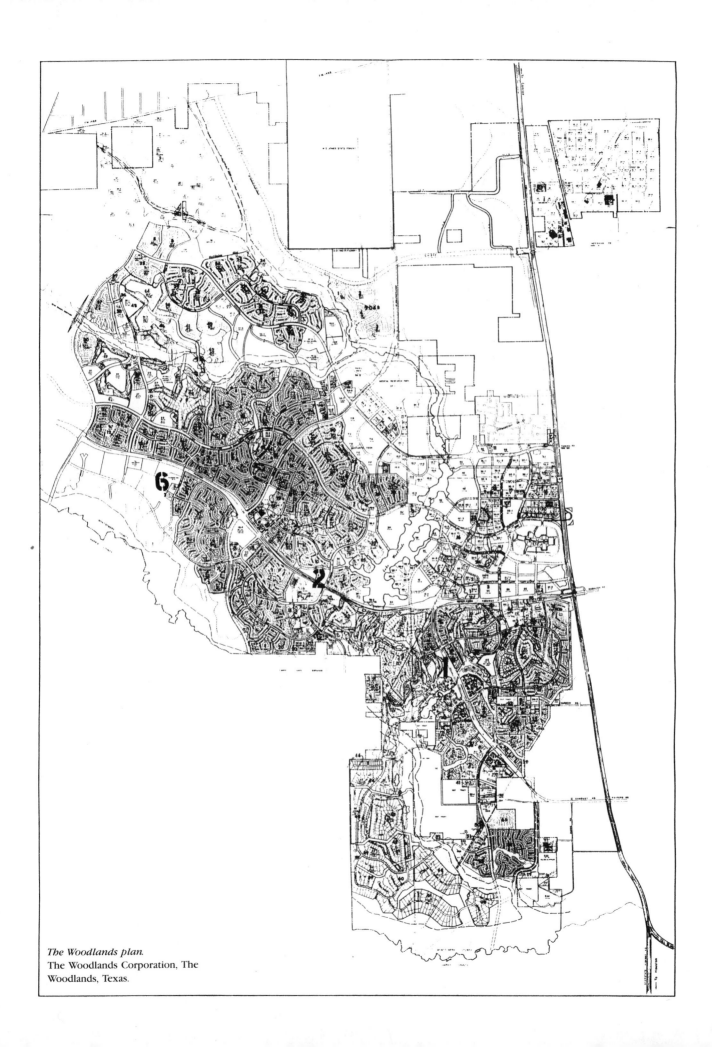

The Woodlands plan.
The Woodlands Corporation, The
Woodlands, Texas.

McHarg called this methodology "physiographic determinism"—based on the proposition that development should respond to the intrinsic opportunities and constraints that the landscape presents. Although the "Design Synthesis" maps produced by WMRT followed the natural imperatives of soils and vegetation, William Pereira's initial work, extended by the work of in-house planners, proposed an orderly pattern of circulation and land use derived conceptually from Columbia. WMRT incorporated these patterns into its proposed plans. The result was an organizational model based loosely on Columbia's villages, and a similar road system of curving loops and culs-de-sac, yet with the detailed layout derived from the site's characteristics and tolerances.

The Woodlands town center was a mall (under construction in 1993), surrounded by hotels, business parks, and cultural and recreational facilities, and located near Interstate 45 along the community's eastern boundary. The rest of the site was divided into seven villages of roughly 2,000 acres each and university, business, industry, and research campuses. Roughly 25% of the community's 25,000 acres was retained in open space, much of that in the Panther Creek and Spring Creek floodplains and four golf courses. The circulation system was a net of arterial roads running roughly east-west and north-south, about two miles apart. Closed loops extended from the arterial

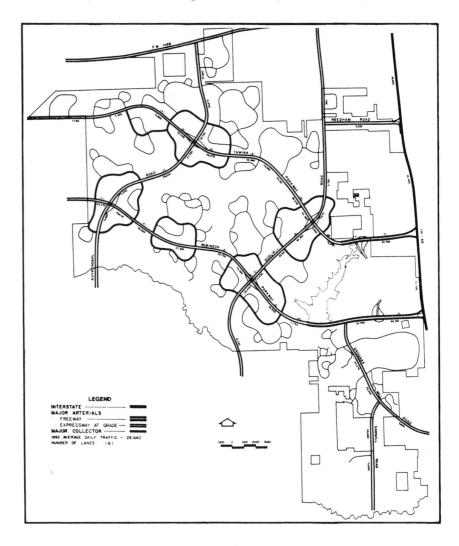

Circulation diagram, The Woodlands. Wallace McHarg Roberts and Todd, *The Ecological Plan,* The Woodlands Corporation, 1974, unpublished.

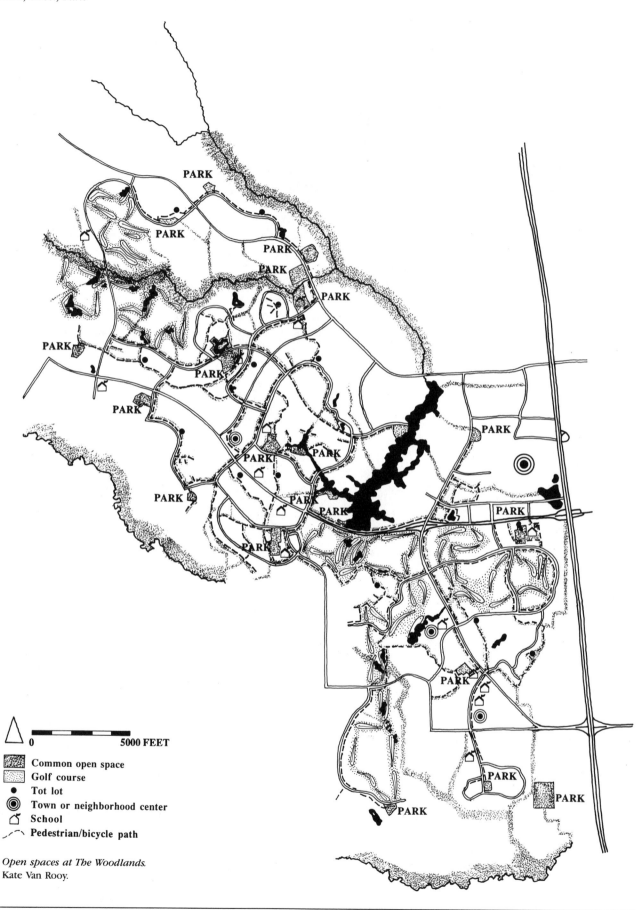

△
0 ▬▬▬▬▬ 5000 FEET

▨ **Common open space**
▦ **Golf course**
● **Tot lot**
◎ **Town or neighborhood center**
⌂ **School**
⌐-⌐ **Pedestrian/bicycle path**

Open spaces at The Woodlands.
Kate Van Rooy.

roads through each village and back out again. Main arterials followed the site's ridges, and smaller roads fed the developable sites between drainage channels, in the manner of intertwined fingers. Houses typically faced minor loops and culs-de-sac. Responsive to the land, the pattern was simple and memorable—image, identity, and orientation were clear.

The Woodlands Corporation has refrained from drawing a master land use plan. Their policy has been to work within the guiding framework of the ecological plan, while retaining land use flexibility. Grogan's Mill Village, the first area to be constructed, provides the best example of the early planning intentions. Most of the parks and natural open spaces at Grogan's Mill were located behind houses, deep within housing areas. Most notably, a woodland path along a north-south open space corridor connects a church, elementary school, and neighborhood park at one end, with the athletic center and village shopping center at the other. This provides a direct walking route, whereas vehicular connections are more circuitous. Grogan's Mill Village Center proved to be economically unsuccessful, continually struggling to fill retail spaces. Later villages were modified in size and location with fewer, but larger, village centers installed alongside arterial roads. Changes were made to parks and open space design as well. The corporation discovered that parks attract buyers to a neighborhood. They are now, professionally designed and located on prominent sites adjacent to roads. Waller ponds, a form of seasonal ponds found throughout the site, were often smaller than the one-acre minimum size for legal wetlands. These are now being dug deeper to create year-round "amenity areas,"[47] scenic locations for higher-priced housing.

The residential landscape of Grogan's Mill met George Mitchell's aspirations for a forested character. Although streetscapes were fairly open from house to house, significant patches of vegetation were periodically preserved, and culverted ditches along the roads contributed to the rough, natural qualities. Behind the houses was a dense backdrop of forest. This was achieved both by limiting the amount of clearing that builders could do on their sites and preserving corridors of common open space beyond the shallow rear yards. Drainage swales, paths, and tot lots were located within

Grogan's Mill Village, The Woodlands.
C. Girling.

these forested commons. Over the years, residents of Grogan's Mill have enhanced the forested backyard spaces through a hands-off approach. Most have limited their landscaping to small decks under the trees, and few have planted grass or gardens.

To emphasize the forested image, road corridors throughout the site were designated as greenbelts. Primary walking and bike paths were then located within the roadway greenbelts, a logical and efficient approach that the designers hoped would encourage bicycle usage.[48] Unfortunately, the result proved less than satisfactory from the perspective of both recreation and transportation. The pathways are extensive but, by following roadways, do not always provide direct, grade-separated linkages from homes to schools or shopping centers. Paralleling drivers, bikers and pedestrians must go from cul-de-sac to collector to arterial and back, crossing several high-speed roads along the way, to reach most destinations. The circuitous routes and risks to safety discourage all but the most determined bikers and pedestrians. The paths are used for low-speed recreational riding, but serious bikers have taken to the streets. The paths were intended to "fit" the natural surroundings, winding in and around trees, but the meandering trails do not make good alternative transportation routes. In fact, they become dangerous at modest bicycle speeds. As for being places to go for a Sunday stroll, they are less than ideal, necessitating walkers to follow roadways, with traffic moving past at 50 miles an hour.

Outdoor activity at The Woodlands centered on private or semiprivate recreation facilities. A private club, The Woodlands Athletic Center, pro-

Bear Branch of Panther Creek, The Woodlands.
C. Girling.

vides aquatics, fitness programs, tennis, and gymnastics; the YMCA provides a similar range of programs plus ball sports; The Woodlands Country Club, also private, has four golf courses, tennis, aquatics, fitness programs, and an elegant club house. The home owners' association, The Woodlands Community Association (WCA) manages all the parks and open space facilities in the community, with most geared toward active recreation. Park activities typically include outdoor pools (three), tennis courts, basketball courts, ball fields, picnic and play facilities. Tot lots and miniparks are located within housing enclaves and are sometimes associated with ponds and drainages; however, they are not extensive. Most recently, the WCA has been involved in constructing two new soccer and ball fields and organizing sports programs on behalf of the community. It is important to note that the WCA, funded from home owners fees, provides these services primarily for its members—the residents of The Woodlands. Parks and open space in this project, as in most MPCs, are fundamentally different from those that exists in cities—WCA retains the right to restrict nonresident use.

WMRT recommended that high-intensity recreation areas should complement, but not infringe upon, the natural open spaces,[49] so the road corridors, parks, and golf courses were a distinct set of outdoor spaces. They were not physically connected to the natural areas, such as streamways, wetlands, and major forested areas, which were to be protected from both development and human access for their habitat value. Significant wildlife corridors resulted, particularly along the Spring Creek, Panther Creek, and Bear Branch floodplains. Although important from the standpoint of wildlife

Bear Branch of Panther Creek, flooded.
C. Girling.

protection, the opportunity they provide for environmental education has been overlooked. The Woodlands has no nature center, nor any trails to these natural areas. Some of the undeveloped areas of the site, which also remain in their natural state, have been marked with "no trespassing" signs. Human access and environmental education has been denied for 20 years.

In 1985 the corporation abandoned its commitment to McHarg's original recommendations. While the "Ecological Plan" is still referenced in their guidelines, it has eliminated the use of natural drainage and is now using underground drainage systems that carry storm water into wide, straight-sided ditches. The corporation is less stringent in its interpretation of clearance restrictions, allowing all but trees over six inches in caliper[50] to be removed. Excepting the residents of Grogan's Mill, most of the population of The Woodlands experiences a suburban landscape that is very similar to the themed landscapes of other master-planned communities. One local landscape architect commented that nearby Kingwood appears to have more natural areas than the newer sectors of The Woodlands.[51] In areas developed in the 1980s and 1990s, large, traditionally styled homes front on picturesque curving streets. Front yards are characterized by trimmed lawns, which encircle a mandatory 40% natural area. This area is commonly interpreted to be a few native trees left standing in a bark chip bed. Often annuals have been added to the bed for seasonal color. Perhaps as the vice-president of Community Planning said,[52] the Houston area was not ready for The Woodlands, and what that market needed was a more conventional solution. It is ironic that at a time when professions dealing with land

Residential street in Cochran's Crossing, The Woodlands.
C. Girling.

planning and development are looking to prototypes like The Woodlands for well-designed, functioning surface drainage systems, especially those integrated with other open space, The Woodlands has taken an about-face in favor of an engineered system.

Two decades of master-planned community development has resulted in some very positive open space planning practices. Because of nationally mandated environmental impact analyses, most new community developers now recognize and set aside natural areas, especially wetlands. Linear systems, such as drainage corridors, are also commonly preserved and incorporated into the open space system. While preserving natural areas for many wildlife species, these areas also provide residents with opportunities to experience raw nature close to home. In many cases, trails within natural areas also provide recreational routes for walkers and bikers; however, few offer viable alternative transportation routes. In extremely large developments like Irvine Ranch and The Woodlands, off-street connections were created to connect one village to the next. Although the system never achieved its original goals, at Irvine it is possible to bike on off-street paths from Woodbridge to Newport Beach, six miles away. The Woodlands advertises 61 miles of off-street trails, and by aligning trails with the major arterials, it is possible to bike or hike from the far reaches of Cochran's Crossing to Grogan's Mill, also six miles away. However, at both places automobiles still dominate; walking and biking are addressed primarily as recreation. Golf courses provide a large percentage of the open space in MPCs, a situation that could be seen as inequitable and environmentally insensitive. The inequity derives from the fact that not all residents play golf. Those who do not are commonly denied access. On the other hand, people choose which community they will purchase a home in, and more golfers than average will live in MPCs with golf courses. Golf course designers are beginning to respond to the call for environment-sensitive designs and maintenance programs, and some are now incorporating natural areas into the course.[53]

Some MPC developers utilize environmental planning processes derived from McHarg's work and create communities for a diversity of households, with jobs and services close at hand. These considerations add up to very sound planning according to the standards of national planning associations.[54] The primary criticisms of such communities is that their gross densities are still very low and they are very automobile oriented. Set within edge-city landscapes, they contribute to regional problems. In a region the size of Orange County in California, well-planned communities improve the daily lives of residents, but do not alleviate the serious regionwide problems of traffic congestion, air and water pollution, and continued outward growth. Planned communities contribute to these problems in the same way that unplanned, incremental subdivisions do.

Although well planned by contemporary standards, MPCs only scratch the surface of environmental or social problems. They address short-term needs and desires, while ignoring long-term and incremental impacts. They certainly improve the recreational possibilities for the residents and provide children and other nondrivers with greater independence and opportunities within their neighborhoods. However, California households currently make an average of 12 vehicle trips per day from their homes,[55] whether to escape, to see people, or simply because they need supplies.

Once they get into their cars to commute to work or to go shopping, the community open space plan has little significance to their lives.

In the 1990s regional planners began to encourage community designers to create models that can reduce impacts on regional landscapes. State and regional planning authorities began asking cities and their metropolitan regions to reduce automobile use by reducing the necessity to drive and by making mass transportation more palatable. Hence, the neotraditional planning movement swept the planning professions. Spearheaded by architects Andres Duany and Elizabeth Plater-Zyberk, it borrows urban design principles from traditional American towns in which walking works. Those principles are applied to new community designs in an effort to reduce automobile dependency. To address water pollution problems, planning agencies are looking seriously at natural drainage systems. Recognizing that marshes and wetlands are highly effective water purifiers and that they also assist with flood control while providing wildlife habitat, many contemporary new community designers use them as integral parts of the water systems. These working open spaces are becoming the new "backbone" of planned communities.

NOTES

1. "Entice 'Em with Advertising," *Professional Builder* **39,** No. 3 (March 1974), 102–107.
2. The Irvine Company, *Newport Coast Exhibit* (flyer) (Newport Beach, CA: The Irvine Company, n.d.).
3. Clare Cooper Marcus, Carolyn Francis, and Colette Meunier, "Mixed Messages in Suburbia: Reading the Suburban Model Home," *Places* **4,** No. 1 (1988):24–37.
4. Ibid.
5. Ibid.
6. John Stilgoe, *Borderland Origins of the American Suburb 1820–1939* (New Haven, CT: Yale University Press, 1988), p. 168–185.
7. Anne Vernez Moudon, ed., *Master-Planned Communities: Shaping the Exurbs in the 1990s, University of Washington, Urban Design Program* (proceedings of a conference) (Seattle: College of Architecture and Urban Planning, University of Washington, 1990), p. 53.
8. Michael J. Weiss, *The Clustering of America* (New York: Harper & Row, 1988).
9. A "master plan" refers to a planning document that commits to the layout and land use assignments of an area. A comprehensive planning process is employed to create the most symbiotic plan and avoid undue negative impacts.
10. The necessity for new towns to have an employment base has been stressed by many authors. Clear discussions of this can be found in Gideon Golany, *New Town Planning—Principles and Practice* (New York: Wiley Books, 1976); and Raymond Burby and Shirley F. Weiss, *New Communities U.S.A.* (Lexington, MA: Lexington Books, 1976).
11. Michael J. Weiss, *The Clustering of America.*
12. Anne Vernez Moudon, *Master-Planned Communities,* p. 10.
13. Ibid.
14. Ibid.
15. The complete absence of discussion of social theory in books like Moudon's and in published descriptions of MPCs suggests that social theory was replaced by market research to provide the foundation for community organization in these communities. See Moudon, *Master-Planned Communities,* p. 10.
16. Moudon, *Master-Planned Communities,* p. 10.
17. Robert Riley, "Speculations on the New American Landscapes," *Landscape* **24,** No. 3 (1980):4.
18. Marcus, Francis, and Meunier, "Mixed Messages in Suburbia"; and Moudon, *Master-Planned Communities,* p. 12.
19. David Guterson, "No Place Like Home," *Harper's* **285,** No. 1710, (November, 1992):55–64.

20. Robert Fishman, *Bourgeois Utopias: The Rise and Fall of Suburbia* (New York: Basic Books, 1987) Ch. 7.
21. Ibid., p. 190.
22. Joel Garreau, *Edge Cities Life on the New Frontier* (New York: Doubleday, 1991), p. 42–47.
23. Urban Land Institute, *Irvine: the Genesis of a New Community* (Washington, DC: Urban Land Institute, 1974), p. 38–49.
24. Fishman, *Bourgeois Utopias,* p. 184.
25. This information was gained from a transcript of a presentation by Mike LeBlanc, The Institute of Pacific Basin Affairs, Dominican College, San Rafael, California, June 1991.
26. This term refers to the exurban cities surrounding Los Angeles. It was used by Irvine Company vice chairman, Raymond Watson, in Moudon, *Master-Planned Communities,* p. 19.
27. Much of this contemporary information comes from the authors' observations during the summer of 1991, and discussions with landscape architect Bob Jacob at SWA Group, Laguna Beach.
28. Kevin Lynch's urban design principles of identifying districts with clear boundaries, and creating nodes of activity connected by public paths, were the source of these concepts. See Moudon, *Master-Planned Communities,* p. 50.
29. Written by the author, Cynthia Girling, for this book.
30. Guterson, "No Place Like Home."
31. Robert Thayer, Jr., *Gray World, Green Heart: Technology, Nature and the Sustainable Landscape* (New York: John Wiley & Sons, 1994).
32. Sim Van der Ryn and Peter Calthorpe, *Sustainable Communities* (San Francisco: Sierra Club Books, 1986).
33. Ian McHarg, *Design with Nature* (New York: John Wiley & Sons, 1992).
34. Similar results are reported by Thayer, *Gray World, Green Heart.*
35. Van der Ryn and Calthorpe, *Sustainable Communities.*
36. Paula Kochler French, "The Communal Landscape," *Landscape Architecture* **67** (November 1977):503–508; and Thayer, *Gray World, Green Heart.*
37. See Garrett Hardin and John Baden, *Managing the Commons* (San Francisco: W.H. Freeman and Co., 1977).
38. Ian L. McHarg and Jonathan Sutton, "Ecological Plumbing for the Texas Coastal Plain," *Landscape Architecture* **65,** No. 1 (January 1975):78–89.
39. Ian McHarg's firm, Wallace, McHarg, Roberts and Todd (WMRT), authored several studies for The Woodlands Corporation, including: "An Ecological Inventory" (1971) and "The Ecological Plan" (1974). Photocopies of these are available from the Community Planning Department of The Woodlands Corporation. The Woodlands, TX 77380.
40. In 1968 the New Communities Program began under the administration of the United States Department of Housing and Urban Development. The New Communities Administration provided federal guarantees to lenders and direct grants to local governments to assist with the extensive planning and infrastructure costs involved in the development of new communities. The program funded 17 new communities from 1968 to 1975, ranging from Roosevelt Island, New York, with a planned population of 18,000, to The Woodlands, Texas, with 150,000 planned. See Gideon Golany, *New Town Planning: Principles and Practices* (New York: Wiley Books, 1976, p. 300) and Carlos C. Campbell, *New Towns: Another Way to Live,* (Reston, VA: Reston Publishing Company, 1976).
41. This first plan was prepared by Houston architect Cerf Ross.
42. George T. Morgan and John O. King, *The Woodlands: New Community Development, 1964–1983,* (College Station: Texas A & M Universiy Press, 1967).
43. The Mitchell Energy Corporation, the parent corporation, received commitments for a $50 million grant from HUD. The developer never received the full grant, and what was received was often delayed. See Morgan and King, *The Woodlands.*
44. Studies in the initial inventory included geology and groundwater, surface hydrology, limnology, pedology, plant ecology, wildlife, and climatology.
45. Wallace, McHarg, Roberts, and Todd, "An Ecological Inventory," p. 79.
46. This process was summarized in Wallace, McHarg, Roberts and Todd, "The Ecological Plan," pp. 5–7.
47. The Woodlands Corporation, "Recreational Standards," an internal document dated February 1993.
48. This information was gained from interviews the author held with Robert Heineman, vice president for Community Planning, The Woodlands Corporation, in February 1993.

49. Wallace, McHarg, Roberts and Todd "The Ecological Plan," p. 37.
50. Signifying that tree trunks measure six inches in diameter, five feet above the ground.
51. The local landscape architect, Kathy Poole, was at the time an employee of SWA in Houston and was involved in the design of master-planned communities.
52. From an interview with Robert Heineman, The Woodlands Corporation, February, 1993.
53. J. William Thompson, "LA Forum," *Landscape Architecture* **83,** No. 9 (September 1993):60–64.
54. See critiques in Moudon, *Master-Planned Communities,* Part Two.
55. Peter Calthorpe, *The Next American Metropolis: Ecology, Community and the American Dream* (New York: Princeton Architectural Press, 1993), p. 20.

7
CENTERS AND NETWORKS
The New Suburbs

Some dictionaries still define *suburb* as "an outlying district of a city, especially *residential.*" The definition lags behind reality. Contemporary suburbs are no longer domestic dormitories tied by an umbilical cord to the city—they are no longer *sub*-urban. "Technoburbs" are self-sufficient urbanized areas, equipping themselves with employment, services, supplies, and cultural amenities. The disaggregated and often disorganized layout of these outer cities was the product of zoning practices and the availability of freeways and electronic communications, both of which encouraged rapid outward growth. The populations that these new suburbs house and employ are liberated, on the one hand, yet imprisoned by cars, phones, and computers. Between 1983 and 1990, increased vehicle trips per household accounted for 25% of growth in highway travel and average commuting distances increased by 25%.[1] Much of this increase can be attributed to growth of the outer suburbs, where commutes range between 8 and 20 miles and people commonly spend one to two hours per day traveling to and from work. In valiant efforts to use the time lost to the freeway, these commuters begin and end their workday, in the car, with cellular phones on their shoulders and paperwork spread out on the empty passenger seat.

> One might sum up the structure of the technoburb by saying that it goes against every rule of planning. It is based on two extravagances that have always raised the ire of planners: the waste of land inherent in a single family house with its own yard, and the waste of energy inherent in the use of the personal automobile. . . . Yet the technoburb has become the real locus of growth and innovation in our society. And there is real structure in what appears to be wasteful sprawl, which provides enough logic and efficiency for the technoburb to fulfill at least some of its promises.[2]

Suburban cities are now recognized as major contributors to the severe environmental problems of urban areas, including resource waste and concurrent trash disposal crises, air and water pollution. Many metropolitan areas are not going to meet upcoming deadlines for clean air and water mandated by the Environmental Protection Agency. Facing penalties, they have begun to seek mechanisms to reduce automobile-generated air pollution—quelling outward growth and modifying land use patterns to reduce automobile dependency. As of 1991, Washington State has required its cities to implement urban growth limits and the state of Oregon, which has had urban growth limits since the 1970s, recently mandated all communities of more than 25,000 to implement land use regulations and transportation plans geared toward reducing reliance on automobiles and encouraging alternative forms of transportation.[3] In Eugene, Oregon, a draft plan includes designating its existing downtown as a Transit Oriented Development District, in which parking requirements are reduced and higher density development is encouraged. Though outward growth continues around many metropolitan areas, planners are beginning to implement programs to alter the patterns of growth and decrease personal vehicle use over the next few decades.

Pollution and land consumption are recognized problems of urban expansion; however, there are social problems as well. One of the primary criticisms of edge cities is that they provide few of the physical elements that engender a sense of community among residents.[4] They lack common sources of civic pride and cohesion, such as civic buildings, plazas, parks, and monuments. Proponents contest that people find community in other ways, through work associates, religious groups, and even the recreational clubs they belong to.[5] They believe that, although privately owned, shopping malls and theme parks provide excellent community meeting places. A wealth of activities besides shopping, which is now largely recreational, occur at the nation's 3,500 regional malls, ranging from art shows and music concerts to 4H displays. In many communities the mall is the primary teenage hangout. Community recreation has become an important part of many mall programs, with skating rinks, cinemas, and food fairs becoming increasingly popular. In Edmonton, Alberta, the West Edmonton Mall, with its hotels, a copy of New Orleans's Bourbon Street, cinemas, an amusement park, skating rinks, and even some shopping, has become a destination resort for western Canada. In Eugene, Oregon, senior citizens living in isolated adult housing complexes are driven to the Valley River Center mall so that they can walk the mile of corridor for exercise.

Public open spaces, those owned by the public and created in the public interest for all manner of public activities, are missing in the edge cities. The American democracy has, until recently, had a parallel in the openness and equal accessibility of major public open spaces. These spaces, which claim and mark the center of cities—Central Park, Boston Common, Golden Gate Park—are places about which all citizens feel proud and possessive. They are a part of each individual's experience in the city. In the planned communities that constitute much of the outer cities, common, not *public,* green space abounds. Such spaces are the equivalent of dispersed community parks; however at the accumulated scale of the whole outer city, civic space and buildings rarely exist.[6] Town squares and city parks have been replaced by malls as the only places to go to experience a vibrant and diverse crowd. Recognizing a vacancy, in the mid-1980s a few town planners developed different models, new communities that reintegrated civic spaces.

HOMETOWNS, VILLAGES, NEIGHBORHOODS—REPLAYED

By the late 1980s and early 1990s popular and professional magazines were flooded with articles about the new suburban planning trends.[7] The most publicized were models by town planners Andres Duany and Elizabeth Plater-Zyberk (DPZ) from Miami and Peter Calthorpe from San Francisco. DPZ promoted a concept that it called "traditional neighborhoods,"[8] often erroneously called "neotraditionalism" by journalists, and Calthorpe promoted a concept called "Pedestrian Pockets."[9] There were numerous similarities between the two. The designers blamed suburban ills on exclusionary zoning, which distributed single land uses across vast areas and created a destructive dependency on the automobile. DPZ proposed that new suburban or exurban developments should be modeled after the traditional American town of the eastern seaboard, with dense and complex development patterns and pedestrian-oriented streets. These planners theorized that by making communities more walkable, the number of automobile trips per household would be drastically reduced and, ultimately, the social life of the community would improve. In a similar vein, Peter Calthorpe, who was influenced by the severe traffic congestion in the San Francisco Bay area, proposed not only small-scale towns with walkable streets and centers that provided jobs and shopping, but also regional rapid transit to connect them to each other and the central city. Only an alternative that seemed better than the personal automobile would get people out of their cars, he argued.

An Idea Whose Time Has Come. Again.

Publicity brochure for Laguna West, Sacramento, California.
Photographed by Don Satterly.

Developers throughout the nation welcomed these ideas as the trends to pursue in the 1990s. The nostalgia for traditional towns was recognized to be immediately salable as nature-based themes became commonplace. The missing "city" side of the suburban equation was asserting itself. Slogans such as "Laguna West: Your New Hometown" (California), "Fisher's Landing: A Town to Come Home To" (Washington), and "Main Street: Remember Spending the Day in Town, Just for Fun?" (New Jersey) emphasized collective nostalgic memories of small town life and close-knit families. As "family values" became a palliative of the Bush administration, developers reinforced nostalgic visions of family life with images such as a traditional family relaxing in front of a traditionally styled home on an old-fashioned front porch. For many in the development industry the traditional towns idea was just a catchy slogan, reinforced by wood-railed porches and a relaxed country decor, but for a select group of town planners the idea went deeper.

Centers: Traditional Neighborhoods

While developers appealed to people's nostalgia for the good life of times past, planners and urban designers looked to historical towns and urban neighborhoods for clues to what was missing in the suburbs. Designers, often believing that physical design can help to improve social conditions, sought order and hierarchy to delineate strong centers with urban qualities, such as outdoor shopping streets and civic buildings enfronting public squares. The rules had changed. In America's traditional towns, the hierarchy of society was visible, where church and state occupied monuments at the town's center, the wealthy lived in elegant homes on nearby hills, and the poor and middle classes lived in lowlands or across the tracks. Unlike the major cities of the nation that had hired designers like Daniel Burnham and Frederick Law Olmsted to lay out a city plan and design related parks systems in the late nineteenth and early twentieth centuries, few suburban cities had done any visionary planning. Architect and planner Daniel Solomon commented, "Since 1965, the urban structure of the American city has been reduced to a rudimentary organization of land-use blobs, freeways, and arterials. . . . [The] other area of planning is what is generally called design review [and] deals with subjects like window trim, roof pitches, or shades of driftwood stain. . . . Between the vagaries of land-use blobs and the minutia of design reviews, there is an enormous chasm into which the whole heritage of the American town has fallen."[10] That chasm is the deliberate urban design of communities.

Duany and Plater-Zyberk's traditional neighborhoods took the planning and development communities by storm after the widespread promotion of Seaside (begun in 1982), a new resort community in Florida. The design for Seaside was based on principles of town design derived from DPZ's field studies of traditional American towns and studies of turn-of-the-century urban designers, notably, architect Raymond Unwin and city planner and landscape architect John Nolen. From old town Alexandria, Williamsburg, Marblehead, Princeton, and Nantucket, Duany and Plater-Zyberk concluded that what attracted people to these places was a diversity of people, activities, and architecture within an orderly town plan. Streets felt comfortable to pedestrians because they were narrow, enclosed with interesting building walls and lined with trees. Community order was clarified by directly connecting neighborhoods with important town centers, parks, and monu-

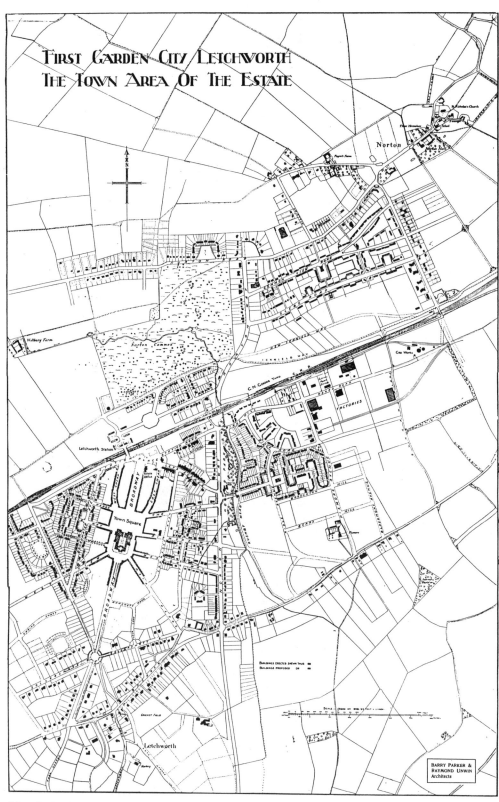

Plan for Letchworth Garden City.
From Raymond Unwin, *Town Planning in
Practice,* London: T. Fisher Unwin, 1909,
foldout enclosure.

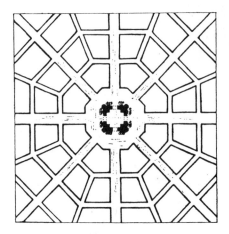

"Theoretical web-shaped plan for a town."
From Raymond Unwin, *Town Planning in Practice,* London: T. Fisher Unwin, 1909, p. 236.

ments, and neighborhoods were distinctive and finite in size—people could easily traverse them on foot, and each neighborhood contained a complex mix of land uses and building types.

Duany and Plater-Zyberk's work makes frequent reference to Raymond Unwin's town planning principles articulated in his 1909 *Town Planning in Practice.*[11] Unwin was particularly intrigued with Camillo Sitte's organic approach to town planning, whereby the characteristics of the site played a dominant role in determining the town's layout. Unwin supported these ideas for the residential areas of a town, concluding that the character of the site provided the best opportunities to express a town's unique qualities. He differed from Sitte when it came to the layout of the town's center and its major roads, and proposed the spider web as the diagram from which he would begin to lay out a town.

Unwin believed that towns needed a center, or a series of related centers, which contained the town's important public buildings and outdoor meeting places, all artfully designed in a composition that was a clear expression of the community. Town and neighborhood centers should be placed on the most advantageous sites, he argued, then connected with the most important roads. This arrangement formed the skeleton of the town. The neighborhood streets would then follow the land's contours and logically subdivide the land into simple building plots. The layout of the town would have a clear, readable order but would also be closely tied to the landscape, giving each town a unique character.

Although Duany and Plater-Zyberk borrowed these simple principles of town layout from Unwin, John Nolen's built towns had a more direct influence.[12] Nolen, a landscape architect by training and one of the fathers of the city-planning profession, studied America's historical towns and applied principles of layout learned from them to his new towns, the most famous of which were built between 1909 and 1930. His interest in town design stemmed in part from the contemporary sentiment that small towns and communities held the greatest promise for housing a rapidly urbanizing population. Like urban historian Lewis Mumford, he proposed that with the availability of automobiles, trains, air travel and radio, telephone, and film communications, life in small communities could be as fulfilling, yet safer and healthier than life in cities. Nolen was critical of gridiron town plans applied without attention to the existing elements and landscape character. The "acme of absurdity,"[13] according to Nolen, was when San Francisco applied a grid over its hilly terrain. Instead, Nolen promoted a hybrid of radial, grid, and natural patterns to order town plans. As a landscape architect, fitting the town to its site came first, and he often saved the most scenic features for parks and open space.

Kingsport, Tennessee, and Mariemount, Ohio, were planned by John Nolen in 1918 and 1916.[14] Kingsport was built to supply business for the new Carolina, Clinchfield, and Ohio Railroad constructed through resource-rich but underdeveloped southeastern Tennessee. Developed by the Kingsport Improvement Corporation, it was intended to be a seat for local industry as well as a profit-making venture. Characteristic of Nolen's work, the plan is significant for its relationship between the street plan and the site. The town was sited on the banks of the Holston River, with the railway as its southern boundary. The business sector was a grid running upslope between the railway and the residential districts. The heart of the community was Broad Street, connecting the railroad station to the prominently sited civic center. The city hall, library, hotel, and several churches

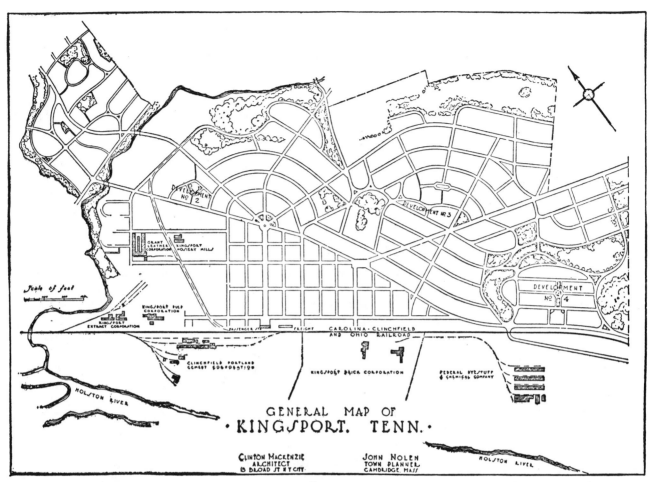

General Map of Kingsport, Tennessee.
John Nolen Town Planner. From John Nolen,
New Towns for Old, Boston: Marshall Jones
Company, 1927, p. 53.

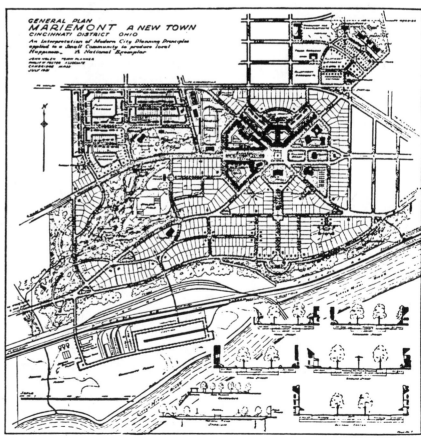

Plan of Mariemont, Ohio.
John Nolen Town Planner. From John Nolen,
New Towns for Old, Boston: Marshall Jones
Company, 1927, p. 122.

encircled this radial center of town. From this point all the primary neighborhood streets radiated. Distinct neighborhoods were located on higher lands north of the business district, each with a curving but orderly plan, and separated from nearby neighborhoods by riparian corridors and generous parklands.

Mariemont, Ohio, is the other town model frequently referenced by DPZ. A new satellite town outside of Cincinnati, Mariemont was modeled after Unwin and Parker's Letchworth. Its founder was Mary M. Emery, a wealthy industrialist who wanted to create a healthy, attractive community for workers of suburban Cincinnati. Typical of Nolen's other plans, it had a strong central focal point linked by a boulevard to the railway station. An octagonal plan for the Town Center with wide, straight radial boulevards merged into a softer, curvilinear configuration in the neighborhoods. The residential streets bore a distinct resemblance to the picturesque models of upper-income neighborhoods designed by the Olmsted Brothers, with spacious, curving, tree-lined streets and large Tudor-styled homes. However, at Mariemont, these large mansionlike buildings were, in actuality, attached houses and apartments. Although many had tiny private yards, large allotment gardens were often located behind apartment housing. A vast park system, following a stream, separated neighborhoods while simultaneously linking outlying residential areas to the commercial center. Nolen and Unwin believed that town plans had to have a simple, clear order, with a town center containing all the major civic and business functions. All major roads should lead to the center. Both designers used parks and natural open space to separate distinctive residential neighborhoods with roads following the land's contours. Each neighborhood had a small center of its own. The Unwin diagram titled "A Method of Zoning" provides a clear point of departure from which to understand DPZ's plans. Its general principles of town design apply equally well to these designers' plans.

Whereas Unwin, Nolen, and America's historical towns have provided design inspiration for Duany and Plater-Zyberk, their arguments in favor of a change to traditional new towns were a reaction to contemporary conditions. Their new town proposals suggested repairs to today's dysfunctional suburbs. In his frequent public lectures, Andres Duany scathingly criticized the work of land use and transportation planners whom he blamed for many of the ills of contemporary suburban areas. Zoning practices nationwide have mandated single-function land uses spread illogically over vast areas of the suburban landscape, with the result that suburban residents have to make frequent automobile trips over great distances, in multiple directions, to accomplish their daily tasks: going to work, taking children to school and after-school activities, shopping, banking, and assorted errands. Duany cites a statistic that suburbanites in Orlando, Florida, made an average of 13 automobile trips a day to and from their homes.[15] But, he said, zoning was not the only culprit. Transportation planners, the subject of much of his wrath, were equally to blame. The standard hierarchical post-1950s road system, where local dead-end residential streets fed into collector streets, into arterials, and finally into highways and freeways, were equally to blame. Not only were these roads designed exclusively for cars, encouraging high speeds and disregard for pedestrians, but their layout prohibited taking the shortest route from home to school or store. In his show-and-tell lectures given to public officials, Duany used aerial photos of numerous circumstances where residents live or work only hundreds of feet from services but were prohibited by design from walking to them.

Chapter 7. Centers and Networks: The New Suburbs

Let us take as an example the professor who may live [in a planned suburb in Kendall, Florida]. That professor, if he teaches at the community college nearby, could get there easily enough. It's well within walking distance. However, he can't, there is a drainage ditch to bridge, then a huge parking lot. It doesn't even occur to this person to walk. That professor instead gets in his car, goes out into the curvilinear street maze, down to the great collector street, enters the college parking lot, and parks at what turns out to be a couple of hundred feet from his home. The same itinerary is forced on a person who lives close to the shopping center. Or on a kid who goes to a church school nearby.[16]

The traditional town model fixes these problems, said Duany, by consciously making direct connections between homes and services, schools, churches, and places of work. These town plans eliminate "pods," which are single-use, dead-end functions, whether they be community colleges, business parks, shopping centers, or walled residential communities. Instead, DPZ encouraged modified grid patterns whereby residential streets interconnect and offer a variety of routes for driving and walking from place to place. Most neighborhood services were located in high-density, mixed-use commercial centers, with shops at the street level and housing on the second or third floors. Office areas were handled similarly, as a type of neighborhood, linked very directly and by the shortest route to the residential areas.

Like both Unwin and Nolen, DPZ is interested in creating orderly town plans. Its plans, like its predecessors', are clearly hybrids between radial plans, grids, and organic landscape-based plans. While these may begin with

Town center for Tanin, Alabama.
Andres Duany and Elizabeth Plater-Zyberk Architects and Town Planners.

grids, the center of which is the town square and commercial center, these are altered in response to the site's predominant characteristics. Town centers recall Unwin's spider web with radial streets leading to nearby neighborhoods. Grid orientations are altered or pieces removed to align with landforms or defer to open space elements. The designers' intentions in making such adjustments are less to decrease the impact of development on the site, than to use the underlying landscape character to determine community form, harking directly back to the lessons of Raymond Unwin and Camillo Sitte. In part owing to the unique design process by which most DPZ town plans are conceived in a week or less, they stop short of conducting thorough environmental analyses prior to developing conceptual town plans. With sketchy understandings of the sites' natural processes, they use the most obvious natural characteristics, such as the alignment of waterways or topography to give character to the town and its neighborhoods.

Duany and Plater-Zyberk *design* towns. From the beginning, they have a vision of what the community they design will look like. To achieve this vision, the master plan is accompanied by an "urban code"—a cross between subdivision ordinances and design guidelines—which direct other architects in the design of specific buildings and sites. These detailed rules about the use, size, proportion, spacing, openings, and closures of buildings and similar issues of size, scale, and appointment of streets and parks are a direct reaction to what DPZ believes are the disastrous results of Euclidean zoning—single-use and oversimplified rules without design direction.

DPZ plans establish "types" of development that may occur on a land parcel. Within each type the list of alternative uses is extensive and very mixed by today's standards. For example, a building might have retail on the ground level, with offices and residential above, or the same site may have hotels, rooming houses, restaurants, or studios. By allowing a broad range of uses within one type, diversity is encouraged within each zone and change is possible over time. For example, as a neighborhood matures, a residence may evolve into a studio, restaurant, or several apartments. At the same time, spelling out site development principles such as building set-backs and heights, relative locations of buildings, yards and parking, principles of solar access, and even historical precedents for style, the DPZ code promotes visual compatibility. The architects frequently refer to old town Alexandria, Virginia, and Georgetown in Washington, D.C., where the streetscape is consistent despite the variable functions of shop, office, or home and individualized details in the gardens and on facades. For example, in DPZ town centers, buildings must be set on the property line at the street to form a street wall. These designers believe that this relationship is crucial to creating bustling shopping areas. Shop windows and doors line the street and invite people in, while the two- to three-story wall creates an enclosed and comfortable sidewalk space. It is equally important not to break the street wall—too much discontinuity leads to the impression that stores and services are too far apart for walking—so the codes set limits on the amount of unbuilt space along the street.

Streets and other public spaces are covered in DPZ codes and designed schematically through cross sections and perspective sketches. Scale and proportion are of utmost concern. When streets are too wide, says Duany, pedestrians become uncomfortable in them. Similarly, when buildings get too high, or walls too plain, pedestrians feel dwarfed and bored. DPZ codes call for either arcades or trees and fences to define the pedestrian zone. Picket fences are often required, because they add to the traditional town

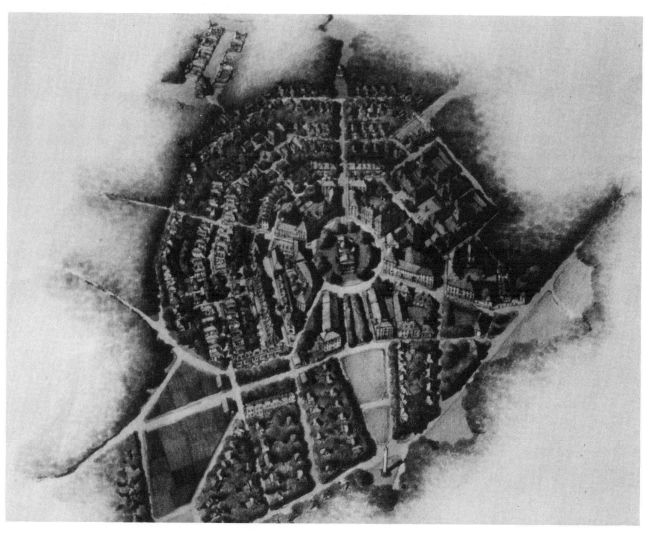

A village near Annapolis, Maryland.
Andres Duany and Elizabeth Plater-Zyberk
Architects and Town Planners.

quality as well as define the street edge. They allow visibility into front yards, yet are a clear statement of the line between private and public. The DPZ code is based on a combination of pragmatic, spatial, and cultural values.

DPZ has also developed a unique process for new community planning, a hybrid of visionary urban design and participatory planning.[17] A team of designers, land-planning experts, and local officials is gathered for a one-week, on-site design "charrette" to create the first plan for the community. The charrette team often tour the site and surrounding area together to initiate the process. At the end of an intense week of work, the conceptual plan and accompanying imagery are complete. The nature of the project and site will often determine the kinds of information the team collects prior to the charrette; however, the basics typically include natural systems data, regulatory data, and a program. The degree to which accurate, in-depth site data is collected varies. On some projects, such as Kentlands, only readily available information was assembled, such as data on topography, soils, and flood zones. On other projects, such as Nance Canyon and Haymount, where clients had a particular concern about environmental issues,

Portions of the urban code for a village near Annapolis, Maryland.

Duany and Plater-Zyberk, Architects and Town Planners. From Alex Krieger and William Lennertz, eds., *Andres Duany and Elizabeth Plater-Zyberk: Towns and Town-Making Principles.* New York: Rizzoli, 1991, pp. 30, 31.

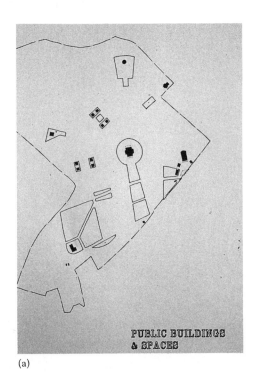

PUBLIC BUILDINGS & SPACES

(a)

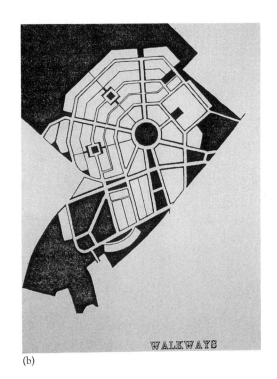

WALKWAYS

(b)

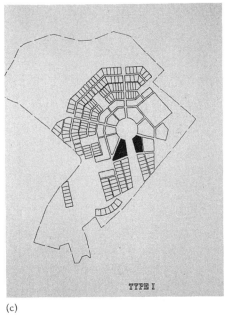

TYPE I

(c)

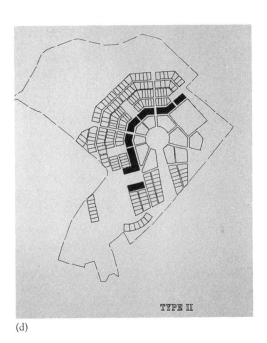

TYPE II

(d)

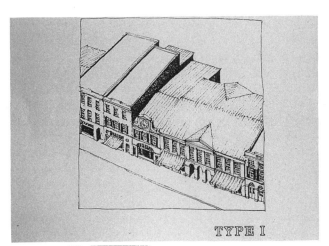

TYPE I

(i)

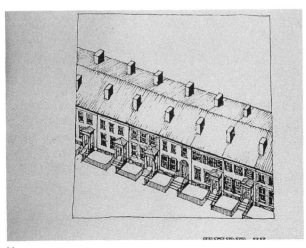

(j)

KEY:

(a) Public Buildings and Spaces

(b) Walkways

(c) Type I

(d) Type II

(e) Type III

(f) Type IV

(g) Type V

(h) Public Buildings

(i) Type I

(j) Type II

(k) Type III

(l) Type IV

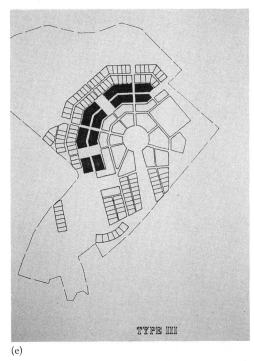

TYPE III

(e)

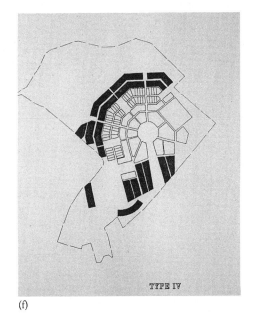

TYPE IV

(f)

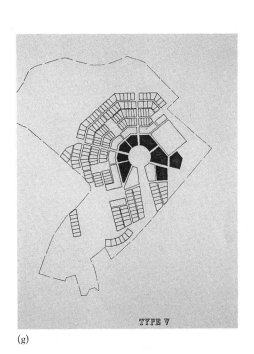

TYPE V

(g)

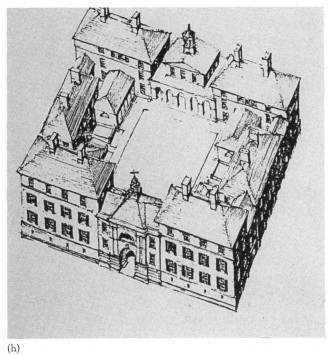

(h)

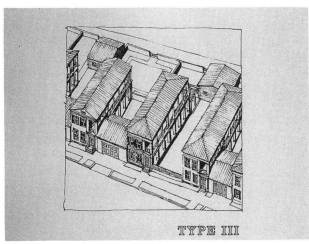

TYPE III

(k)

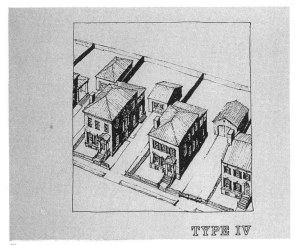

TYPE IV

(l)

more in-depth natural systems studies were completed ahead of time. At Haymount, for example, bald eagles nested along the Rappahannock River running through the site. Specific studies of their habitat needs led to a decision to retain most of the river frontage in a natural state. In many cases some environmental expertise is retained on the charrette team to influence the decision-making process.

DPZ's traditional neighborhood concept proposed that suburban developments be small in area and concentrated around a multiuse service, work, and residential center. Plans were based on an orderly arrangement of streets and centers, with streets being the focus of public activity. The main community fabric was a set of civic components: schools, libraries, post offices, and town halls, all located on public squares or greens within the neighborhood centers. These were directly linked by attractive tree-lined streets. Because all residents would live within easy walking distance (a quarter mile) of these neighborhood centers, the street was a strolling and meeting place, further enhanced by people sitting on front porches and stoops ready to chat with passing neighbors. The image is compelling, but proof of DPZ's theories will come only if developers are willing to build "traditional neighborhoods," home buyers follow suit and purchase the houses, and residents behave the way DPZ predicts they will.

Kentlands

Joseph Alfandre, a developer of "mediocre subdivisions,"[18] converted to DPZ's traditional towns in 1988 as he was embarking on the project now called Kentlands. His fond recollections of his own childhood in Bethseda, Maryland, convinced him that Duany and Plater-Zyberk had an idea he could sell. In a week-long charrette with Alfandre, DPZ and its team developed a concept of making the site's historical mansion and farm buildings the town's civic center, and styling neo-Georgian and neo-Federal houses around it along narrow brick-paved streets. Full-page advertisements in *The Washington Post* described the community in fairy-tale style:

> Once upon a time, all great neighborhoods were built like Kentlands. Yards were framed with stone planters and picket fences. Steps were laced with wrought iron railings. Porch swings swung over solid brick floors. Fake siding and phony veneers were non-existent. As were dead-end streets and feeder roads. The streets were laid out in a grid pattern and were narrow to slow down traffic. Sidewalks took you to school, to church, to the store, and to your best friend's house. Everything was within a five minute walk.[19]

The site was a 356-acre former farmstead located on the edge of Gaithersburg, Maryland, an "edge city" northwest of Washington, D.C. It was partially forested and had a lake and approximately 25 acres in wetlands. An adjacent property was a bird sanctuary owned by the National Geographic Society. The developer planned to build 1,600 housing units, a regional mall with 1.2 million square feet of space, a "main street" commercial area with an additional 900,000 square feet of commercial and office space, a library, elementary school, day care center, two churches, and a recreation club.

The wetlands on the site seemed to divide it into two halves and made connecting the community's parts difficult. The designers turned this into an advantage by designating five neighborhoods—Old Farm Neighborhood, Gate House Neighborhood, Hill District, Lake District, Midtown, and

A Place Like Kentlands Comes Along Only Once Every 200 Years.

If you're partial to old towns like George-town and Williams-burg, you'll be totally taken with Kentlands.

Because Kentlands is built along the same lines. Its narrow two-lane streets crisscross to form blocks instead of dead ends. Its sidewalks take you to school, to the park, to the store, and to church.

And like the old towns, it has landmarks. On the public square, a turn-of-the-century mansion is being restored for the community. Across the street is a block-long village green. An 11-acre lake and great stands of trees frame the landscape.

And on every Kentlands block are the stateliest new homes in Gaithersburg. Some offer separate garages with living quarters on top. Others are graced with white picket fences. There are lazy front porches, wrought iron railings, and quaint alleyways that enclose courtyards.

Special below-market financing is available from the B.F. Saul Mortgage Company. We'll even buy your present home from you through our Guaranteed Sales Program.

Prices range from the mid-$200s to the $500s for single-family homes. From the $170s to the $300s for townhomes. And from the $120s to the $160s for condominiums. Apartments rent from $715 to $1,200.

Rocky Gorge Communities, C-I/Mitchell & Best, Joseph Alfandre Homes, and Bozzuto have homes for you to see. And the Kentlands Information Center is open daily from 10 to 6. Call 301-948-8353. And join us.

Unless you want to wait another 200 years.

Exclusive Financing Rate 5.88%	RATE	MONTHLY PAYMENTS
	5.88%	$1,112 Year 1
8.42% Annual Percentage Rate	6.88%	$1,235 Year 2
	7.88%	$1,363 Year 3
	8.88%	$1,496 Years 4-30

KENTLANDS
GAITHERSBURG, MARYLAND

Kentlands, Gaithersburg, Maryland.
From a sales brochure by Alfandre Homes,
circa 1992.

The plan of Kentlands. (1) Old Farm District; (2) Gatehouse District; (3) Hill District; (4) Lake District; (5) Midtown; (6) Downtown.
Andres Duany and Elizabeth Plater-Zyberk
Architects and Town Planners.

Downtown—separated by the wetland greenbelts between them. Each was characterized by its own grid-based plan, a mix of housing types following either Federal or Georgian motifs, and a focus on a civic feature. They were connected by the primary roads of the community, leading from center to center. The Gate House neighborhood, located on the southwest portion of the site, focused on a traffic circle around which were the school, a church, a day care center, and town houses. The Old Farm Neighborhood included the historical estate buildings, which were planned to house a cultural center for Gaithersberg, including a conference center, artists' studios, a post office, public gardens, and a restaurant. For the time being they house the sales offices for the developer and several builders and the office of the town architect, two employees from Duany and Plater-Zyberk's office. Midtown and Downtown, the street-related commercial district and the mall, remain undeveloped but are promised to be the shopping and working areas for the community.

Unfortunately, despite the very small size of the development, Duany's five-minute walking rule[20] was not consistently applied in Kentlands. Only a fraction of the residences will be within a five-minute walk of the civic and commercial centers. The majority of houses were put in the Gate House Neighborhood and the Hill District, both of which are a ten-minute walk from the mall site. These neighborhoods are closer to an existing commercial area at the intersection of two roads bordering the site. Paradoxically, the relationship between these Kentlands neighborhoods and the existing commercial area is the one that Andres Duany glibly criticizes. To get to the nearby commercial area with fast-food restaurants, convenience stores, and the like, residents of Kentlands have to drive, although this area is a five-minute walk from the most populated neighborhoods. The edges of the property along Darnestown Road and Quince Orchard Road (across which are numerous cul-de-sac subdivisions) are high planted berms, at the base of which is a low wall. Exit points are limited and no sidewalks exist, although the need is evident from the dirt paths within the green verges. Although the community is walkable internally, the architects, developers, and the city of Gaithersburg have overlooked important off-site connections. Following the model of earlier MPCs, they seem to have made the assumption that walking need not occur outside the strongly delineated boundaries of Kentlands.

DPZ plans have had two distinctly different types of public open space: streets, squares, and parks were the civic spaces that formed the skeleton of the plan, and natural open space was used to surround and separate neighborhoods. Aesthetics rather than function was the primary criterion for

Section through Darnestown Road, Kentlands.
Kate Van Rooy.

A park in the Old Farm neighborhood, Kentlands.
C. Girling.

both the design and location of Kentland's open spaces. Parks were designed in a "traditional" character to complement the neo-classical design of civic buildings—typically geometric lawns encircled by stately trees. Their location was at the center of the community; the confluence of radial streets and their primary purpose seemed to be a grand lawn in front of a significant building. They were primarily suited to passive activities such as walking, sitting, or informal games, and, except for the school yard, playgrounds and fields for active recreation were not planned.

Kentlands had several different street types, with their designs related to the adjacent land uses; however, all streets felt narrower and more consistently enclosed than their contemporaries in nearby developments. Narrow town-house streets had the front porches and stairs built right on the property line, next to a narrow sidewalk which was directly adjacent to the curb. In nearby single-family housing areas, houses were set back 15 feet, leaving

*A street in the Gatehouse neighborhood,
Kentlands.*
C. Girling.

enough space for stairs and a small garden between the house and the
sidewalk, while maintaining a strong presence of porch and entry on the
street. Between the sidewalk and the street there was a narrow planting
strip with trees. On many of the streets at Kentlands, sidewalks were paved
with brick. The rich color and texture of this material contributed significantly to the close and friendly quality of residential streets.

Natural open space was the field upon which the positive structure of
the town was placed. Used as greenbelts to separate neighborhoods or
towns, it was dealt with as a natural backdrop and rarely grappled with as a
design or management issue. At the Kentlands, a portion of the original 25
acres of wetlands was preserved in common ownership. Having accomplished this significant task, DPZ did not create clear guidelines as to how
the community should deal with the natural areas. Although DPZ prescribed in detail the relationships between buildings, their gardens, and

Wetlands area, Kentlands.
C. Girling.

streets or alleys, no direction was given for designing the edge between town and natural preserve. Nor was there explicit instruction about how to maintain or restore natural ecosystems in and around developed sites. In the summer of 1992, red surveying tape marked the natural areas as off-limits and there was no indication that they would be successfully incorporated into the community vision. The town architects, DPZ employees, did not know how these edges would be treated, nor who would construct the community's trail system.[21] In several areas, development had changed the drainage patterns so dramatically that forest cover was dying because of standing water. In another case, a "forest preserve" had been cleared of underbrush and a brick path terminated in a circle of unknown purpose in the midst of threatened trees—the area was being irrigated. Apparently, rather than preserving these areas, the developers and residents had succeeded in damaging them. The fault lies, at least to some degree, with the town planners who had provided insufficient education of the site's users.

Avalon Park

Elizabeth Plater-Zyberk observed that DPZ's plan for Avalon Park was a weaving of the grided town plan with its traditional elements of open space: street, square, and park, and preserved natural systems: streamways, wetlands, and detention basins.[22] The subject of much controversy, this proposed 5,705-acre Orlando, Florida, development is sited beyond the city's urban services boundary. State law requires that communities prebuild infrastructure before such a new development is occupied, so the cost of infrastructure will presumably be borne by the developer. City and county planners objected to the plan on the basis that a major new development just beyond the urban services boundary of the city would guarantee low-density sprawl between the two, effectively erasing the growth planning they were trying to implement. The developer argued that county planners underestimated growth for the east sector of the county and that they

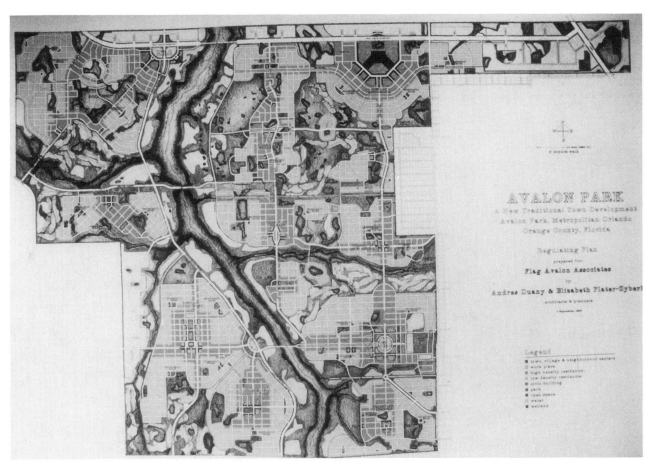

Avalon Park territory plan.
Andres Duany and Elizabeth Plater-Zyberk
Architects and Town Planners.

favored an expansion of the urban service boundary. As of the spring of 1993, a resolution had not been reached.

Called a "territory" design by DPZ, Avalon Park was composed of two towns and three smaller villages. The towns and villages of Avalon Park were distributed along orthogonal roads that extended the historical road patterns of the surrounding areas. Greenbelts following the Econlockhatchee River, which passes midway through the site, and its floodplains, streams, and wetlands separated the towns and villages. Each town and village would have a center, with a combination of offices and shopping surrounded by higher-density housing. Towns and villages were subdivided into two to four neighborhoods. At the core of each neighborhood a small center was planned, with a general store, park or square, and bus stop.

One-fifth of the site, 1,095 acres, was reserved for open space purposes. Four primary types of open space were proposed which, DPZ said, were "graduated" for human use. What was not clear was the kinds of use the designers envisioned and the design parameters for such uses. At one end of the scale were squares, located at the town and village centers and depicted as plazas or formal gardens surrounded by arcaded commercial buildings. Neighborhoods also had modest squares at the center. Playgrounds were small spaces located very near to residences, and parks were natural areas within neighborhoods, presumably with easier access than greenbelts. The illustrations of public spaces for Avalon Park showed no people or facilities for recreation, and although a detailed "urban code" was developed, there

191

Neighborhood center, Avalon Park.
Andres Duany and Elizabeth Plater-Zyberk
Architects and Town Planners.

Neighborhood playground, Avalon Park.
Andres Duany and Elizabeth Plater-Zyberk
Architects and Town Planners.

was no comparable document covering the design of green spaces. Natural areas such as the parks and greenbelts remained vague designations on the plans, often bordered by retention ponds or golf courses—relationships that deserve careful attention because of potential pollution problems.

This plan, as well as several other more recent projects by Duany and Plater-Zyberk, indicate that they have, either by interest or necessity, begun to incorporate vast natural areas into their territorial plans. The designation of sensitive areas as natural preserves demonstrates progress from typical new community designs of 10 years ago; however, numerous models for more sophisticated landscape design and management exist, such as Reston, with its open space management plan, and The Woodlands, with its design guidelines for natural areas. As demonstrated by problems surfacing at the Kentlands project, the next step for DPZ will be to designate the transitions that must be made between developed and natural areas of their towns, much as they prescribe the design of the street and facade. Without such careful attention, small natural areas are doomed to cultivation, and larger ones are likely to become misunderstood, even resented disruptions to the fabric of the town. The Woodlands Ecological Plan provides a model for a needed addition to their town plans—an open space code accompanied by management guidelines.

NETWORKS: TRANSPORTATION AND OPEN SPACE

The surface and subsurface networks of a community—the roads, trails, sewers, utilities, and water supply—also called infrastructure, constitute as much as 80% of the developers' costs. Their cost-effectiveness has always been a fundamental consideration of community design. Why, then, is there so much waste in the conventional design of modern suburbs? Why do these engineered streets contribute to traffic congestion? These road systems, along with dispersed, single-purpose land use patterns, have been blamed for the unprecedented use of personal automobiles by suburbanites and the resulting severe traffic congestion now common in the edge cities. Robert Cervero[23] argued that much of the increase in suburban traffic that occurred in the 1980s could be attributed to the significant buildup of jobs around the fringe areas of metropolitan centers. With 49% of American workers holding white-collar jobs, many of which are now located on suburban office campuses, commuting patterns have changed. In 1980, 40% of work-trips in the United States were suburb-to-suburb trips, whereas only half that many were suburb-to-central-city trips.[24] Orange County, California, is perhaps the worst example, where commuting patterns have become completely unpredictable. Traffic is consistently heavy on all major roads and freeways, and traffic jams can occur anywhere at any time. When traveling by car from one suburban community to another, one is advised to add an hour to normal travel time to accommodate tie-ups. Provision of mass transit to the most populous outer cities is one solution, and although some cities, such as Seattle, have consistently rejected mass transit, San Diego and Los Angeles have initiated new systems. Cervero, who is skeptical of the pat mass-transit solution, recommends single-occupancy auto disincentives, such as caps on available parking, combined with dramatic increases in business- and government-led transportation management programs to orchestrate car and van-pooling programs for job regions.

Urban planners in many of the nation's metropolitan areas have argued for higher levels of integration between transportation planning and land use planning:

> Little more need be said about the importance of balancing jobs and housing as well as intermixing land uses as the most fail-safe cure for regional traffic woes. Although perhaps today an overused phrase, the central message behind balanced growth remains as sound and unequivocal as ever. Travel is a direct function of how we organize our communities, and if we physically segregate activities and fail to zone certain areas for a mixture of uses, chronic traffic breakdowns are inevitable.[25]

A number of cities, such as San Diego, Sacramento, Seattle, and Portland, have all instituted land use planning programs linked to transportation planning. All of these communities are investigating various forms of transit-oriented developments in which new high-density, mixed-use developments will be encouraged around public transit stations. In all cases the twofold purpose of these incentive programs is to concentrate growth and reduce the total usage of personal automobiles.

Peter Calthorpe's Pedestrian Pocket concept is a vision for well-designed suburban settlements linked to regional rapid transit systems.[26] An architect, town planner, and part-time professor at the University of California, Berkeley, he came to the conclusion that to affect change in the growth patterns of metropolitan areas, new types of development were needed. He proposed Pedestrian Pockets, compact communities located beyond the urbanized portion of a metropolitan area, with public transit connections to the urban center and to one another. Although roadways would exist, they would theoretically provide a less efficient network. Each community would have some specialized commercial endeavor, such as a shopping center, back office development, cultural center, or light industry, providing a significant number of jobs to local residents. Together the network of communities would offer balanced regional growth while consuming less land. Calthorpe's vision was that the tight-knit form, an orientation toward public outdoor space, and the provision of complete retail and business services in the community would enable people to spend more of their lives within one locale, ameliorating contemporary commuting patterns. In addition, the well-coordinated design of streets, plazas, parks, playgrounds, bikeways, walkways, school yards, and community centers would encourage more walking and outdoor activity, thus reducing use of cars and potentially increasing social interaction.

Much of Peter Calthorpe's previous work was characterized by a strong environmental ethic, the most notable examples being his innovative passive solar project, the Bateson Building in Sacramento, and Marin Solar Village. The content of an exurban village was first explored in the Marin Solar Village project, which had five residential neighborhoods of apartments and single-family houses, a commercial village center, a transit center, office complex, mushroom farm and truck gardens, and a light industry complex housed in old aircraft hangars. The layout resembled the Radburn plan, with bays and culs-de-sac projecting into green space, which buffered different land uses, such as agriculture, commerce, and residences, and provided separated pedestrian circulation throughout. Common lands for recreation, movement, and agriculture existed at all scales of development, from housing cluster to neighborhood to village. Reflecting the communal

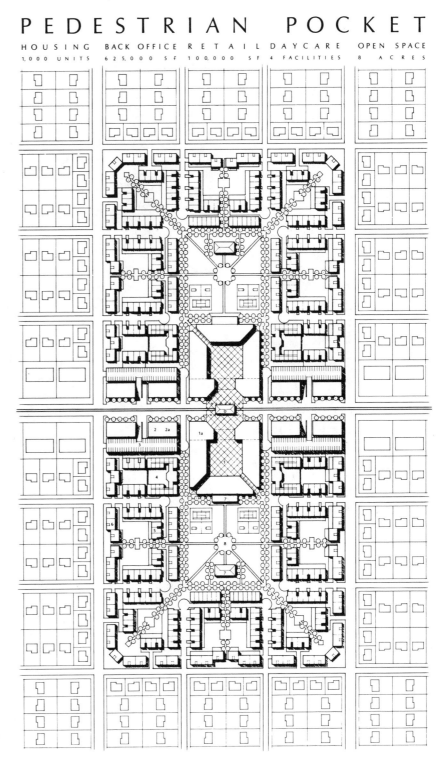

PEDESTRIAN POCKET

HOUSING   BACK OFFICE   RETAIL   DAYCARE   OPEN SPACE
1,000 UNITS   625,000 SF   100,000 SF   4 FACILITIES   8 ACRES

The Pedestrian Pocket.
Peter Calthorpe and Mark Mack,
unpublished paper, 1987.

tenor of the times, it was proposed that collective activity would occur at
several levels, ranging from small groups of householders who would share
yards, playgrounds, and gardens, to the community as a whole, which would
operate cooperative farms and other productive enterprises.[27]

The Pedestrian Pocket was a denser and far more orderly plan than
Marin Solar Village. Calthorpe had turned away from organic layouts and

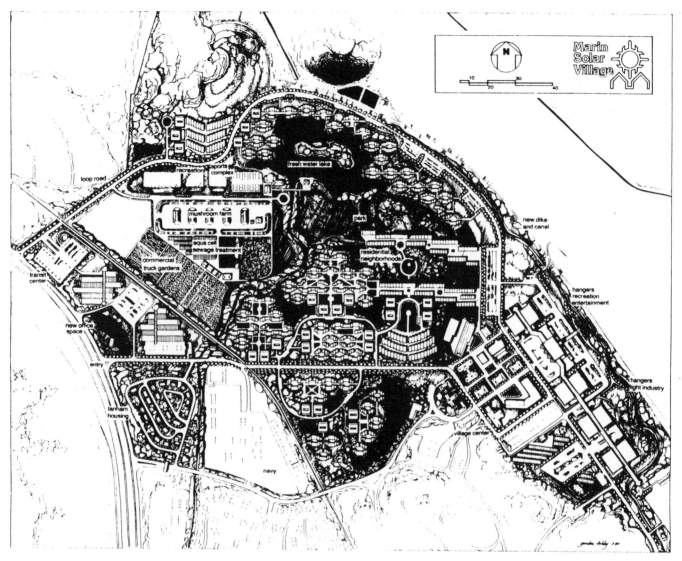

Marin Solar Village plan.
From Sim Van der Ryn and Peter Calthorpe, *Sustainable Communities,* San Francisco: Sierra Club Books, 1986, p. 66.

looked more toward urban models. Nonetheless, there were remnants of Marin Solar Village in the Pedestrian Pocket: the backbone of interconnected open space, the clustering of attached housing around common yards, the village center as the heart of commercial activity, and a transit link to the metropolitan area. At the same time, his attention shifted from broad concerns about sustainability and alternative energy to a more focused perspective on reducing automobile dependency and automobile-driven development patterns.

> Given the social, economic, and environmental forces of our time, some new synthesis of [automobile, pedestrian, and transit] systems is necessary. The problem is to introduce the needs of the pedestrian and transit into the auto-dominated regions of our metropolitan areas, not to return to the fiction of small-town America.[28]

Calthorpe distinguished his work from Andres Duany and Elizabeth Plater-Zyberk's Traditional Neighborhoods with his proposals for alternative, regional transportation systems. Calthorpe's energy-conserving perspective

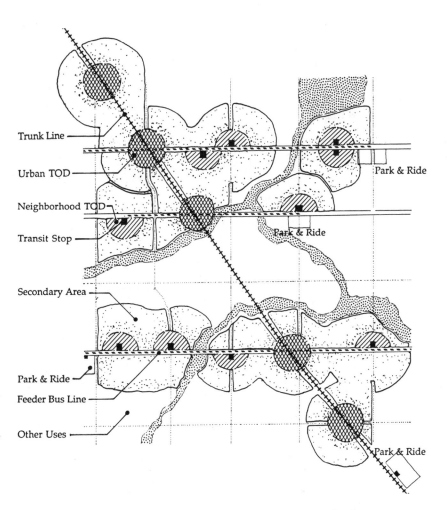

Trunk Line

Urban TOD

Neighborhood TOD

Transit Stop

Secondary Area

Park & Ride

Feeder Bus Line

Other Uses

Park & Ride

Park & Ride

Park & Ride

Networks of Transit Oriented Developments for Sacramento County. Calthorpe Associates, San Francisco, California. (Also see Howard's Social Cities, p. 58.)

mandated that walking and biking routes in a community had to connect to mass-transit stations, whereas Duany and Plater-Zyberk were skeptical of the rapid-transit solution and focused on walking within the new community.

Calthorpe's proposals for creating transit-related satellite communities have influenced metropolitan planning throughout the Pacific states. After a well-publicized design charrette at the University of Washington in Seattle, Doug Kelbaugh published *The Pedestrian Pocket Book,* describing Calthorpe's concept as well as the results of the charrette. Planners in several West Coast cities immediately began to consult with Calthorpe and to use the concept. The idea of transit-related growth was not new, and it echoed both Ebenezer Howard's rail system and America's early interurban rail lines, which had opened the suburbs. What Calthorpe had done was to modernize the vision of these types of communities and to establish a set of planning principles to guide their design.

Several aspects of the Pedestrian Pocket appealed to planners. By tying higher-density development to rapid transit and, at the same time, limiting the area of the dense development using the quarter-mile rule, necklaces of dense development could support rapid transit lines which needed higher populations for adequate ridership. By limiting the location and impact of these high-density areas to the less desirable lands along transportation corridors, the surrounding lands would be reserved for much lower-density development. Pedestrian Pockets also supported centralized shopping, offices, and community services tied to a rapid transit system.

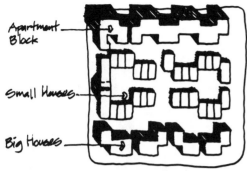

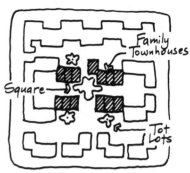

A. The overall plan includes a variety of Housing types and forms.

B. Single and double units are placed on the perimeter for street and urban orientation.

C. Family housing is clustered at the interior, a children's play area is nearby.

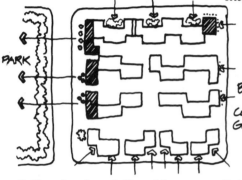

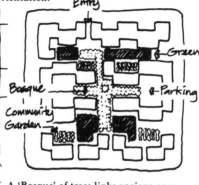

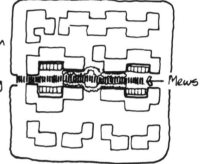

D. Shops face the parkside and front doors face the streets to enhance pedestrian activity.

E. A 'Bosque' of trees links various open spaces; greens, community gardens, entries and parking.

F. The Mews reinforces the Sacramento tradition of mid-block alleys.

Diagrams for Somerset Parkside Housing.
From Sim Van der Ryn and Peter Calthorpe, *Sustainable Communities,* San Francisco: Sierra Club Books, 1986, p. 9.

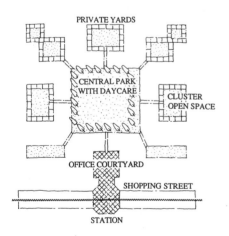

Pedestrian Pocket open spaces.
Peter Calthorpe and Mark Mack, unpublished paper, 1987.

Lying somewhere between Radburn's backbone of green space and DPZ's straight streets and landmarks are Calthorpe's town plans. The Pedestrian Pocket included a structured network of programmed outdoor spaces with gradients of privacy ranging from intimate yards to very public gathering places. The layouts strongly resembled patterns that Calthorpe used in urban housing projects such as Somerset Parkside Housing. There, on a single block in downtown Sacramento, he created four semi-public courtyards surrounded by two-story family housing, all enclosed within a perimeter wall of three- and four-story apartment buildings. Each unit had a small private yard, and each faced a courtyard intended for play, gardening, or relaxation. The courtyards had the scale and enclosure of suburban back yards, yet were interconnected, each with a different purpose and design. Similar courtyard housing schemes formed the building blocks for the Pedestrian Pocket's housing areas.

The diagram of the open space network for the Pedestrian Pocket was the skeleton of the community plan. At the heart of the community was a spine of public space extending from park to civic square. Spaces along the spine, including private yards, cluster open spaces, neighborhood parks, and office courtyards, were each designed for a specific set of activities and linked by walkways. Children's play, family games, swimming, and sunning were taken out of the private yard and placed in the public domain. Rather than being isolated recreation, linear outdoor activities—walking, running and biking—connected stationary activities and daily events, such as trips to the market, taking the children to school, and getting to work. Calthorpe stated, "Mobility and privacy have increasingly displaced the traditional commons, which once provided the connected quality of our towns and cities. Our shared public space has been given over to the car and its accommodations, while our private world has become bloated and isolated."[29] His intent in the Pedestrian Pocket was to overcome the isolation of the autonomous suburban yard through a return to the commons.

Sacramento County

In their ongoing revision of the Sacramento County General Plan, county planners adopted Calthorpe's concept of high-density nodes within the suburban fabric as one solution to their most pressing problems: "urban sprawl, escalating traffic congestion, non-attainment of regional air quality standards, and growing demands for housing opportunities which meet the needs of an increasingly diverse population."[30] In 1989 the county engaged Calthorpe Associates, with Minter and Associates, to develop design guidelines for "Transit-Oriented Developments" (TODs), an adaptation of Pedestrian Pockets. The new General Plan [31] incorporated these TODs as special planning areas within the urban growth limits. Like Pedestrian Pockets, these were higher-density, mixed-use developments occurring at transit interchanges and intended to become local centers. They maximized use of existing urbanized lands while reducing use of nonurban lands, linking land use with transit planning, reducing auto trips and, thus, air pollution, and providing a diversity of housing types. Although the Land Use Element of the proposed General Plan indicated sites for TODs, it was not enforced. Planners knew that they could not force the proposal on the development community; rather, it was offered as an incentive program, whereby mixed uses and higher densities would be the benefits of adopting the program. The "TOD Design Guidelines"[32] were intended to clarify the program's goals and guide design, while giving developers flexibility in interpretation. They introduced the TOD concept, explained its intended purposes, and also spelled out criteria for qualification as a TOD: location adjacent to transit, minimum and maximum size, required and allowable land uses.

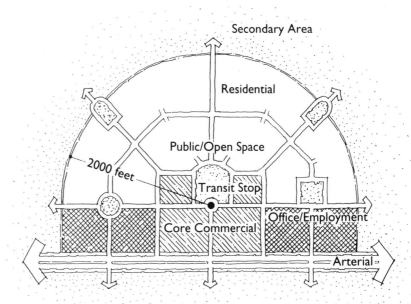

Diagram for the Transit Oriented Development.
From Calthorpe Associates, Mintier and Associates, "Transit Oriented Development Design Guidelines," Sacramento County Planning and Development Department, Sacramento, California, unpublished.

Unlike Radburn and most of Calthorpe's previous residential work, the TOD was not a superblock. Pedestrian and vehicular circulation were purposefully united, with streets becoming important parts of the linkage system between elements of open space. Pedestrian routes not visible from a street were discouraged, in a response to safety and security concerns of the general public, particularly heightened in California. Scholarship has confirmed that streets that are frequented and overlooked by residents are safer than those inhabited only by cars.[33] Calthorpe added to this proposition his own vision of a series of linked parks and civic spaces leading to a town center. In TODs, the streets became an integral part of the public open space network by being the primary intercommunity linkages, shared equally by pedestrians and cars.

Laguna West

Concurrent with the development of the TOD guidelines, Calthorpe Associates was involved with several private developers who were pursuing the Pedestrian Pocket concept. The design of Riverwest Developments' Laguna West so closely paralleled work on the guidelines, that its plan provided the basic diagrams for TODs. In 1989 developer Phil Angelides asked Calthorpe Associates to redesign the final phase of a 2,500-acre subdivision his firm was developing. He had become convinced that criticisms of suburban developments like the ones he had been building were justified, and was attracted to Calthorpe's Pedestrian Pocket concept.[34] Coined the first "Pedestrian Pocket," Laguna West was hailed by the local press, planners, and the building industry. Although the model was significantly different from Sacramento's typical low-density walled subdivisions, with streets "wide enough to land jets on,"[35] and although it failed to meet numerous county regulations, it moved rapidly from design to an approved plan reflecting the county government's general support for the concept.

The Laguna West plan was structured by its open space network. Symmetrical axes radially divided the site and provided the primary open space

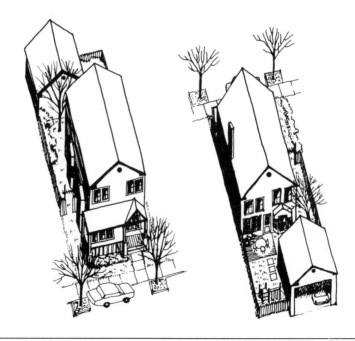

A house and yard at Laguna West.
Kate Van Rooy.

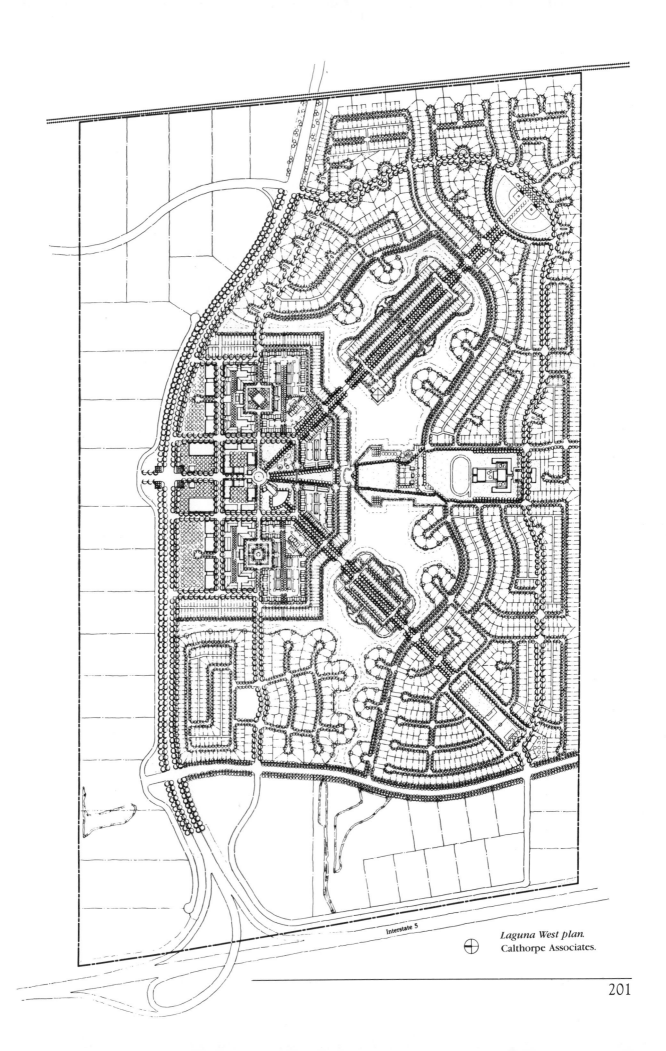

Interstate 5

⊕ *Laguna West plan.*
Calthorpe Associates.

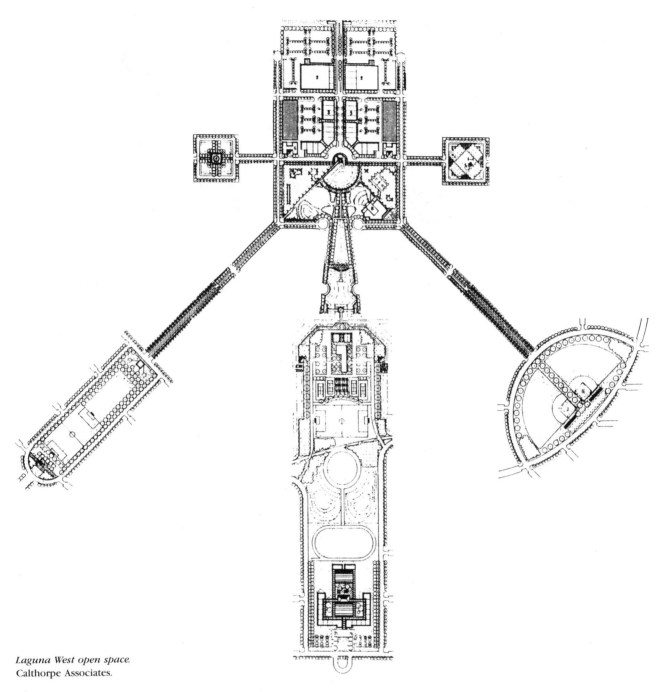

Laguna West open space.
Calthorpe Associates.

linkages. The central north-south axis, a linear park, formed the spine of the community. Beginning in the village green, which contained the town hall, community amphitheater, and day care center, it extended south to the community playing fields and recreation center and, at the southern extreme, to the elementary school. Diagonal boulevards, lined with double rows of trees and separated walking and biking paths, made connections from the town center to the outlying residential areas. Each began at the village green and terminated at a neighborhood park. Similarly, two minor streets led to parks within the town center. The heart of the community was the very point at which all these arms converged, an open plaza at the village green, where park and shopping converged.

The Village Green at Laguna West.
Calthorpe Associates.

Residential street, Laguna West.
Peter Keyes.

Consistent with the shift of attitude seen in the TOD Guidelines, Calthorpe here challenged the necessity of entirely separating vehicles and pedestrians. He adopted streets as the primary linear components of the public open space network, forming direct connections from home to park to town center. All streets were designed for both pedestrians and vehicles, with separated, shaded sidewalks, parallel parking, and parks periodically punctuating the routes. Houses with porches were placed within 12 feet of the street, and garages were tucked behind them. People were being enticed to leave the car in the garage and walk to town. It will be many years before the results of this experiment are known. The population of the community must rise dramatically before the town center will be built, and critics question whether residents will then be willing to modify their automobile-dependent lifestyle.[36]

Rather than mimicking the picturesque, as do most of the surrounding subdivisions, landscape imagery for Laguna West was derived from the ordered agricultural landscapes of California's central valley. Recalling the site's most recent past, a grided landscape of fields and shelter belts, the axial street layouts were punctuated by rows of sycamore and Lombardy poplar. To reflect the region's arid condition and to conserve water, landscape architect Ken Kay chose a palette of drought-tolerant plants such as black locust, live oak, hackberry, and olive for the major streets and public lands. In the landscape design guidelines, residents are encouraged to limit turf grass and choose drought-tolerant plants from the plant lists provided.[37]

The artificial lake was the final component of the public open space plan, providing scenic views and recreation in the form of nonmotorized boating. Its perimeter, roughly 50% public land, was circumnavigated by a

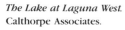

The Lake at Laguna West.
Calthorpe Associates.

continuous pedestrian and bike path. A marketing feature open to much criticism in these times of drought, the lake was defended by the developers and architects as consuming no more water than would the great expanses of turf required for a golf course.[38] This lake could have been a large gray water-recycling enterprise, receiving surface runoff from the site, partially cleansing those waters with aquatic plants to consume nutrient overloads and fountains to aerate the water, returning it to public lands and residents for irrigation. Instead, all of the water for this 72-acre lake is supplied from deep underground aquifers—the water source that has been so devastated by agricultural practices and urbanization in California's central valley—while surface drainage is carried off the site in underground sewers. Compounding this oversight was the lack of attention given to the wetland area, which also could have provided a unique opportunity for on-site water purification. Possibly a last minute deletion from lands zoned "highway commercial," the wetland was isolated and bounded by pavement: Interstate 5 to the west, commercial sites to the north and south, and a collector road to the east. Although an obvious opportunity functionally, aesthetically and educationally the wetland was ignored in the open space plan. By being so excluded, it will likely become a nuisance in the eyes of both developers and residents.

Also missing from this project were off-site connections for pedestrians and bicycles.[39] None were indicated to the north, and to the west Interstate 5 forms a barrier. The only crossing of the railway boundary along the east is Laguna Boulevard, which has sidewalks and designated bike lanes but will also become a heavily traveled arterial when the freeway connection at I-5 is complete. To the south two residential streets dead-end into the adjacent property, indicating the intention for future connections. All major open space linkages were terminated well within the property, discouraging their connection to adjacent properties and giving this development a walled character, derived from the continuous edge of backyard fences. This is a similar problem to the one DPZ had at Kentlands. Calthorpe has given careful attention to linking communities via transit; however, the potential for open space to provide a similar function has been neglected.

Gold Country Ranch

Laguna West exhibited some of the fundamental urban design principles of transit-oriented development, but overlooked issues of off-site pedestrian and bicycle connections, water quality, and the integration of a wetlands area. Calthorpe's more recent work addresses those weaknesses. In *The Next American Metropolis,*[40] he included principles of "Ecology and Habitat": hard-and-fast urban growth boundaries as in Oregon; protection and integration of natural areas in the community, including the protection of existing streams and wetlands; use of indigenous and drought-tolerant plants; and energy conservation in site and building design. Calthorpe proposed that a healthy future for the American metropolis lies in the "ecology of communities," in which principles of ecology guide growth. Diversity, interdependence, scale, and decentralization should be applied to both human and natural dimensions and all scales of community design. Gold Country Ranch, a proposed new town of 10,000 people in the Sierra foothills, was a project to which Calthorpe applied his Ecology-Habitat guidelines. Located on a 7,750-acre cattle ranch between the towns of Marysville and Grass

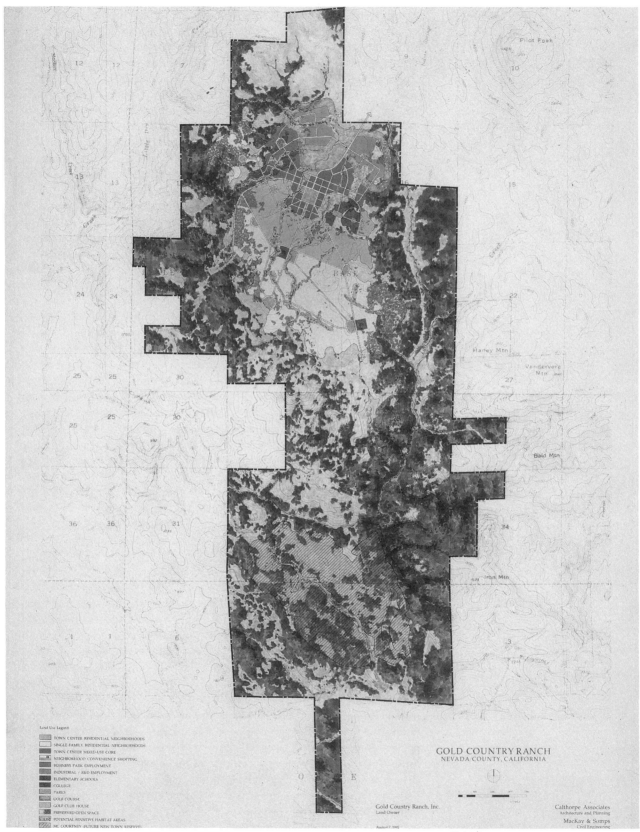

Land Use Legend

TOWN CENTER RESIDENTIAL NEIGHBORHOODS
SINGLE-FAMILY RESIDENTIAL NEIGHBORHOODS
TOWN CENTER MIXED-USE CORE
NEIGHBORHOOD CONVENIENCE SHOPPING
BUSINESS PARK EMPLOYMENT
INDUSTRIAL / R&D EMPLOYMENT
ELEMENTARY SCHOOLS
COLLEGE
PARKS
GOLF COURSE
GOLF CLUB HOUSE
PRESERVED OPEN SPACE
POTENTIAL SENSITIVE HABITAT AREAS
MC COURTNEY (FUTURE NEW TOWN RESERVE)

GOLD COUNTRY RANCH
NEVADA COUNTY, CALIFORNIA

Gold Country Ranch, Inc.
Land Owner

Calthorpe Associates
Architecture and Planning
MacKay & Somps
Civil Engineering

August 7, 1992

Gold Country Ranch plan.
Calthorpe Associates.

Valley, it was designed to replicate a small, independent town, similar to historical Nevada City, 10 miles away. The siting of Gold Country Ranch contradicted Calthorpe's guideline to develop within urban growth boundaries; however, supporting documentation[41] argued that the region grew at a rate of 4.8% from 1980 to 1991, and that construction of a new community would deter expansion of nearby historical towns. In this era of electronic networks, small new communities located well away from metropolitan areas on less productive lands may very well relieve expansion pressures on other populous areas. Calthorpe Associates reports that people relocate to Nevada County from all over the state. To prevent unplanned expansion of Gold Country Ranch itself, urban development would be restricted to the most level sites and surrounded by extensive greenbelts. Seventy-four percent of the site was retained as agriculture and forest, forming permanent greenbelts around the two town sites.

The character of the streets, houses, and shopping areas promises to be similar to that of Laguna West, but the setting varies dramatically. The proposal emphasizes preservation of wetlands, riparian corridors, and forested slopes, which include pedestrian, equestrian, and bicycle trails. The whole natural open space network will link parks, schools, shopping areas, and the community college to each other and, in the opposite direction, to the surrounding greenbelt. Although not providing a full explanation, the plan also mentions integrating detention ponds, secondary water treatment, and use of reclaimed water for both urban and agricultural irrigation. The preliminary draft plan was based on a 10-year-old environmental impact report, prepared for a previous development proposal, and environmental studies done by Harland Bartholomew and Associates for the county's General Plan update. These were supplemented by current aerial photographs; however, no environmental experts were consulted. As a result, the proposals for extensive natural area preservation remain very conceptual. Assuming a site-specific environmental analysis is completed to confirm the assumptions made, the intentions of both the ranchwide land use plan and the Spenceville Town Center Plan are commendable. The plan indicates a complex, yet coordinated, network of natural preserves, natural recreation corridors, and developed open space, both green and paved. Linked together, these offer unending possibilities for circulation, recreation, and environmental education.[42]

In his design guidelines, reminiscent of the FHA guidelines for subdivision design, Calthorpe has made recommendations for designing the transitions between natural and developed areas. In another transit-oriented development proposal, Dry Creek Ranch,[43] Calthorpe Associates recom-

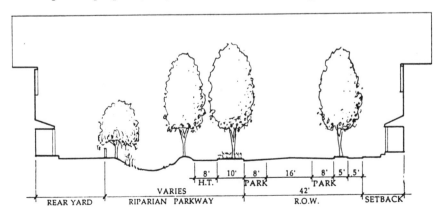

Street at riparian parkway.
From Calthorpe Associates, MacKay and Somps, "Design Guidelines for Dry Creek Ranch," 1991, unpublished report.

SPENCEVILLE TOWN CENTER
ILLUSTRATIVE PLAN

GOLD COUNTRY RANCH
NEVADA COUNTY, CALIFORNIA

November 2, 1992

Calthorpe Associates
Architecture and Planning

Spenceville town plan.
Calthorpe Associates.

mended locating connector and minor residential streets adjacent to open
space corridors to increase both visibility and public accessibility of such
natural commons. Cross-section drawings show a planting strip with street
trees adjacent to the road, followed by an eight-foot-wide walk, the riparian
corridor and a backyard fence making the other edge. Where the riparian
corridor aligned a major arterial street, it was much wider and had paths

adjacent to the road and the backyard fence. In this case paths can be of different grades or for different purposes, and they can create a clear line between the maintained landscape of yards and the untouched natural landscape. The plan for Gold Country Ranch also shows many streets adjacent to riparian corridors, and it is hoped that similar guidelines will be designed to assure resolution of these difficult edge conditions.

With his conceptual model, the Pedestrian Pocket, Peter Calthorpe developed an integrated transportation and land planning strategy for reconfiguring the suburban landscape. Central to this idea has been a key conception of the Radburn plan, that public open space should be the backbone of a community, and of the Garden cities concept, that networks of small cities should be linked by mass transit.

> We must return meaning and stature to the physical expression of our public life. From streets and parks to plazas, village squares, and commercial centers, the Commons defines the meeting ground of a neighborhood and its local identity. Rather than isolated and residual spaces, the Commons should be brought back to the center of our communities and re-integrated into our daily commercial life. Public spaces should provide the fundamental order of our communities and set the limits to our private domain. Our public buildings should be proudly located to add quality, identity, and focus to the fabric of our everyday world.[44]

Emphasizing the urgent need for higher-density suburbs, Calthorpe has also blended accepted principles of urban residential design with sophisticated open space strategies. He is convinced that with provision of services and employment, and high quality open space design, suburbanites will adapt to higher-density living. In addition, if walking is pleasant and convenient, and public transportation is efficient, he believes people will begin to reduce their dependency on cars.

RE-ENVISIONING THE SUBURBS

Metropolitan areas are facing structural, financial, and ecological crises that are, in part, attributable to expansive suburbanization. Their planners and managers are looking toward Traditional Neighborhoods and Pedestrian Pockets as carrots for developers who could contribute to larger efforts to reconfigure suburban areas. San Diego, Sacramento, and Portland have adopted growth management plans based on Calthorpe's transit-oriented developments. Neotraditional planning, a nationwide movement based on DPZ's urban design principles, has permeated the language and work of most urban planners. Innumerable examples of smaller redevelopment projects that are attempting to make neighborhood streets, commercial areas, even former shopping malls, look and feel like the streets of old Arlington, Virginia, and Georgetown, District of Columbia, are reported in architecture, landscape architecture, planning, and popular magazines.[45] These efforts are reactions to public recognition of the negative impacts of unplanned, incremental suburbanization. The ability to realize proposals like Peter Calthorpe's will be achieved only if metropolitan regions contribute to the necessary fabric. Regionwide land planning must be instituted and tied to transportation planning; natural resources planning must be tied to recreational planning; and engineered drainage systems must be reevaluated and tied to efforts to preserve and restore urban waterways.

With or without regionwide systems firmly in place, developers who are interested in seeing their industry contribute to environmental sustainability must forge ahead and pursue proposals such as Traditional Neighborhoods and Pedestrian Pockets, because they show at a local scale how to design more self-sufficient communities. The simple habit of walking, rather than always hopping into a car, will transform the life of the community. DPZ and Calthorpe have developed viable concepts that still need to mature and to be tested in the marketplace. Both DPZ's territorial plans and Calthorpe's networks of TODs are visions of how suburban areas might be ordered—they have given form to suburbs. Both accommodate natural systems as separated preserves, but neither reflects a full understanding of how to integrate natural systems as the lifeblood of any landscape, urbanized or not. This is the work of the next decade.

NOTES

1. 1991 U.S. Department of Transportation Study, source unknown.
2. Robert Fishman, *Bourgeois Utopias: The Rise and Fall of Suburbia* (New York: Basic Books, 1987), p. 190.
3. Oregon Land Conservation and Development Commission, *1991 Transportation Planning Rule for the Statewide Planning Goal 12* (Salem: Oregon Land Conservation and Development Commission, 1991).
4. Peter G. Rowe, *Making a Middle Landscape* (Cambridge, MA: MIT Press, 1991), p. 48.
5. Gurney Breckenfeld, "Downtown Has Fled to the Suburbs," *Fortune* **87,** (October 1972):80–87, 156–162.
6. Stephen Carr, Mark Francis, and Leanne Rivlin, *Public Space* (New York: Cambridge University Press, 1992), p. 67; and Peter Calthorpe, *The Next American Metropolis: Ecology, Community, and the American Dream* (New York: Princeton Architectural Press, 1993), p. 23.
7. *Time, Harper's, Fortune, Professional Builder, Progressive Architecture, Landscape Architecture, Places, UTNE Reader,* and *The Urban Ecologist,* to name only a few, ran articles about new suburban planning trends.
8. Alex Krieger and William Lennertz, eds., *Andres Duany and Elizabeth Plater-Zyberk: Towns and Town-Making Principles* (New York: Rizzoli, 1991).
9. Doug Kelbaugh, *The Pedestrian Pocket Book: A New Suburban Design Strategy* (New York: Princeton Architectural Press, 1989); and Peter Calthorpe, *The Next American Metropolis,* p. 44.
10. Daniel Solomon, *ReBuilding* (New York: Princeton Architectural Press, 1992), p. 26.
11. Raymond Unwin, *Town Planning in Practice* (New York: Princeton Architectural Press, 1909).
12. John Nolen, *New Towns for Old: Achievements in Civic Improvement in Some American Small Towns and Neighborhoods* (Boston: Marshall Jones Company, 1927).
13. Ibid., p. 14.
14. Ibid.; see also Robert Stern, *The Anglo-American Suburb* (London: Architectural Design, 1981).
15. Andres Duany and Elizabeth Plater-Zyberk, "The Second Coming of the American Small Town," *The Wilson Quarterly* **16** (Winter 1992), 19–51.
16. Andres Duany, "Traditional Towns," *Architectural Design* **59,** No. 9/10 (1989), p. 60–64.
17. Ellen Schoshkes, *The Design Process* (New York: Whitney Library of Design, 1989), p. 226–253.
18. Eve Kahn, "Model Community That Isn't," *The Wall Street Journal* (June 1, 1992), A10.
19. Advertisement in *The Washington Post* (May 30, 1992).
20. The DPZ-authored "Traditional Neighborhood Ordinance" published by the Foundation for Traditional Neighborhoods promotes a maximum five-minute walk to neighborhood stores.
21. This information was gained from an inverview with Mr. Mike Watkins in the DPZ office at Kentlands in June 1992.
22. From a telephone interview between Cynthia Girling and Ms. Plater-Zyberk in 1991.

23. Robert Cervero, *Suburban Gridlock* (New Brunswick, NJ.: Center for Urban Policy Research, 1986), Chapter 1.
24. Ibid., p. 29.
25. Ibid., p. 228.
26. Peter Calthorpe and Mark Mack, "The Pedestrian Pocket" (Unpublished paper 1987); and Kelbaugh, *The Pedestrian Pocket Book.*
27. Sim Van der Ryn and Peter Calthorpe, *Sustainable Communities* (San Francisco: Sierra Club Books, 1986), pp. 59–83.
28. Peter Calthorpe, "The Post-Suburban Environment," *Progressive Architecture* **3**, No. 91 (1991):84, 85.
29. Kelbaugh, *The Pedestrian Pocket Book,* p. 19.
30. Calthorpe Associates, with MacKay and Somps, *Transit-Oriented Development (TOD) Design Guidelines* (Unpublished. Sacramento, CA: Sacramento Planning and Development Department, July 1990), p. 1.
31. Sacramento County Planning and Development Department, *General Plan Revised Draft* (Unpublished. Sacramento, CA: Sacramento County Planning and Development Department, December, 1992).
32. Calthorpe Associates, *TOD Design Guidelines.*
33. Jane Jacobs, *Death and Life of Great American Cities* (New York: Random House, 1961), and Mark Francis, "The Making of Democratic Streets," in Anne Vernez Moudon ed., *Public Streets for Public Use* (New York: Columbia University Press, 1987), p. 31.
34. Gary Delsohn, "The First Pedestrian Pocket," *Planning* **55,** No. 12 (December 1989):20–22.
35. Ibid.
36. Michael Leccese, "Next Stop: Transit-Friendly Towns," *Landscape Architecture* **80,** No. 7 (July 1990):47–53.
37. Ken Kay and Associates, *Laguna West Landscape Design Guidelines,* (Unpublished. 1991).
38. From one of many discussions that Cynthia Girling had with Peter Calthorpe between 1991 and 1993. Also see Cynthia Girling, "The Pedestrian Pocket: Reorienting Radburn," *Landscape Journal* **12,** No. 1 (Spring 1993):40–50.
39. Girling, "The Pedestrian Pocket: Reorienting Radburn."
40. Peter Calthorpe, *The Next American Metropolis,* p. 72.
41. Calthorpe Associates, "Gold Country Ranch, a Mixed-Use, Pedestrian-Oriented Small Town in Nevada County," (Unpublished. For Gold Country Ranch, Inc., December 29, 1992); and Calthorpe, *The Next American Metropolis,* p. 160.
42. The Gold Country Ranch proposal includes a Boy Scout camp and associated interpretive trails.
43. Calthorpe Associates, with MacKay and Somps, "Dry Creek Ranch Project Book" (Unpublished. 1991).
44. Calthorpe, *The Next American Metropolis,* p. 23.
45. Daralice Boles, "Reordering the Suburbs," *Progressive Architecture* **70**, No. 5 (May, 1989):78–91; Lloyd Bookout "Neotraditional Town Planning, Cars, Pedestrians, and Transit," *Urban Land* **51,** No. 2 (February 1992) pp. 10–15; Andres Duany and Elizabeth Plater-Zyberk "The Second Coming of the American Small Town"; Jane Holtz Kay, "The Green vs. the Grid," *Landscape Architecture* **79**, No. 8 (October 1989):74–79; Philip Langdon, "Beyond the Cul-de-Sac," *Landscape Architecture* **79,** No. 8 (October 1989):72, 73; Vernon Mays, "Neighborhoods by Design," *Progressive Architecture* **73,** No. 6 (June 1992):92–102; and Robert Gerloff, "Rediscovering the Village," *UNTE Reader* **51,** (May/June, 1992), pp. 93–96.

8
SUBURBIA 2000

In seeking to create a landscape of greater opportunity, it is important to examine suburban successes and to explore where new directions might take us. Models from the past century provide ample precedent for understanding the fundamental role of open space in the context of suburban community design. They offer clues both to how so much recent development went wrong, and to how these flaws can be corrected. Traditional definitions of designed open space emphasized the role of the public park and park systems. These now need to be supplemented by the inclusion of all aspects of the public and private landscape, including streets, sidewalks, yards, driveways, vacant and natural lands. Open space structures the physical form and pattern of communities. It is a central component in understanding and conceiving the suburban landscape, in maintaining a healthy environment, and in structuring the pattern and pace of suburban life at all levels. Increasingly, open space is the subject of landscape reclamation and discovery.

Suburban development has typically occurred on a parcel-by-parcel basis, with little comprehensive planning. Open space considerations have tended to be either internal to a particular development (playgrounds, commons, or park) or at a regional scale (county park or preserve.) As suburban areas mature, critical linkages between home, park, local services, and natural areas are found to be missing. Now is an opportune time to look again at open space, that which was consciously created, carelessly left over, or thoughtlessly omitted. Most suburbs were created with a disproportionate emphasis on the individualistic private home. At the time, developers and policymakers failed to realize that the design, distribution, and pattern of land uses were also powerful determinants to creating desirable communities. Although new development will continue unabated, validating the search for new suburban models, it is equally important to devise strategies for retrofitting the immense investment we have already made in the suburbs. As the outer cities take on a life of their own, they are ripe for reconsideration.

RETROFITTING SUBURBS: BELLEVUE, WASHINGTON

Bellevue, Washington, is a community that is reclaiming its natural systems through the coordinated design of an entire open space system and its pivotal surface drainage program. Prior to World War II, Bellevue was a small settlement in a hilly, forested landscape across Lake Washington from Seattle. When it was incorporated in 1953, it was rapidly becoming a community of low-density subdivisions. By the early 1980s, Bellevue was a sprawling suburban community much like the incremental suburbs described in Chapter 4. Bellevue, "City of the Future,"[1] was dominated by cars, with expansive ranch-style homes on quarter-acre lots along broad, curving streets that led to Safeway, K Mart, and the Bellevue Mall, all amid seas of parking "downtown." In the mid-1970s, Bellevue again began to experience increased development pressure. The population grew 400% from 1960 to 1970, owing in large part to the annexation of adjacent developing areas. Concurrent outward expansion required the city to expand its roads, sewers, and utilities. The city government reevaluated its subsurface drainage system and made a decision to change from an underground piped system to a less expensive surface drainage system—at that time probably envisioned as a system of ditches and channels.

Conventional methods of removing surface water and controlling floodwaters in urban areas involve vast networks of underground sewers, which feed into channelized streams or rivers and, eventually, into natural waterways. These systems are very expensive. The cost of building and maintaining them is financially crippling many city governments and, despite the expenditures, under extreme flood conditions they often fail. They also contribute to water pollution, carrying pollutants such as oil and other fluids from vehicles, innumerable toxic chemicals used in daily urban life, pesticides, herbicides, and fertilizers to the natural streams and rivers into which they empty. Cleanup efforts in the 1970s and 1980s forced industrial polluters to drastically reduce point source pollution, but many urban areas were left with only modest improvements. By the late 1980s it was evident that every urban dweller and every vehicle contributed significantly to water pollution—that "nonpoint source" contamination was also a major factor in urban water pollution. It became evident that water would have to be cleaner before it reached the sewers, or it would have to be cleaned between the sewer outfalls and the rivers, lakes, or oceans into which it was being dumped. The city of Eugene, Oregon, stepped up street-cleaning efforts and immediately saw results. The city then began a public education campaign to notify people that everyone contributed to the pollution of the beloved Willamette River when they used fertilizers and pesticides, or poured chemicals and toxic materials into the storm sewers. Fish symbols were stenciled next to catch basins as reminders.

Environmental crises and the Clean Water Act of 1987 are forcing engineers to look at alternative methods for removing storm waters from urban areas. Floodplains are being protected in order to serve their natural purpose of retaining floodwaters, and wetlands are being returned to their natural water purification role. For storm-water management, The Woodlands, Texas, has proved that only modest interventions to natural drainage systems are needed to prevent excessive flooding.[2] Bellevue had the political and physical structure in place to develop such a system by the mid-1970s, but it took citizen involvement to secure the city's commitment to creating a natural water management and open space system. In 1976 a regional shopping mall was proposed at the fringes of the city of Bellevue. There was tremendous opposition, both from the downtown merchants and from local residents. Litigation by the city stopped the development, but in the process of fighting the mall, Bellevue had taken a hard look at itself. The citizens made some decisive and—for the mid-1970s—rather radical policy changes.[3] They decided to focus commercial development in the downtown area, to intensify the center, and to discourage dispersed commercial and office development. Active citizens urged the city to write environmental policies promoting the protection of land and water resources within the city. Combined with the earlier decision to revert to a surface storm drainage system, this effort led to new planning strategies and extensive waterway and wetland acquisition. The city's goals included meeting federal clean water standards by 1990, upgrading fisheries, maintaining a natural stormwater system capable of handling a 100-year flood, acquiring and rehabilitating wetlands (especially Mercer Slough between the city and Lake Washington), preserving habitat for upland species, and increasing the use of native plants citywide. In effect, the citizens were making their suburb more urban, while simultaneously bringing nature to the fore.

The two city agencies most directly influenced by these policies were the Storm and Surface Water Utility and the Parks and Recreation Department. Essentially, these two agencies work with the same land and resources, but they utilize them in different ways. The Storm and Surface Water Utility administers the 10 drainage basins in Bellevue. Because this agency has primary responsibility for water resources and a budget for land acquisition, it holds extensive natural or seminatural lands along waterways.[4] Much of the same land has at least some educational or recreational value, and this is where the Parks Department comes into play. Its mandate is "to develop a *system* of open spaces."[5] Included in this system are everything from downtown parks and plazas to recreational parks, playfields and playgrounds, interpretive areas with trails, and, finally, sensitive natural areas with limited human access. Many of the trails and interpretive areas are, in fact, elements of the storm-water system—the storm-water component managed by that utility, and the recreational or educational component managed by the Parks Department. Conceptually, open space in Bellevue is understood to be a continuum, from the refined design of Downtown Park to the sensitive sanctuary of Mercer Slough. The objective is to have the continuum connected physically as well, integrating recreation, education, and alternative transportation.

A typical residential street, Bellevue, Washington.
C. Girling.

A small wetland behind housing, Bellevue, Washington.
C. Girling.

Bellevue still looks like a typical suburban community. The downtown redevelopment has just begun, with a few very "urban" projects in a sea of strip malls and asphalt. Medium-density housing is appearing around the fringes of downtown, but much of the community is single-family homes on large fenced lots. It all looks very commonplace, until you notice the natural streams running along the edges of roadways and hidden behind housing developments, or you discover Lake Hills Greenbelt Park, a lowland flood zone that contains no buildings but, in their place, open agricultural fields crossed by bike paths that emerge from the adjacent forest. Elsewhere you see a boardwalk constructed along the edge of a roadway to provide passage while preserving a small wetland area. Bellevue is a city in transition, a city creating a future for itself as it evolves from a domestic suburb to an outer city—a little sister to Seattle. The work being done to preserve, restore, and concurrently use the natural resources within the urbanized area has made Bellevue a nationally recognized leader in suburban planning and storm-water management. It is successfully reenvisioning itself from the 1950s "City of the Future" to the current "City in a Park"—and may soon become the "City in Nature."

THE FUTURE OF YARD, STREET, AND PARK

Community development is an ongoing process. The early suburbs discussed previously, such as Riverside and Radburn, are still people's homes,

RUNOFF CHANNEL

LOCAL STREET

The Cottonwood Neighborhood, a proposal by Lyle Grant.

but they are not the same as when they were built. They have changed and matured with the times. Many have embraced values from the last few decades and added active recreation to the once pastoral landscape. Riverside residents are well aware of their community's historical status and have a general respect for Olmsted's plan, yet they are struggling with how to include modern recreational needs, such as tennis and basketball courts. Suburban communities now under construction will also evolve. The hope is that through thoughtful planning, their changes will be carefully guided, so that their maturity brings improvement. The task of the community planner is not to design a static product, but to set the framework for a process of change that improves the quality of a place with age. To construct such a framework, it is important to imagine the possibilities. What else might the suburban yard be? How might we reconceive of the street? What might the parks and open spaces of a community become?

Yard

Few landscapes inspire such passions as the American lawn. We love the spacious verdure, but hate the watering, mowing, and fertilizing needed to maintain its beauty. We love the democracy of the open streetscape, but being increasingly security conscious, we wall off the neighborhood instead. Despite increasing evidence that lawns have harmful environmental consequences, we give them up with great reluctance. Richard Wolkomir, in a *Smithsonian* article, has called American's "lawnoholics."[6] In order to create and maintain the ideal lawn at its desired color, texture, and height we have brought the full weight of modern science to the task. Chemicals encourage or inhibit growth, water is redistributed and polluted, terrain is denuded, and machines mow incessantly. Contemporary lawn culture has reached its peak with this "industrial lawn," made possible by a multibillion-dollar industry.[7] In due course there have been adverse effects on environmental quality. Lawns have displaced local ecosystems nationwide with green, but static, chemical-dependent carpets. They can even begin to sound venomous when we learn that grass clippings account for three-quarters of all yard waste and the second largest source of solid waste in the nation!

One rational alternative, a counterpoint to the industrial lawn, is the "freedom lawn." The authors of *Redesigning the American Lawn: A Search for Environmental Harmony* exhort us to adopt "an ecological approach to designing and caring for our lawn, preserving some of the lawn's cherished values while diminishing some of its contributions to local, regional and global environmental crises."[8] This does not mean abandoning the lawn, only limiting its dimensions, altering its constituent elements, and modifying its maintenance. The freedom lawn has a diversity of plants, eschews the chemical fix, and is selectively mown (preferably by hand). As much as possible it is site specific, yet still adheres to lawn conventions. It is both traditional and innovative. The name is catchy and clever, having a patriotic ring and an open-ended set of allusions. The freedom lawn implies a liberation from labor and community restraint; it conjures up a return to individualism and a shift away from provincial conformity. Desert suburbs provide examples. In these locales, drought has caused people to abandon the green during dry summer months in favor of the more natural grassland gold. Others are exploring more radical alternatives. Artfully arranged rocks, gravel, and cacti are becoming more common. The xeriscape movement that

A front yard in Palm Springs, California.
Kenneth Helphand.

promotes choosing appropriate plantings to minimize water use is gaining supporters. Community pressure to conform to yard norms is lessening, and there are more individuals subverting the convention of the lawn. As these small fragments, the yards that create the mosaic we call the suburban landscape, are altered, the additive picture will be different.

Yards have great promise. Neighborhood walks in Eugene, Oregon, reveal a grass roots movement toward reimagining the possibilities of the yard. Lawns are being converted to vegetable gardens or planted with native materials, ranging from wildflower meadows to cactus deserts. Some become personal and idiosyncratic displays. As front yards change, a new streetscape emerges, one that is more villagelike and projects a sense of individualized craft. On the other hand, in new subdivisions it is business as usual. Although the tiny, green yard attracts attention, it is important to note that it is now competes with the garage and driveway for space and identity, as the stability of family and home competes with mobility. In their promotion of alternative suburban design, DPZ and Calthorpe use small, modest yards in their projects. Their illustrations show front yards as gardens that fill the narrow space between the house and sidewalk. The back is composed of a small patio for outdoor eating or reading and a patch of lawn for play. At Calthorpe's Laguna West, residents were discouraged from planting large lawns and encouraged to utilize native drought-tolerant plants.[9] In older communities, there is talk among municipal officials[10] of removing requirements to pipe roof drains to storm sewers by encouraging permeable

An alternative street planting in Eugene, Oregon.
C. Girling.

*A creek reclamation and "greenstreet"
proposal by Jeanine Strickland.*

surfaces over dry wells to retain rainwater, and landscape filters on planting strips to remove impurities before they reach the street. In the near future lawns and gardens may be allowed to absorb roof and driveway runoff and contribute to aquifer recharge, rather than storm runoff.

Street

Suburban streets are also ripe for reclamation. They offer vast areas of public space with innumerable other prospects in addition to moving traffic and storing cars. For example, Donald Appleyard has offered "A Charter of Street Dwellers Rights," which does not exclude vehicles, but seeks to achieve a balance, regarding the street as an organic entity with a multitude of functions and possibilities. Each street can be an extension of home as refuge *and* a rich social environment. The street, he wrote, should be a safe sanctuary; a livable, healthy environment; a place for play and learning; a neighborly territory; a community; a green and pleasant land; and a unique and historical place.[11] Street reclamation can capture portions of territory from automotive dominance and offer new configurations of activity and experience. With limited or no mass transportation and a settlement pattern of dispersed activities, those who do not drive, children especially, are currently disenfranchised in the suburban landscape. As Anne Vernez-Moudon has stated, suburbs have been designed not with places to walk *to*, but places to walk *in*, the shopping mall being the preeminent example.[12] Seeking companionship, social stimulation, and a provoking environment, it is no surprise that suburban teens make the mall their predominant hangout. Suburban streets are subject to national traffic standards that treat pedestrians as impediments to the free flow of cars. How can this attitude be inverted? Richard Untermann, for one, has examined these standards and proposes their revision to include sidewalks on all streets, the reinstatement of planting strips, and diminished speeds, rather than perpetuating the

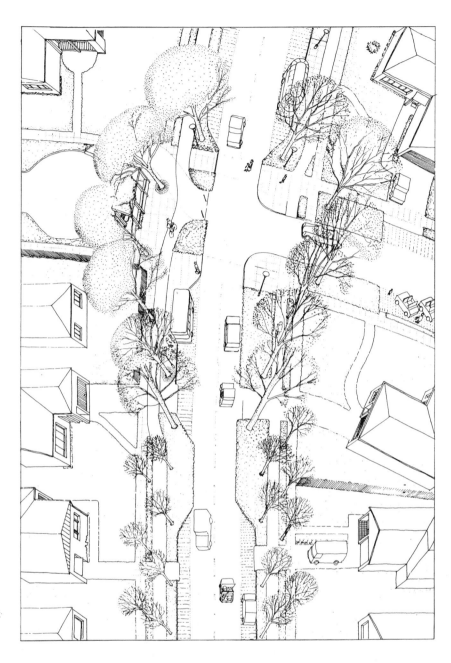

A 1950 suburban street re-designed.
From Peter Bosselmann, "Redesigning
Residential Streets," Anne Vernez Moudon,
ed., *Public Streets for Public Use,* New York
Columbia University Press, 1987, p. 329.
Reprinted with permission of the publisher.

wider, smoother, and straighter standard of traffic engineers that prevents
easy public, pedestrian use. He states that "roads within master-planned
communities are still too wide. There is no need to waste so much land on
pavement. Narrow roads function quite effectively and slow traffic down in
residential areas."[13] Denser land use patterns coupled with mixed uses
reduce travel distance and further encourage pedestrians. At the site-
specific level the walking environment itself needs to be a rich landscape
experience. Peter Bosselman's redesigned residential street offers one vision
of street reclamation with a narrowed street, abrupt turns, and the use of
trees as gateways and chokers and to define segments of the street.[14] Most
important, his vision includes a return of eclectic human activity to the
street.

Cul-de-sac streets and their appendages, driveways, offer vast protected areas of possibility. The driveway, the smallest increment in the suburban street network, links each residential lot to the cul-de-sac, creating a distinct suburban street variant.[15] The typical driveway runs perpendicular from the street, one per house. In contemporary subdivisions, these have grown to be three vehicles wide, dwarfing the lawn and yielding a net effect of door-to-door concrete. Other possibilities exist, such as driveways shared between two houses. California architects Dan Solomon and Peter Calthorpe have both used green driveways, narrow runners of concrete within a lawn. At the very least these vast paved surfaces can become decorated carpets at the foyer of the yard, as depicted in frequent advertisements for concrete pavers in *Landscape Architecture*. In many communities, streets as well as subdivisions are cul-de-saced. They are dead-ended and internally oriented, most often with connections made only at one end, to the collector street. With a minimum of effort and area, pedestrian linkages can be made through the cul-de-sac's bulbous terminus. Connections such as this occur at Columbia, Maryland, but this community is a rare exception. Culs-de-sac can be mini-streets serving many homes or part of another hybrid such as the *woonerf*, a Dutch concept that combines pedestrian and vehicular spaces to create a hybrid yard space.[16] Here the boundaries between driveway, street, play space, storage, and work area are softened. Within a *woonerf* automobiles defer to pedestrians, and the entire area—its spatial organization, plantings, materials, and services—favor the pedestrian. Many suburban streets are already halfway to being a *woonerf*, having the necessary low traffic flows to begin with. (In Holland the rate was 100 to 300 vehicles per hour.) Perhaps we can cultivate multipurpose street designs, such as *woonerf*, that experiment with the ambiguities of ownership, territorially, and function already suggested by the yardscape of the cul-de-sac.

A wooonerf in Breda, the Netherlands. Kenneth Helphand.

An alternative open space: stormwater filtration through the common space at Ecolonia, the Netherlands.
Ron Kellett.

At a grander scale, boulevards and parkways have great potential to integrate recreational and open space functions; unfortunately, however, most are image without substance, offering nothing more than "entry statements" and a ceremonial greening of the street. In every edge city there are thousands of acres of right-of-way planted with grass and trees, mowed, watered, and fertilized until they look as sterile as they are. Where such rights-of-way are restored to a natural state, as at The Woodlands, they provide migration routes for creatures other than the esteemed automobile. Where the cul-de-sac offers an opportunity for a suburban *woonerf*, arterials and collectors can become corridors of forest or meadow for cars, people, and wildlife.

Park

There are lessons in park history. Promoters of traditional neighborhoods insist that the centrally located square, common, or park—the site for civic buildings and landmarks in a community—must be reinstated in the suburbs. Without such spaces, they say, it is virtually impossible to have any communal life. New communities may very well benefit from an accessible, orderly arrangement of public spaces; however, the contemporary suburb presents other possibilities that demand imaginative responses. Suburbs have nascent gathering places in unconventional locations: in super market checkout lines, on fast-food drive-in strips, at school doorways, at video stores, in parking lots, and at shopping malls. These must be looked to for the potential they offer as open spaces. Such nontraditional places may offer the most promise for places of socialization. Why not "mall-parks" to replace those vast unused sectors of parking lots? The interiors have already assumed many traditional Main Street and downtown public square functions, albeit in a privatized form. But what of making parks in areas that are potential places of congregation, within the vast parking reserves surrounding shopping centers of all scales? Commerce and open space are not antithetical, as successful urban public spaces have demonstrated. However, it would be foolish to simply lift urban models and relocate them in the suburbs. There are aspects of suburban open space that differ from the urban experience.

The idea of the park itself is undergoing redefinition. Theme parks and malls, currently part of the suburban vocabulary, are pervasive contemporary metaphors.[17] These models reconsider the verities of the urban park as a respite from nature. Parks are thought of as part of the urban continuum, as places for play, as great "buildings," or, by the cynical, as hopelessly nostalgic romantic relics. The fundamental definitions and meanings of "nature" have been called into question. This ideological quest has a design counterpart. A new environmental aesthetic is emerging, one that looks to processes as well as places, to habitat and not just viewpoints, and beyond single functions to complexities.[18] Ultimately, this aesthetic, which will help shape the look of the land, is a revised view of human-nature relationships. As ideas and forms change, so too will the suburb. Such change may signal a return to original visions of being closer to nature, albeit a more complex nature of process. On the urban side, there will be an intensification and diversification of the community of people. Both meanings of suburban open space will be present, a stronger sense of community and a feeling that nature is close at hand. Symbolic expressions are significant: just as town squares express community values, so too do undisturbed woodlots.

Reconceived open space patterns are an aspect of landscape reclamation, the rediscovery of places ignored, devalued, or abused, of seeing the potential in a landfill, alley, ditch, or wetland. These can be pragmatic parks, serving a purpose as part of the community infrastructure and offering recreational and out-of-doors experience. Often, additional land acquisitions are less crucial than a shift of vision and attention, for vast areas of land are already in public or single ownership. (A major exception is the need for additional lands to provide access or linkages in a systemic network.) Retrofitted to a community, underutilized and derelict land presents a possibility to create structure where little existed. Utility corridors and industrial reserves offer the most immediate gains, but in every community sewer easements, ditches, and platted but unbuilt roads, to name a few examples, are awaiting a new role in the open space continuum. With the implementation of urban growth boundaries, all cities can have greenbelts, certainly a more desired prospect than the current beltways for automobiles. Perhaps it is time for automobile beltways to be inspired by the earlier parkway ideal of green automobile corridors that served as roads for transportation, but also as recreational routes and linkages between larger components of a park system. At the more prosaic local level, the connection may be as simple as linking adjacent culs-de-sac. Charles Little has said, "The impulse behind the greenway networks is to *integrate* land uses rather than separate them—to *join* the urban and the rural into a kind of normative American countryside."[19] The greenway movement, and it has become that, is essentially suburban in its sensibility.

Storm water filtration system through a residential open space. A proposal by John Schmidt.

In the maturing suburban circumstance, part of the challenge is how to maintain that sense of being at the edge, able to partake of both city and nature. The role here for the suburban park is key. On the one hand, it might be a town square or a community or neighborhood park with all the recreational facilities people need. On the other hand, as part of a network it can provide linkage to natural patches and corridors, to nature close to home, rather than an hour's drive away. The basic boundaries of the metropolis are changing, and in the process new transportation systems will be constructed, densities will intensify, new land use relationships will be formed.

The overlap of function and the hybridization of spaces may be a characteristic of suburban places. A distinctive contribution of the suburbs has been the creation of new combinations. Thus, inside homes and schools there are multipurpose rooms, recreation rooms, family rooms, or "great" rooms. These are more than merely kitchens with television sets, but spaces that combine traditional uses and new technologies and habits. The characteristics are not new, but the particular constellation of physical artifacts and uses is distinctively suburban. Outside, driveways are used as patios, backyards as playgrounds, streets as squares, and parks as refuges. Streets are more than thoroughfares; with imagination, they can become public gardens, linear parks, or urban forests. Similarly, storm sewers need not be pipes underground. They can be swales, streams, and wetlands, all of which will bring the suburbs closer to the best of both worlds.

The future of the suburbs lies in both community action and individual initiative. It is imperative to recognize, and work with, the individualistic component in American values and ideology. The suburbs, as an expression of this ideology, offer some helpful signs, each modest, but collectively powerful, especially if they are encouraged and not thwarted by unnecessary regulation. With a few modest changes to taste and regulation, yards can contribute to urban health, for they are permeable biomass. Similarly, by giving up a few car trips per week and a few minutes worth of speed, we can reduce the predominance of cars on streets and increase their contribution to the variety of public open space. Concurrently, streets can become alternate transportation routes—for feet. Acres and acres of parks and greenways need only modest changes in management practices or, in some cases, modest regrading and planting to contribute wildlife habitat and water recharge and cleansing. As lawns become meadows, wildlife returns and a whole new wonderful world is accessible to suburban children and their elders. Suburbs no longer need to be the middle ground between city and country. They are their own kind of nature—a nature equally part of the city and the wilds.

NOTES

1. Descriptive phrase coined by the city government.
2. Anne Spirn, *The Granite Garden: Urban Nature and Human Design* (New York: Basic Books, 1984), p. 66.
3. City of Bellevue, Washington, *Comprehensive Plan* (1974).
4. City of Bellevue, Washington, Storm Water and Drainage Utility, *Comprehensive Drainage Plan* (1988).
5. City of Bellevue, Washington, Parks and Recreation Department, *Parks, Recreation and Open Space Plan* (1987).

6. Richard Wolkomir, "Mownomaniacs Take the Sword to the Sward," *Smithsonian* **21**, No. 2 (May 1990):166.

7. Herbert Bormann, Diana Balmori, and Gordon Geballe, *Redesigning the American Lawn: A Search for Environmental Harmony* (New Haven, CT: Yale University Press, 1993), pp. 60–63.

8. Ibid, p. 55.

9. Ken Kay and Associates, *Laguna West Landscape Design Guidelines* (1991).

10. City of Eugene, Oregon, Department of Public Works, *Comprehensive Stormwater Management Plan* (1992).

11. Donald Applyard, *Livable Streets* (Berkeley: University of California Press, 1981), p. 150.

12. Anne Vernez-Moudon, ed., *Public Streets for Public Use* (New York: Columbia University Press, 1987), p. 2.

13. Richard K. Untermann, "Can We Pedestrianize the Suburbs?" in Anne Vernez-Moudon, ed., *Public Streets for Public Use*, p. 4.

14. Peter Bosselman, "Redesigning Residential Streets," in Anne Vernez-Moudon, ed., *Public Streets for Public Use*, pp. 321ff.

15. Richard MacCormac "Suburban Syntax," *Architectural Review* **178**, No. 10 (October 1985):53, 54.

16. Royal Dutch Touring Club, *Woonerf* (ANWB: The Hague, 1980); and Donald Appleyard, *Livable Streets*, p. 249.

17. Michael Sorkin, *Variations on a Theme Park* (New York: Hill and Wang, 1992).

18. Anne Spirn, "The Poetics of City and Nature: Towards a New Aesthetic for Urban Design," *Landscape Journal* **7**, No. 2 (Fall 1988): 108–126; Laurie Olin, "Form, Meaning and Expression in Landscape Architecture," *Landscape Journal* **7**, No. 2 (Fall 1988):149–168; and Catherine Howett, "Systems, Signs, Sensibilities: Sources for a New Landscape Aesthetic," *Landscape Journal* **6**, No. 1 (Spring 1987):1–12.

19. Charles Little, *Greenways for America* (Baltimore: Johns Hopkins University Press, 1990), p. 134.

REFERENCES

"A Complete House for $6,990." *Architectural Forum* **86**, No. 5 (May 1947):70–73.

Abbot, Carl. *Portland Planning, Politics and Growth in a Twentieth-Century City.* Lincoln, NE: University of Nebraska Press, 1983.

Abrams, Janet. "La Forma Della Citta: Due Progetti di Andres Duany & Elizabeth Plater-Zyberk" (The Form of the [American] City). *Lotus International* **50** (1986):6–35.

"After 25 Years Experimenting, Bill Leavitt Bets on Two Bargains in Quality for 1955 . . . and the Levitt's Jubilee House Reconsiders the Answers to Eight Important Questions." *House and Home* **6**, No. 5 (November 1954):136–139.

Alanen, Arnold, and Joseph A. Eden. *Main Street Ready-Made: The New Deal Community of Greendale, Wisconsin.* Madison: The State Historical Society of Wisconsin, 1987.

Alexander, Christopher, Sara Ishikawa, and Murray Silverstein. *A Pattern Language: Towns, Buildings, Construction.* New York: Oxford University Press, 1977.

"ALSA Merit Awards." *Landscape Architecture* **72**, No. 5 (September/October 1992): 99.

Appleyard, Donald. *Livable Streets.* Berkeley: University of California Press, 1981.

Archer, John. "City and Country in the American Romantic Suburb." *Journal of the Society of Architectural Historians* **42**, No. 2 (May 1983):139–156.

Babcock, Richard F. *Legal Aspects of Planned Unit Residential Developments, with Suggested Legislation Part II: Suggested Legislation and Commentary Technical Bulletin No. 52.* Washington, DC: Urban Land Institute, May 1965.

Babcock, Richard F., and Fred P. Bosselman. *Exclusionary Zoning: Land Use Regulation and Housing in the 70s.* New York: Praeger, 1973.

Bailey, James. *New Towns in America: The Design and Development Process.* New York: John Wiley & Sons, 1973.

Bair, Frederick H. *The Open Space Net Report No. 230.* Chicago: American Society of Planning Officials, January 1968.

Baldassare, Marc. *Trouble in Paradise: The Suburban Transformation in America.* New York: Columbia University Press, 1986.

Beaverton [Oregon] City Planning Commission. *Preliminary Development Plan for Beaverton*, n.d.

Bernstein, Leonard. *Trouble in Tahiti.* New York: G. Schirmer, Inc., 1953.

"Biggest Homebuilders of 1954." *House and Home* **7**, No. 1 (January 1955):40.

"Biggest New City in the US." *House and Home* **2**, No. 6 (December 1952):80–91.

"Bill Levitt's Third Big Town." *House and Home* **14**, No. 2 (August 1958):72–85.

Billing, John C. "Terrorism and the Secure Landscape." *Landscape Architecture* **76**, No. 4 (July/August 1986): 58–63.

Birch, Eugenie Ladner. "Radburn and the American Planning Movement: The Persistence of an Idea." *APA Journal* **46**, No. 4 (October, 1980):424–439.

Boles, Daralice. "Reordering the Suburbs." *Progressive Architecture* **70**, No. 5 (May 1989):78–91.

Bookout, Lloyd. "Neotraditional Town Planning: Cars, Pedestrians, and Transit." *Urban Land* **51**, No. 2 (February 1992):10–15.

Boorstin, Daniel. *The Americans: The Democratic Experience.* New York: Random House, 1973.

Bormann, F. Herbert, Diana Balmori, and Gordon T. Geballe. *Redesigning the American Lawn: A Search for Environmental Harmony.* New Haven, CT: Yale University Press, 1993.

Bosselman, Peter. "Redesigning Residential Streets." In *Public Streets for Public Use,* edited by Anne Vernez-Moudon. New York: Columbia University Press, 1991.

———. "Redesigning American Residential Streets." *Built Environment* **12**, Nos. 1/2 (1986):98–106.

Breckenfeld, Gurney. "Downtown Has Fled to the Suburbs." *Fortune* **87** (October 1972):80–87.

———. *Columbia and the New Cities.* New York: Ives Washburn, Inc., 1971.

Brooks, Richard Oliver. *New Towns and Communal Values: A Case Study of Columbia, Maryland.* New York: Praeger Publishers, 1974.

———. "Interpretation: Social Planning in Columbia." *American Institute of Planners Journal* **37**, No. 11 (November 1971):373–379.

Brown, Denise Scott. "Wright in the Rear-View Mirror." *The New York Times* (12 September 1993):sec. 2, p. 56.

Brown, Patricia Leigh. "A House for a Life That Used to Be." *The New York Times* (3 September 1992): B4.

Brownell, Baker, and Frank Lloyd Wright. *Architecture and Modern Life.* New York: Harper & Brothers, 1938.

"The Builder's House 1949." *Architectural Forum* **90**, No. 4 (April 1949):81–101.

Burby, Raymond, and Shirley F. Weiss. *New Communities U.S.A.* Lexington, MA: Lexington Books, 1976.

Burchell, Robert, and James W. Hughes. *Planned Unit Development: New Communities American Style.* New Brunswick, NJ: Center for Urban Policy Research, Rutgers University, 1972.

Cairns, Malcolm and Gary Kessler. "Protecting a Prototype: Guidelines for Riverside, Illinois." *Landscape Architecture* **77**, No. 4 (July/August 1987):62–65.

Calthorpe Associates. *Gold Country Ranch, a Mixed-Use, Pedestrian-Oriented Small Town in Nevada County.* 29 December 1992. Unpublished.

Calthorpe Associates, McKay and Somps. *Dry Creek Ranch Project Book.* 1991. Unpublished.

———. *Transit Oriented Development (TOD) Design Guidelines.* Sacramento [California] Planning and Development Department, July 1990. Unpublished.

Calthorpe, Peter. *The Next American Metropolis: Ecology, Community, and the American Dream.* New York: Princeton Architectural Press, 1993.

———. "The Post-Suburban Environment." *Progressive Architecture* **3**, No. 91 (1991):84–85.

Calthorpe, Peter, and Mark Mack. "The Pedestrian Pocket." 1987. Unpublished.

Campbell, Carlos. *New Towns: Another Way to Live.* Reston, VA: Reston Publishing Company, 1976.

Carpenter, Edward. "Brave New town." *Industrial Design* **11**, No. 3 (March 1964):62–67.

Carr, Stephen, Mark Francis, and Leanne Rivlin. *Public Space.* Cambridge, MA: Cambridge University Press, 1992.

Carson, Rachel. *Silent Spring.* Greenwich, CT: Fawcett Publications, 1962.

Cautley, Marjorie Sewell. "Planting at Radburn." *Landscape Architecture* **21**, No. 1 (22 October 1930):23–29.

Cervero, Robert. *Suburban Gridlock.* New Brunswick, NJ: Center for Urban Policy Research, 1986.

————. "Unlocking Suburban Gridlock." *Journal of American Planning Association* **52** (Autumn 1986): 389–406.

Christensen, Carol A. *The American Garden City and the New Towns Movement.* Ann Arbor, MI: University of Michigan Research Press 1986.

Christie, Alden. "Radburn Reconsidered." *Connection* 7 (25 May 1964):37–41.

City Club of Portland. *Creating Community in Suburbia: New Options for a Gresham Neighborhood.* 14 May 1991. Unpublished.

City of Bellevue [Washington] Storm Water and Drainage Utility. *Comprehensive Drainage Plan.* 1988. Unpublished.

City of Bellevue [Washington], Parks and Recreation Department. *Parks, Recreation and Open Space Plan.* 1987. Unpublished.

City of Bellevue [Washington]. *Comprehensive Plan.* 1974. Unpublished.

City of Eugene [Oregon], Department of Public Works. *Comprehensive Stormwater Management Plan.* 1992. Unpublished.

Collins, George R. "Broadacre City: Wright's Utopia Reconsidered." In *Four Great Makers of Modern Architecture: Gropius, Le Corbusier, Mies van der Rohe, Wright,* edited by Adolf K. Placzek. New York: Da Capo Press, 1970.

"Community Patterns." *Architectural Forum* **44**, No. 4 (April 1936):244–247.

Craig, Lois. "Suburbs." *Design Quarterly* **132** (1986):1–32.

————. "Houses at Liberty: Picturing Suburban America." *Design Quarterly* **138** (1987): 20–29.

Creese, Walter L. *The Search for Environment: The Garden City Before and After.* Baltimore: Johns Hopkins University Press, 1992.

————. *The Crowning of the American Landscape: Eight Great Spaces and Their Buildings.* Princeton: Princeton University Press, 1985.

Cronin, William. *Nature's Metropolis: Chicago and the Great West.* New York: W. W. Norton, 1991.

Delsohn, Gary. "The First Pedestrian Pocket." *Planning* **55**, No. 12 (December 1989):20–22.

Dent, David J. "The New Black Suburbs." *The New York Times Magazine* (14 June 1992): 18–25.

Dingus, Anne. "Any Place but Texas." *Texas Monthly* **21** (August 1983):144–148.

Dobriner, William. *Class in Suburbia.* Englewood Cliffs, NJ: Prentice-Hall, 1963.

Dolce, Philip, ed. *Suburbia: The American Dream and Dilemma.* Garden City, NY: Anchor Books, 1976.

Donaldson, Scott. *The Suburban Myth.* New York: Columbia University Press, 1969.

Downing, Andrew Jackson. *Rural Essays.* New York: Geo. A. Leavitt, 1869.

————. *A Treatise on the Theory and Practice of Landscape Gardening* (with a supplement by Henry Winthrop Sargent). 6th ed. New York: A. O. Moore, 1859.

Duany, Andres. "Traditional Towns." *Architectural Design* **59**, Nos. 9/10 (1989):60–64.

Duany, Andres, and Elizabeth Plater-Zyberk. "The Second Coming of the American Small Town." *The Wilson Quarterly* **16**, No. 1 (Winter 1992):19–51.

————. *Traditional Neighborhood Ordinance.* Miami, FL: Foundation for Traditional Neighborhoods, 1989.

Dullea, George. "The Tract House as Landmark." *The New York Times* (17 October 1991):B1.

Dunlop, Beth. "Breaking the Code." *Architecture* **79**, No. 4 (April 1990):80–83.

————. "Coming of Age." *Architectural Record* **177**, No. 8 (1 July 1989):96–103.

Edwards, Arthur M. *The Design of Suburbia.* London: Pembridge Press, 1981.

Eichler, Edward P., and Marshall Kaplan. *The Community Builders.* Berkeley: University of California Press, 1970.

Eliot, Charles. *Charles Eliot: Landscape Architect.* Boston: Houghton Mifflin, 1902.

Engst, Elaine D., and H. Thomas Hickerson. *Urban America: Documenting the Planners.* Ithaca: Cornell University Libraries, 1985.

"Entice 'Em with Advertising." *Professional Builder* **39**, No. 3 (March 1974): 102–107.

Fabos, Julius Gy., Gordon T. Milde, and Michael Weinmayer. *Frederick Law Olmsted, Sr.: Founder of Landscape Architecture in America.* Amherst: University of Massachusetts Press, 1968.

"The Fastest-Selling Houses in the USA." *House and Home* **4**, No. 2 (August 1953):126–130.

Fein, Albert, ed. *Landscape into Cityscape: Frederick Law Omsted: Plans for a Greater New York City.* Ithaca: Cornell University Press, 1967.

Feiss, Carl. "Broadacre City Revisited: FLW's Restatement, with Embellishments." *Progressive Architecture* **40** (July 1959):181–188.

Finrow, Jerry. *Champignon Memorandum.* (23 October 1990). Unpublished.

Fishman, Robert. "The Rise and Fall of Suburbia." *Design Quarterly* **153** (Fall 1991):13–16.

———. *Bourgeois Utopias: The Rise and Fall of Suburbia.* New York: Basic Books, 1987.

———. *Urban Utopias in the Twentieth Century.* New York: Basic Books, 1977.

"Five Prize Neighborhoods." *House and Home* **11**, No. 3, March 1957, 116–121.

Forman, Richard T. T. & Godron, Michel. *Landscape Ecology.* New York: John Wiley & Sons, 1986.

Frances, Mark, Lisa Cashdan, and Lynn Paxson. *Community Open Spaces.* Washington, DC: Island Press, 1984.

French, Paula Kochler. "The Communal Language." *Landscape Architecture* **67** (November 1977):503–508.

Gans, Herbert. *The Levittowners: The Ways of Life and Politics in a New Suburban Community.* New York: Pantheon Books, 1967.

Gantenbein, Douglas. A Central Park for Seattle Suburb." *Progressive Architecture* **70**, No. 2 (February 1989):28.

Garreau, Joel. *Edge City: Life on the New Frontier.* New York: Doubleday, 1991.

———. "Edge Cities." *Landscape Architecture* **78**, No. 8 (December 1988):51–75.

Geddes, Robert. "Jefferson's Suburban Model." *Progressive Architecture* **70** (May 1989):9.

Gehry, Frank. "Beyond Function." *Design Quarterly* **138** (1987):2–11.

Gerloff, Robert. "Rediscovering the Village." *UTNE Reader* **51** (May/June 1992): 93–96.

Gill, Brendan. *Many Masks: A Life of Frank Lloyd Wright.* New York: G. P. Putnam's Sons, 1987.

Girling, Cynthia. "The Pedestrian Pocket: Reorienting Radburn." *Landscape Journal* **12**, No. 1 (Spring 1993):40–50.

Golany, Gideon. *New Town Planning—Principles and Practices.* New York: Wiley Books, 1976.

———, ed. *Strategy for New Community Development in the United States.* Stroudsburg, PA: Dowden Hutchinson & Ross, 1975.

Goldberger, Paul. "A New Form, an Enduring Sameness." *The New York Times* (27 October, 1986).

Gottdiener, Mark. *Planned Sprawl: Private and Public Interest in Suburbia.* Beverly Hills, CA: Sage Publications, 1977.

Granz, Galen. *The Politics of Park Design.* Cambridge: MIT Press, 1982.

Groth, Paul. "Lot, Yard, and Garden: American Distinctions." *Landscape* **30**, No. 3 (1990):29–35.

Guterson, David. "No Place Like Home: On the Manicured Streets of a Master-Planned Community." *Harper's* **285**, No. 1710 (November 1992):55–64.

Hamblen, Matt. "The Kentlands Charrette: Producing a Town Plan in a Week." *Urban Land* **47**, No. 9 (September 1988):10–15.

Hardin, Garrett. "The Tragedy of the Commons." *Science* **162** (13 December 1968):1243–1248.

Hardin, Garrett, and John Baden, ed. *Managing the Commons.* San Francisco: W. H. Freeman and Co., 1977.

Hayden, Dolores. *Redesigning the American Dream.* New York: W. W. Norton, 1984.

Hecht, Melvin E. "The Decline of the Grass Lawn Tradition in Tucson." *Landscape* **19**, No. 3 (May 1975):3–10.

Heckscher, August. *Open Spaces: The Life of American Cities.* New York: Harper & Row, 1977.

Heidrich, Robert W. "A Village in a Park: Riverside, Illinois." *Historic Preservation* **25**, No. 2 (April/June 1973):28–33.

Helphand, Kenneth I. *Colorado: Visions of an American Landscape.* Niwot, CO: Roberts Rinehart, 1991.

———. "McUrbia: The 1950s, and the Birth of the Contemporary American Landscape." *Places* **5**, No. 2 (1989):40–49.

———. "Mille Intrepretazione." *VilleGiardini* **202** (December 1985):50–53.

———. "The Western City Park." *Parks in the West and American Culture*, Institute of the American West, Sun Valley, Idaho. (1984):5–6.

———. "Environmental Autobiography." *Childhood-City Newsletter* **14** (December 1978):8–17.

Henderson, Susan. "Llewellyn Park, Suburban Idyll." *Journal of Garden History* **7**, No. 3 (September 1987):221–243.

"Here Are Six Easy Lessons in Land Planning." *House and Home* **12**, No. 2 (August 1957):160–164.

Herrera, Philip. "The Instant City: Corporate Builders of New Towns." *Fortune* **75** (1 June 1967):135–138.

Hertzen, Heikki von, and Paul D. Speiregen. *Building a New Town: Finland's Garden City, Tapiola.* Cambridge, MA: MIT Press, 1971.

Hester, Randolph, and Mark Francis. *The Meaning of Gardens.* Cambridge, MA: MIT Press, 1990.

Hoppenfeld, Morton. "A Sketch of the Planning-Building Process for Columbia, Maryland." *American Institute of Planners Journal* **33**, No. 6 (November 1967):398–409.

Hough, Michael. *City Form and Natural Process: Towards a New Urban Vernacular.* New York: Routledge, 1984.

Houseman, William. "The Many Sides of Life in a Planned Community." *House Beautiful* **126**, No. 10 (October 1984):106–107, 172, 174.

"How Levittown Disproves the Cynical Prophets." *House and Home* **12**, No. 5 (November 1957):54.

How to Landscape the Home Grounds. Painesville, OH: The Storrs & Harrison Co., 1928.

Howard, Ebenezer. *Garden Cities of To-Morrow.* Edited by F. J. Osborn. Cambridge, MA: MIT Press, 1965.

Howett, Catherine. "Systems, Signs, Sensibilities: Sources for a New Landscape Aesthetic." *Landscape Journal* **6**, No. 1 (Spring 1987):1–12.

Hubbard, Henry. "Land Subdivision Regulations." *Landscape Architecture* **16**, No. 1 (October 1925):53–54.

Hubka, Thomas C. *Big House, Little House, Back House, Barn: The Connected Farm Buildings of New England.* Hanover, NH: University Press of New England, 1984.

Huxtable, Ada Louise. "'Clusters' Instead of 'Slurbs'." *The New York Times Magazine* **9** (February 1964):37–44.

Jackson, J. B. "The Vernacular Landscape is on the Move . . . Again." *Places* **7**, No. 3 (1991):24–35.

———. "Nearer Than Eden." *The Necessity for Ruins*, 19–36. Amherst: University of Massachusetts, 1980.

Jackson, Kenneth. *Crabgrass Frontier: The Suburbanization of the United States.* New York: Oxford University Press, 1985.

Jacobs, Jane. *Death and Life of Great American Cities.* New York: Random House, 1961.

Kahn, Eve. "Model Community That Isn't." *The Wall Street Journal* (1 June 1992):A10.

Katz, Donald. *Home Fires.* New York: Harper Collins, 1992.

Kay, Jane Holtz. "The Green vs. The Grid." *Landscape Architecture* **79**, No. 8 (October 1989):74–79.

Keating, Ann Durkin. *Building Chicago: Suburban Developers and the Creation of a Divided Metropolis.* Columbus: Ohio State University Press, 1988.

Kelbaugh, Doug. *The Pedestrian Pocket Book: A New Suburban Design Strategy.* New York: Princeton Architectural Press, 1988.

Kelly, Barbara M. *Expanding the American Dream: Building and Rebuilding Levittown.* Albany: State University of New York Press, 1993.

Ken Kay and Associates. *Laguna West Landscape Design Guidelines.* May 1991. Unpublished.

Knack, Ruth Eckdish. "Repent Ye Sinners Repent." *Planning* **55,** No. 8 (August 1989):4–8.

Kowinski, William Severini. "Suburbia: End of the Golden Age." *The New York Times Magazine* (16 March 1980):16–19ff.

Kraay, Joop H. "Woonerven and Other Experiments in the Netherlands." *Built Environment* **12** Nos. 1/2 (1986):20–29.

Krasnowiecki, Jan. *Legal Aspects of Planned Unit Residential Development, with Suggested Legislation. Part 1: The Legal Aspects, Technical Bulletin No. 52.* Washington, DC: Urban Land Institute, 1965.

Krieger, Alex, and William Lennertz, eds. *Andres Duany and Elizabeth Plater-Zyberk: Towns and Town-Making Principles.* New York: Rizzoli, 1991.

Krueckeberg, Donald A., ed. *Introduction to Planning History in the United States.* New Brunswick, NJ: Center for Urban Policy Research, 1983.

"Lake Anne Village Center: A Planned Community Nucleus." *Progressive Architecture* **47**, No. 5 (May 1966):17–24.

Langdon, Philip. "Beyond the Cul-de-sac." *Landscape Architecture* **79**, No. 8 (October 1989): 72–73.

———. "A Good Place to Live." *The Atlantic Monthly* **261**, No. 3 (March 1988): 39–60.

Lautner, Harold. *Subdivision Regulations: An Analysis of Land Subdivision Control Practices.* Chicago: Public Administration Service, 1941.

Leccese, Michael. "Next Stop: Transit-Friendly Towns." *Landscape Architecture* **80**, No. 7 (July 1990):47–53.

———. "Brave Old World." *Landscape Architecture* **78**, No. 8 (December 1988): 56–65.

Levinson, Barry (director). *Avalon.* Tri-Star Pictures, 1990.

"Levitt's Landia." *Architectural Forum* **94**, No. 2 (February 1951):140–148.

Little, Charles. *Greenways for America.* Baltimore: Johns Hopkins University Press, 1990.

Lowen, Sara. "The Tyranny of the Lawn." *American Heritage* **42**, No. 5 (September 1991):44–55.

Lynch, Kevin. *Managing the Sense of the Region.* Cambridge, MA: MIT Press, 1976.

MacCormac, Richard. "Suburban Syntax." *Architectural Review* **178** (October 1985):53–55.

Mann, Lawrence D. *A Preliminary Inventory of Planned Communities.* Drachman Institute Working Paper, University of Arizona, Tucson, n.d.

March, Lionel. "An Architect in Search of Democracy." *Writings on Wright.* Edited by H. Allen Brooks, 195–206. Cambridge: MIT Press, 1981.

Marcus, Clare Cooper, ed. "The Future of Urban Open Space." *Places* **6**, No. 1 (Fall 1989).

Marcus, Clare Cooper. *The House as a Symbol of Self.* Berkeley: Institute of Urban and Regional Development, University of California, 1971.

Marcus, Clare Cooper, and Wendy Sarkissian. *Housing as If People Mattered.* Berkeley: University of California Press, 1986.

Marcus, Clare Cooper, Carolyn Francis, and Colette Meunier. "Mixed Messages in Suburbia: Reading the Suburban Model Home." *Places* 4, No. 1 (1978):24–37.

Marsh, Margaret S., and Samuel Kaplan. "The Lure of the Suburbs." In *Suburbia: The American Dream and Dilemma,* edited by Philip Dolce. Garden City, NY: Anchor Books, 1976.

Martin, Edgerton, and Christopher Faust. "Arcadia at the Edge." *Design Quarterly* **156** (Summer 1992):14–20.

Marx, Leo. *The Machine in the Garden: Technology and the Pastoral Ideal in America.* New York: Oxford University Press, 1964.

Masotti, Louis M., and Jeffrey K. Hadden, eds. *The Urbanization of the Suburbs.* Beverly Hills, CA: Sage Publications, 1973.

Mays, Vernon. "Neighborhoods by Design." *Progressive Architecture* **73**, No. 6 (June 1992):92–102.

McCamant, Kathryn, and Charles Durett. *Cohousing.* Berkeley, CA: Habitat Press, 1988.

McHarg, Ian. *Design with Nature.* New York: John Wiley & Sons, 1992.

McHarg, Ian L., and Jonathan Sutton. "Ecological Plumbing for the Texas Coastal Plain." *Landscape Architecture* **65**, No. 1 (January 1975):78–89.

Meehan, Patrick, ed. *The Master Architect: Conversations with Frank Lloyd Wright.* New York: John Wiley & Sons, 1984.

Meinig, D. W., ed. "Symbolic Landscapes: Models of American Community." *The Interpretation of Ordinary Landscapes.* New York: Oxford, 1979, pp. 164–194.

Meyersohn, Rolf, and Robin Jackson. "Gardening in Suburbia." In *The Suburban Community*, edited by William Dobriner. New York: G. P. Putnam's Sons, 1958.

"Mobs Stone Home of First Negro Buyer in Levittown, Pa." *House and Home* **12**, No. 3 (September 1957):45.

Morgan, George T., and John O. King. *The Woodlands: New Community Development, 1964–1983.* College Station, TX: Texas A & M University Press, 1967.

Moudon, Anne Vernez. "The Evolution of Common Twentieth Century Residential Forms: An American Case Study." In *International Perspective on the Urban Landscape*, edited by J. W. R. Whitehand and P. J. Larkham. London: Routledge, 1991.

———, ed. *Master Planned Communities: Shaping the Exurbs in the 1990s. Proceedings of conference. Urban Design Program,* College of Architecture and Urban Planning, University of Washington, Seattle, 1990.

———, ed. *Public Streets for Public Use.* New York: Columbia University Press, 1987.

Muller, Peter O. *Contemporary Suburban America.* Englewood Cliffs, NJ: Prentice-Hall, 1981.

———. *The Outer City: Geographical Consequences of the Urbanization of the Suburbs.* Washington, DC: Association of American Geographers, 1976.

Mumford, Lewis. "The Fourth Migration." In *Planning the Fourth Migration: The Neglected Vision of the Regional Plan Association of America,* edited by Carl Sussman. Cambridge, MA: MIT Press, 1976.

———. "A Modest Man's Enduring Contributions to Urban and Regional Planning." *AIA Journal* **65**, No. 12 (December 1976):19–29.

———. "The Intolerable City: Must It Keep On Growing?" *Harper's* **152** (February 1926):283–293.

Neckar, Lance. "The Park: Prospect and Refuge." *Reflections* 6 (Spring 1989):4–13.

"$9,990 Levitt Houses Boast 70′ lots, Levittown, PA." *Architectural Forum* **95** (October, 1951):217–219.

Nohl, Werner. "Open Space in Cities: Inventing a New Esthetic." *Landscape.* **28**, No. 2 (1985):35–40.

Nolen, John. *New Towns for Old: Achievements in Civic Improvement in Some American Small Towns and Neighborhoods.* Boston: Marshall Jones Company, 1927.

Norcross, Carl. *Open Space Communities in the Market Place, Technical Bulletin No. 57.* Washington, DC: Urban Land Institute December, 1966.

Olin, Laurie. "Form, Meaning and Expression in Landscape Architecture." *Landscape Journal* **7**, No. 2 (Fall 1988):149–168.

Oliver, Paul. *The Village Green.* Arts Council of Britain, n.d.

Olmsted, Frederick Law. "Preliminary Report upon the Proposed Suburban Village at Riverside, Near Chicago, by Olmsted, Vaux & Co." In *The Papers of Frederick Law Olmsted Vol. VI: The Years of Olmsted, Vaux and Company, 1865–1874,* edited by David Schuyler and Jane Turner Censer, 273–290. Baltimore: Johns Hopkins University Press, 1992.

———. "Park in the New American Cyclopedia 1861." In *The Papers of Frederick Law Omsted Vol. III: Creating Central Park 1857–1861,* edited by Charles Beveridge and David Schuyler III, 346–367. Baltimore: Johns Hopkins University Press, 1983.

———. "To Calvert Vaux" August 29, 1868. In *The Papers of Frederick Law Olmsted Vol. VI: The Years of Olmsted, Vaux and Company, 1865–1874,* edited by David Schuyler and Jane Turner Censer, 269–273. Baltimore: Johns Hopkins University Press, 1992.

———. "Memorandum accompanying drawing for C. E. Norton, Cambridge, Mass." February 8, 1868. In *The Papers of Frederick Law Olmsted Vol. VI: The Years of Olmsted, Vaux and Company, 1865–1874,* edited by David Schuyler and Jane Turner Censer, 257–261. Baltimore: Johns Hopkins University Press, 1992.

———. "To Mary Perkins Olmsted August 23, 1868" in *The Papers of Frederick Law Olmsted Vol. VI: The Years of Olmsted, Vaux and Company, 1865–1874,* edited by David Schuyler and Jane Turner Censer, 266–267. Baltimore: Johns Hopkins University Press, 1992.

Oregon Land Conservation and Development Commission. *1991 Transportation Planning Rule for the Statewide Planning Goal 12.* Salem, OR, 1991. Unpublished.

Osborn, Frederic J., and Arnold Whittick. *The New Towns: The Answer to Megalopolis.* New York: McGraw-Hill Book Company, 1963.

Perry, Clarence. "The Neighborhood Unit." *Regional Survey of New York and Its Environs Vol. VII.* New York: Regional Plan of New York and Its Environs, 1929.

———. *Housing for the Machine Age.* New York: Russell Sage Foundation, 1939.

"Planned City Made Grave Error in Plan." *Eugene Register Guard* **13** (March 1989): p. 11.

Pollen, Michael. *Second Nature: A Gardener's Education.* New York: Atlantic Monthly Press, 1991.

Popenoe, David. *The Suburban Environment: Sweden and the United States.* Chicago: University of Chicago Press, 1977.

Rachlis, Eugene, and John E. Marqusee. *The Land Lords.* New York: Random House, 1963.

Ranney, Victoria Post. *Olmsted in Chicago.* Chicago: Open Lands Project, 1972.

Rapoport, Amos. *House Form and Culture.* Englewood Cliffs, NJ: Prentice-Hall, 1969.

"Reston: An Answer to Suburban Sprawl: Urban Living in the Country." *Architectural Record* **136** (July 1964):119–134.

Reston Association. *Open Space Guidelines.* (Updated Spring 1993.) Unpublished.

Riley, Robert. "Speculations on the New American Landscapes." *Landscape* **24**, No. 3 (1980):1–9.

Rochlin, David. "The Front Porch." In *Home Sweet Home: American Domestic Vernacular Architecture,* edited by Charles W. Moore, Kathryn Smith, and Peter Becker, 24–29. New York: Rizzoli, 1983.

Rosenbaum, Ron. "The House That Levitt Built." *Esquire* **100**, No. 6 (December 1983):378–393.

Rosenthal, Jon. "Cluster Subdivisions." *Information Report No. 135.* Chicago: Planning Advisory Service of the American Society of Planning Officials, 1960.

Roth, Darlene. *Frederick Law Olmsted's First and Last Suburbs: Riverside and Druid Hills.* Bethesda, MD: National Association of Olmsted Parks, 1993.

Rouse, James. "How to Build a Whole City from Scratch." Address to the National Association of Mutual Savings Banks, 17 May 1966.

Rowe, Peter G. *Making a Middle Landscape.* Cambridge, MA: MIT Press, 1991.

Royal Dutch Touring Club. *Woonerf.* The Hague: ANWB, 1980.

Sacramento County [California] Planning and Development Department. *General Plan Revised Draft.* December 1992. Unpublished.

Samuelson, Robert J. "The Joys of Mowing." *Newsweek* **117**, No. 17 (29 April 1991):49.

Schaffer, Daniel. *Garden Cities for America: The Radburn Experience.* Philadelphia: Temple University Press, 1982.

Schwartz, Joel. "The Evolution of the Suburbs." In *Suburbia: The American Dream and Dilemma,* edited by Philip Dolce. Garden City, NY: Anchor Books, 1976.

Shoshkes, Ellen. *The Design Process* New York: Whitney Library of Design, 1989.

Simon, Robert. "Planning a New Town—Reston, Virginia." *Proceedings, American Society of Planning Officials Conference.* Boston, 5–9 April 1964.

Smith, Norris Kelly. *Frank Lloyd Wright: A Study in Architectural Content.* Englewood Cliffs, N.J.: Prentice-Hall, 1966.

So, Frank S., David R. Mosena, and Frank S. Bangs. *Planned Unit Development Ordinances: Report No. 291.* Chicago: American Society of Planning Officials, May 1973.

Solomon and Associates, *Toward Community: Residential Design Guidelines of the City of San Jose.* 1986. Unpublished.

Solomon and Associates, Center for Environmental Structure, and Phoebe Wall. *A City of Gardens: Pasadena Design Ordinance for Multi-Family Housing.* 1988. Unpublished.

Solomon, Daniel. *ReBuilding.* New York: Princeton Architectural Press, 1992.

———. "Life on the Edge: Toward a New Suburbia." *Architectural Record* **176**, No. 13 (November 1988):63–67.

Sorkin, Michael. *Variations on a Theme park: The New American City and the End of Public Space.* New York: Hill and Wang, 1992.

———. "Dwelling Machines." *Design Quarterly* **138** (1987):30ff.

Spielberg, Steven (director). *ET: The Extra Terrestrial.* Universal Studios, 1982.

Spirn, Anne. "The Poetics of City and Nature: Towards a New Aesthetic for Urban Design." *Landscape Journal* **7**, No. 2 (Fall 1988): 108–126.

———. *The Granite Garden: Urban Nature and Human Design.* New York: Basic Books, 1984.

Stein, Clarence. *Towards New Towns for America.* Cambridge: MIT Press, 1966.

Stern, Robert A. M., ed. *The Anglo-American Suburb.* London: Architectural Design, 1981.

Stilgoe, John. *Borderland: Origins of the American Suburb, 1820–1939.* New Haven, CT: Yale University Press, 1988.

———. "Town Common and Village Green in New England: 1620–1981." In *On Common Ground,* edited by Ronald Lee Fleming, 7–36. Cambridge: Townscape Institute, 1982.

Stilgoe, John R. "The Suburbs." *American Heritage* **35** (February/March 1984): 20–37.

————. "Hobgoblin in Suburbia." *Landscape Architecture* **73**, No. 6 (November/December 1983):54–61.

————. "Suburbanities Forever: The American Dream Endures." *Landscape Architecutre* **72**, No. 3 (May 1982):89–93.

Sussman, Carl, ed. *Planning the Fourth Migration: The Neglected Vision of the Regional Planning Association of America.* Cambridge: MIT Press, 1976.

Tennenbaum, Robert. "Hail, Columbia." *Planning* **56**, No. 5 (May 1990):16–17.

Thayer, Robert L., Jr. *Gray World, Green Heart: Technology, Nature and the Sustainable Landscape.* New York: John Wiley & Sons, 1994.

————. "Designing an Experimental Solar Community." *Landscape Architecture* **67**, No. 3 (May 1977):223–228.

The Irvine Company. Newport Coast Exhibit Flyer. Newport Beach, CA, n.d.

The Woodlands Corporation. *Recreational Standards.* The Woodlands, TX. Internal document dated February 1993.

Thompson, J. William. "LA Forum." *Landscape Architecture* **83**, No. 9 (September 1993):60–64.

Tuan, Yi-fu. *Dominance and Affection: The Making of Pets.* New Haven, CT: Yale University Press, 1984.

————. *The Good Life.* Madison: University of Wisconsin Press, 1986.

Untermann, Richard K. "Can We Pedestrianize the Suburbs?" In *Public Streets for Public Use,* edited by Anne Vernez Moudon, 123–131. New York: Columbia University Press, 1991.

Unwin, Raymond. *Town Planning in Practice: An Introduction to the Art of Designing Cities and Suburbs.* New York: Princeton Architectural Press, 1909.

Urban Land Institute. *A History of the Irvine Ranch.* Washington, DC: Urban Land Institute, 1974.

————. *New Approaches to Residential Land Development: A Study of Concepts and Innovations, Technical Bulletin No. 40.* Washington, DC: Urban Land Institute January, 1961.

US Federal Housing Administration. *Home Ownership: The FHA Plan.* Washington, DC: Government Printing Office, 1948.

————. *The Structure and Growth of Residential Neighborhoods in American Cities 1939.* Washington, DC: Federal Housing Administration, 1939.

————. *Planning Profitable Neighborhoods, Technical Bulletin No. 7.* Washington, DC: Federal Housing Administration, 1938.

————. *Subdivisions Standards for Insurance of Mortgages on Properties Located in Undeveloped Subdivisions. Circular 5(Form 2059).* Washington, DC: Federal Housing Administration, 15 August 1938.

————. *Property Standards: Minimum Standards for Oregon. Circular 2(Form 2277).* Washington, DC: Federal Housing Administration, 15 December 1938.

————. *Planning Neighborhoods for Small Houses, Technical Bulletin No. 5.* Washington, DC: Federal Housing Administraiton, 1934.

Van der Ryn, Sim, and Peter Calthorpe. *Sustainable Communities: A New Design Synthesis for Cities, Suburbs and Towns.* San Francisco: Sierra Club Books, 1986.

Venturi, Robert, *Complexity and Contradiction in Architecture,* New York: Museum of Modern Art, 1966.

Venturi, Robert, Denise Scott Brown, and Steven Izenour. *Learning from Las Vegas.* Cambridge: MIT Press, 1972.

Vogel, Carol. "Clustered for Leisure: The Changing Home." *The New York Times Magazine* (28 June 1987):12–17ff.

Von Eckardt, Wolf. "The Community: Could This Be Our Town?" *The New Republic* **151**, No. 19 (7 November 1964):17–24.

Wallace, McHarg, Roberts and Todd. *An Ecological Plan.* The Woodlands, TX: The Woodlands Corporation, 1974.

————. *An Ecological Inventory.* The Woodlands, TX: The Woodlands Corporation, 1971.

Wattel, Harold L. "Levittown: A Suburban Community." In *The Suburban Community,* edited by William Dobriner. New York: G. P. Putnam's Sons, 1958.

Waugh, Frank, and Peter J. van Melle. *Foundation Planting.* Edited by Leonard H. Johnson. New York: A. T. De La Mare, 1927.

Weiss, Mark A. *The Rise of the Community Builders: The American Real Estate Industry and Urban Land Planning.* New York: Columbia University Press, 1987.

Weiss, Michael J. *The Clustering of America.* New York: Harper & Row, 1988.

Weiss, Shirley F. "New Towns—Transatlantic Exchange." *Town and Country Planning* **38**, No. 8 (September 1970):374–381.

Wetherell, W. D. *The Man Who Loved Levittown.* Pittsburgh: University of Pittsburgh Press, 1985.

White, Morton and Lucia. *The Intellectual Versus the City: From Thomas Jefferson to Frank Lloyd Wright.* Cambridge, MA: Harvard University Press, 1962.

Whitehand, J. W. R., and Peter J. Larkham. *Urban Landscapes: International Perspectives.* New York: Routledge, 1992.

Whyte, William H. *The Last Landscape.* Garden City, NY: Doubleday, 1968.

————. *Cluster Development.* New York: American Conservation Association, 1964.

————. *The Organization Man.* Garden City, NY: Doubleday, 1957.

Wolfe, Charles R. "Streets Regulating Neighborhood Form: A Selective History." In *Public Streets for Public Use,* edited by Anne Vernez Moudon, 110–122. New York: Columbia University Press, 1991.

Wolkimir, Richard. "Mownomaniacs Take the Sword to the Sward." *Smithsonian* **21**, No. 2 (May 1990):166.

Wood, Robert C. *Suburbia: Its People and Their Politics.* Boston: Houghton Mifflin, 1958.

Woodbridge, Sally. "Village Redefined." *Progressive Architecture* **67**, No. 7 (July 1986):106–107.

Wright, Frank Lloyd. "Broadacre City: A New Community Plan." *Architectural Record* **77** (April 1935):243–254.

————. *The Disappearing City.* New York: Walter Farquhar Payson, 1932.

————. *The Living City.* New York: Bramhall House, 1958.

Wright, Gwendolyn. "Domestic Architecture and the Cultures of Domesticity." *Design Quarterly* **138** (1987):13–19.

Wright, Henry N. "Radburn Revisited." *Architectural Forum* **135**, No. 1 (August 1971):52–56.

Yeomans, Alfred B., ed. *City Residential Development.* Chicago: University of Chicago Press, 1916.

INDEX